AN IMPROBABLE SERIES OF RISKY EVENTS

Minneapolis

First Edition March 2024
An Improbably Series of Risky Events: The Memoirs of Gary Lindberg.
Copyright © 2024 by Gary Lindberg.
All rights reserved.

No parts of this book may be used or reproduced by any means, graphic, electronic, or mechanical, including photocopying, recording, taping or by any information storage retrieval system, without the written permission of the publisher except in the case of brief quotations embodied in critical articles and reviews.

10 9 8 7 6 5 4 3 2 1

ISBN: 978-1-962834-09-4

Cover and book design by Gary Lindberg

AN IMPROBABLE SERIES OF RISKY EVENTS

The Memoirs of Gary Lindberg

Wisdom Editions
Minneapolis

Table of Contents

After I Died 1
Childhood Amnesia. 5
Father 18
Mother 33
Sister 52
Neighborhood. 61
Wife 1: Georgia 73
Wife 2: Karen. 85
Military Life. 95
My Lai Massacre 112
Reentry to Civilian Life. 130
Rocket Man 139
The Glensheen Murders. 149
The Great Rockwell Heist 155
Sea Serpents and POWs. 162
Wife 3: Gloria. 187
That Was Then, This Is Now. 194
The Blizzard. 204
Mexico. 216
Drug Trafficking 232
Family Matters. 239
Black Hole 250
New Ventures. 262
Books. 279
Elvis 289
Seeing the Beginning in the End. 300
Acknowledgments 303
About the Author 304

To Scott, the end of the Lindberg line

"I've seen things you people wouldn't believe. Attack ships on fire on the shoulder of Orion. I watched C-Beams glitter in the dark near the Tannhäuser Gate. All those moments will be lost in time... like tears in the rain."

—The last words of replicant Ray Batty in *Blade Runner*, perhaps the most moving death soliloquy in cinematic history

Also by Gary Lindberg

FICTION
Ollie's Cloud
The Shekinah Legacy
Sons of Zadok
Deeper and Deeper

NONFICTION
Letters from Elvis
Brando on Elvis
The Roots of Elvis
The Power of Positive Handwriting
The Soul of Humanity
Humanity Coming of Age

After I Died

I was nobody, and I was nowhere. Shards of images without meaning slid through the darkness, some frightening and some just confusing. As I fought to reclaim consciousness from the nothingness, I feared the visions would devour me. A man cried before his head exploded. Hundreds of mutilated corpses lay in heaps in the jungle—all of them children, elderly men and women. Suddenly, hovering helicopters disgorged throngs of dancing teenagers onto a movie screen, and then a snarling leopard jumped at me. A young man pulled me to safety, but instead of relief, I felt overwhelming grief as I recognized this beautiful man but couldn't quite identify him. Suddenly, grief overtook me.

I struggled to open my eyes, hoping to locate my body in some sensible place, but my eyelids resisted. Slowly, they cracked open, and I tried to turn my head, but it wouldn't move. The fear of paralysis shot through me, and I struggled in vain to move my body. I heard strange beeping sounds as shapes floated past. Momentarily, I thought I might have been abducted by aliens, but then one of the wispy figures transformed into an angel—*maybe I was dead!*—and then into a woman in a blue sweater. I tried to get her attention, but I was speechless, my restrained limbs useless. And I was hot—unbearably, claustrophobically sweltering beneath a blanket.

After an eternity, it seemed, a woman approached and blithely asked if I knew where I was. I had no idea, and if I had known, I could not have communicated it.

As if suddenly realizing the idiocy of her question, the woman spoke. "I'm your nurse, Claudia. You're in the hospital—the recovery room. You've had surgery and you're coming out of anesthesia."

Noticing my arms struggling against the restraints, she mercifully explained, "You must be very still for another ten minutes or so. Your operation ran into some difficulties, and the doctor had to wire an external pacemaker down the jugular vein to your heart. Any movement could cause a rupture. That would be very dangerous, so we've had to restrain you for thirty minutes, especially your head. It won't be much longer, I promise."

The word surgery blew some of the fog away. Vaguely, I remembered entering a hospital but had no recollection of why.

"Is there anything I can do for you right now?" the nurse asked.

At last, I was able to form a raspy word, "Hot."

"Oh," the nurse said. "Blink if you want me to remove the blanket."

I blinked and she pulled it off. "It's a warming device called a Bear Hugger. Sometimes it gets *too* warm. I'll be right back."

She left me for a minute and returned with a damp washcloth to cool my perspiring face.

"Your surgeon will be here when it's time to remove the restraints." She placed a button in my hand and said, "Just press this if you need me." For the next ten minutes, that call button was my only connection to the world, and it gave me comfort.

I must have fallen asleep from the residual effects of anesthesia because it seemed like just a minute before a doctor was speaking to me.

"Gary, I'm Doctor Spooner. Can you wake up?"

The name "Gary" startled me. I realized that until the doctor had spoken my name, I could not have recalled it myself. "We're all very glad to have you with us," he said. "You gave us quite a scare in the operating room. We're going to remove the wire from your jugular right now and then get these restraints off you, so be as still as possible for a while, OK?"

They did something and suddenly my ability to move my head and limbs returned, but the fog inside my head had not entirely lifted.

"Do you know why you're here?" Dr. Spooner asked with a scowl of interrogation.

I could not remember who I had been or why I would be in this purgatory, so I just shook my head, mindful of my need to remain still.

"You had open heart surgery, a double bypass. Things got a bit dicey. Instead of the usual three hours, you were on the table for over seven because of some complications."

I would learn later that I had died twice during the surgery, and it had taken a heroic effort by my surgeon and two surgical teams to bring me back.

"Can you tell me your name?"

Spooner began the tedious hospital protocol to check my memory.

I shook my head.

"How about your wife's name?"

I could find no names at all in my mind and suddenly panicked. My brain was bereft of information.

"Can you remember your phone number?" Spooner asked.

Again, I shook my head.

After a longer interrogation, the doctor concluded that my memory had disappeared. "This could just be postoperative delirium or amnesia," he explained. "It happens in some older patients and usually goes away pretty quick."

These were comforting words delivered unconvincingly. After some prodding the next day, Dr. Spooner told me there was a possibility I had gone too long without oxygen and the result could be brain damage.

For three terrifying days, I had virtually no memories. My life had been diminished to what had occurred after the surgery. I recognized visitors but didn't know their names until they said them, and couldn't remember why I knew them, so I just pretended.

Fearing I would never get my life back—all those unremembered personal experiences, all that knowledge—I grew despondent. At seventy-three, I was too old to build a new life from scratch.

The post-surgical pain was intense after having my chest cracked open for nearly eight hours. Every stretched-out muscle ached, and I couldn't walk without two orderlies holding me up. But the worst of it was the fear that my life, undocumented as it was, had been stolen from me. I did not want my life to just evaporate. There is a kind of immortality to stories when passed down.

My wife, Gloria, said I had been given both a second and third chance at life. She thought I had died from a broken heart because five months earlier my son had passed away from cancer and the grief had overwhelmed me. The sudden, joyful return of memory was followed quickly by the horror of remembering the loss of my beloved son, Brendan. Who would ever know my love for my son and the grief of outliving him? Who except those closest to me would ever know the joys and heartbreaks of my life—the adventures and struggles, the successes and failures?

After I died, I accepted a new mission. It would take many years, but eventually I would recollect and document a spectacular series of events spanning Hollywood escapades, magic and music, war atrocities, monster hunts, POW rescue attempts, art heists, myth busting, Mexican drug cartels, mansion mysteries, brutal murders, space exploration, entrepreneurial perils and so much more.

Socrates supposedly said that an unexamined life is not worth living. I am well past the age of Socrates when he died, but I hold as truth the philosopher's warning about an unexamined life. Since I want my life to have been worth living, it seems wise to add up my many deeds and misdeeds to decide if the sum of them has any meaning at all. My hope is that by the end of writing my story I will finally understand what I should have known all along, and that someone will gain an insight or two from reading it.

Stories once remembered are burdens if left untold, so here is my unburdening.

Childhood Amnesia

Childhood amnesia is a term that cognitive psychologists use to describe people's inability to remember events from their early years. The estimated childhood amnesia offset is about 3.5 years. Before then, perhaps mercifully, it is thought that specific incidents cannot be recalled with any meaningful detail. Autobiographical memory is thought to stabilize between five and six years of age. Memories of early events that are pinned to intense emotions appear to be more accessible to recall.

I realized late in life that my earliest memory was most likely implanted by my mother's frequent retelling of a family ritual she had conducted during World War II when I was very young, and my father was on a baby aircraft carrier called the USS Fanshaw Bay. Every night that Dad was away, according to Mom, she would show me a photograph of my father in his white "dixie cup" sailor's hat and ask me to kiss Daddy good night.

For many years, I was certain that I remembered doing this, but now I believe it was just a false memory implanted lovingly into my developing brain by Mom's frequent retellings. It was probably true, though, and thinking now about kissing my absent father brings tears because he will never return from his final journey away from me.

My father in his white "dixie cup" sailor cap.

Even though Dad could not swim, he had joined the US Navy to avoid being drafted into the army. Intensely phobic of rodents since a mouse had crawled up his childhood pantleg and defied exiting, the idea of rat-infested foxholes scared him even more than drowning. He was given two weeks leave to be home when I was born, but we didn't see each other again until after the War.

My first authentic, intact memory occurred before I turned three. My parents had purchased a modest duplex at 2732 Garfield Avenue South in Minneapolis, just one house away from the large Salem Lutheran Church, now SpringHouse Ministry Center. My mother's parents rented the upper floor to chip in on mortgage payments. Through the eyes of my toddler self, I can vividly relive that first memory and the strong feelings it provoked.

I was seated in a stroller pushed from behind by my beautiful five-foot-one mother. I knew Mom was behind me because I could hear her happy voice speaking to a neighbor as we passed. It must have been summer because I was wearing a little white T-shirt outdoors. Straps over my shoulders connected to baby-blue shorts.

My naked knees and calves extended downward into white stockings stuffed into brown leather boots I had already outgrown. Because I was a blonde, fair-skinned Swede, my mother made sure that I was uncomfortably greasy with sun block.

Mom and me on one of our stroller walks.

As we made a sudden left turn at the end of the block, one of the stroller's front wheels yelped like an anxious chihuahua, and I glanced into the yard of the corner house. There, playing in the grass, was a cute little girl chasing a big ball that suddenly careened toward my stroller. Mom stopped for a moment, and the girl approached, smiling curiously. I knew immediately that she was older than me by at least a year, but I couldn't stop the flood of unfamiliar emotions. I didn't yet know the expression "love at first sight," but this beautiful creature—her name was Alice, I learned later—was my first romantic interest.

Then, as suddenly as the emotional tide had rolled in, a rogue wave of self-consciousness replaced it—an epiphany that this pretty and mature little girl was allowed to gallop freely through her yard while I was imprisoned in my stroller like an infant. As I looked fondly at Alice's tanned legs and my pale-skinned and bony appendages, the embarrassment of my ugliness and lack of suitable age overwhelmed me. As I started to cry, she frowned as if watching an infant throw a tantrum, then laughed and turned away. My humiliation doubled.

Alice and I never became a "thing." Mom soon learned from my obstinance that I didn't want to visit Alice again. She never would have fathomed that I feared this intimidating little girl would taunt me. *You're so white. Your knees are so knobby. Why do they keep you in that stupid stroller—can't you walk?* These words were never spoken, of course, but they echoed inside my head, and they still do. It feels good to write them down.

How I wish I could blame all my insecurity issues on that early, formative experience with Alice, but I can't. I place much more blame on the movies.

By the following year, the summer of 1947, I got my first car and never looked back. With new confidence, I drove down to the corner to show Alice my new vehicle, but she had moved. *That's all right*, I thought. *She was not the kind of girl to be impressed by a flashy automobile.*

My flashy first automobile.

An Improbable Series of Risky Events

* * *

The chronology of my early years is like a shuffled deck of cards in my mind, but I remember a childhood sitting on my parents' laps in dark movie houses munching popcorn and sipping my dad's sugary Cokes. My mother and father, Elaine and Russ, shared a passion for films and would drive an hour to watch one they hadn't seen. According to his parents, my father was a dreamer, but to my mother he was a visionary. Mom accompanied Dad on these movie excursions and was highly critical of poor craftsmanship, which didn't seem to bother my father so long as the plot was intriguing.

Neither of my parents ever considered the age appropriateness of their chosen movies for me, and there were no ratings in those days. Anyway, I'm sure they thought I was just a little scamp and would fall asleep when the popcorn was gone.

I remember being captivated by Walt Disney's *Song of the South*, based on the Uncle Remus stories, and I sang the uplifting song "Zip-a-Dee-Doo-Dah" for months afterward. I even made up my own alternative lyrics that changed with my moods, although the cheery melody made sullenness hard to pull off.

That I can remember the film so vividly confuses me because the movie was released in November of 1946, just after I turned three, and the movie has never been released on any home video format—the equivalent of book banning. The culprits responsible for this removal from the public's eye were critics who harshly characterized the movie's portrayal of African Americans and plantation life as racist. The movie has also never been shown on Disney's streaming platform, Disney+. A decade ago, I tried to find this now-obscure treasure, but it was not available anywhere. How and why, then, was a three-year-old's recollection of this film so vibrant that the grown-up version of that child still hums the perky melody of "Zip-a-Dee-Doo-Dah" to cheer himself up?

Most of my family movie outings, however, were for viewing more adult fare, including a long list of horror and science fiction movies. My father's taste in literature also trended toward genre fiction like westerns and science fiction. His favorite series of novels was based on *Tarzan of the Apes*. He had collected first editions of all eighteen Tarzan novels and read each of them numerous times. I remember reading those deliciously pulpy novels myself when I was about eight and deciding that someday I would write fiction too.

The scary movies gave me nightmares. *The Beast with Five Fingers, The Creeper, Strangler of the Swamp*—even *Abbott and Costello Meet Frankenstein*—all kept me up at night, though I never told Mom or Dad. The risk-reward ratio influenced my decision to stay silent. If I told them I got scared, they would make me feel safer, but they would also stop taking me to the movies. And despite my terror, I loved the experience of horror films, except when I was in my bed at night dreaming that the lower half of a girl grotesquely severed at the waist was walking stiffly toward me. The gruesome fairy tales I had heard growing up—the original, unexpurgated versions with all the gory stuff—did not frighten me as much as the powerful visuals in the shadowy theaters we visited.

Somehow—perhaps because my father was a practicing magician, which taught me how easily people could be fooled— I recognized that someone was making these movies to stoke my fear, and I wanted to know who they were and how they did it. When this occurred, I became destined to become a filmmaker. Since then, I've seldom been genuinely frightened by a movie because my rational mind was usually too busy figuring out how the people behind the camera were scaring me.

This reminds me of the marketing tagline for a 1979 exploitation horror movie called *The Last House on the Left*. In the radio spots, a chilling voice suggested this method by which one could live through the otherwise unsurvivable terror to come: "Keep telling yourself, 'It's only a movie.'"

Just don't ask me about sitting alone in a theater watching Ridley Scott's *Alien* for the first time, or Billy Friedkin's *The Exorcist*. I am not immune to manipulation by excellent craftsmanship.

* * *

As you might imagine, as a five- and six-year-old, I was an avid radio listener. The airwaves of that time were filled with comedy shows and genre mysteries. I loved them all. *Amos 'n' Andy* was a hilarious weekly situation comedy featuring two Black men looking for a better life. They had traveled to Chicago with four ham-and-cheese sandwiches and twenty-four bucks. Andy was a hard worker and Amos a gullible dreamer. Eventually, they launched their own business called the Fresh Air Taxi Company because their only vehicle had no windshield. A friend they met in the big city, George "Kingfish" Stevens, became a recurring character, often luring them into get-rich schemes and tricking them into trouble.

I was about ten when I learned that the radio voices of Amos and Andy were not Black actors but two White men familiar with minstrel traditions. Freeman Gosden played Amos, and his friend Charles Correll played Andy. It was not exactly like learning Santa Claus and the Easter Bunny were not real, but I remember feeling that I had been duped. I had developed a bond with two Black men who were not Black at all. This was probably my first experience with misinformation, an event that me suspicious of many other things in my small world.

The entrepreneurial spirit of Amos 'n' Andy certainly inspired me, though. Over the next two decades I would start fifteen different companies, and some met the same fate as the Fresh Air Taxi Company. All of them, however, taught me important lessons I have never forgotten.

Besides Amos 'n' Andy, there were other inventive comedy series on the radio such as *Fibber McGee and Molly*, *The Abbott and Costello Show*, *Bringing Up Father*, *The Burns and Allen Show* and many others. I was most impressed, though, by the westerns and adventure shows. *The Cisco Kid* series, about a virtuous Mexican wanderer who became a quasi-Robin Hood icon, spanned over 600 episodes. *The Lone Ranger*, about a masked former Texas Ranger with a strict moral code who fought outlaws with his American Indian sidekick, Tonto, presented close to 1,500 adventures. I liked the idealist side of this character and often wore a black Lone Ranger mask around the house, pretending to be this standard-bearer of virtue. I also sometimes listened to other series about other western heroes such as Roy Rogers, Hopalong Cassidy, Gene Autry and Lash Larue, all successful comic book franchises.

Two shows I followed religiously were *Sky King* and *Challenge of the Yukon*. *Sky King* was based on an Arizona rancher and pilot nicknamed "Sky" King. Using his twin-engine Cessna, "Songbird," Sky, his niece and his nephew captured outlaws and spies and saved lost hikers. Like all my other favorite radio personalities, these were good people doing good deeds. *Challenge of the Yukon* was a period adventure series about Sergeant Preston of the Northwest Mounted Police and his lead sled dog, Yukon King. This stalwart team fought evildoers in the Northwest wilderness during the Gold Rush of the 1890s.

Creepier fare also attracted my interest, probably because of my parents' appetite for scary movies. One of my favorite radio series was *The Shadow*, which featured a mysterious man who had "the hypnotic power to cloud men's minds so they cannot see him." The introductory line from most episodes of this show has become iconic in American idiom—"Who knows what evil lurks in the hearts of men? The Shadow knows!" I remember the chill I felt when those disembodied words were followed by an ominous laugh each week in my dark bedroom. The evolving character of the Shadow laid the foundation of the superhero archetype complete with sidekicks, a secret identity and a superpower. I loved that the Shadow operated primarily after dark as a vigilante in the name of justice terrifying criminals into vulnerability.

The radio series *Suspense*, promoted as "radio's outstanding theater of thrillers," featured typical suspense-thriller fare but occasionally veered into science fiction and fantasy. *The Mysterious Traveler* more predictably featured fantasy and science fiction but also presented standard mysteries and suspense. I loved listening to *Murder at Midnight* because of its macabre and often supernatural tales of suspense.

Inner Sanctum Mystery featured stories of mystery, terror and suspense, but its tongue-in-cheek introductions sharply contrasted with the more serious tone of the hosts on shows like *Suspense*. It began as a promotional platform for mystery books published under Simon and Schuster's "Inner Sanctum" imprint and ended each episode with a message about an upcoming novel.

The lack of visuals of the radio shows stimulated my imagination, but by 1949, when my parents bought our first television set, I was enchanted by having actual movies in our living room—even if the screen only measured seven inches diagonally. The National TV-7W01 was truly a marvel and literally brought our family together. We had to sit next to each other to view the tiny monitor just like we always sat close together in the movie houses. The novelty of having TV shows come into our home made the inconvenience of the small screen insignificant. Recently, I installed a 75" flat-screen TV in my living room. In 1949, who could have imagined such a thing? And yet, just last night, I found myself watching a YouTube video on the screen of my iPhone, a picture even smaller than our first TV.

Our first TV set, a National TV-7W01, with a screen slightly larger than an iPhone Pro.

Once the new TV was set up, I could watch *The Lone Ranger*, starring Clayton Moore, a native of Minnesota. There were many other new programs with actors and performers I could not only hear but see. Buffalo Bob and his puppet pal, Howdy Doody, were already in the second year of their twelve-year run. The Ed Sullivan Show brought live music, comedy and dance to us while we ate supper on

TV trays in front of the screen. Dad liked watching *Meet the Press*, now the longest-running program on American television. I think his wartime experience made him interested in what was happening in the world at large. We never missed *The Philco Television Playhouse*, one of the most respected dramatic anthology series of the Golden Age of TV. I loved *Martin Kane, Private Eye*, the earliest successful cops-and-robbers show.

Things were different back then. While researching one of the early *Martin Kane* episodes, which were all sponsored by United States Tobacco Company, I was amused at how brazenly the main character, played by William Gargan, walked into a tobacco shop and discussed pipe tobaccos and cigarettes with the proprietor before moving on to solve the case. Of course, product placement, as it is known today, still occurs. Actors drink Coke products and drive Chrysler SUVs in the shows we watch. But in those early times, subtlety was an unknown and probably unnecessary ingredient in broadcast entertainment.

* * *

My parents unwittingly ensured that my media exposure was deep and complete. Reading comic books became my favorite pastime. Mom bought me every comic that was published—from Disney and Looney Tunes classics to a multitude of superhero comics including *The Justice Society of America*—the first superhero team in comic history. She probably got them at the store where Grandma worked. I eagerly followed the adventures of Superman, Batman, Captain Marvel, Captain America, Plastic Man, Green Lantern, The Human Torch, Mighty Mouse (a superhero version of Mickey) and Wonder Woman.

By the sixth grade, my private collection had over 900 comics, and I set about cataloging each one by taping a typewritten number on the slim spine and recording that number on a matching index card with name, date, volume, series title, list of stories inside and a description of the cover. Yes, obsessive-compulsive, I know. While working through this arduous task, I stayed home "sick" one day to make progress and recruited my sister to help. We spent the day together in my bedroom happily cataloging comics—one of the few times I can recall collaborating with my sister in those early years. Afterward, I had to reassess my belief that having a little sister was useless.

I learned to read very early. My father's collection of wonderful novels and my hundreds of comic books beckoned me to find meaning in the odd squiggles they called letters and words. This came easily to me because of the patient nurturing of my parents. One of my earliest memories is my mother teaching me how to "sound out" a simple word in a children's book. I soon discovered that the words next to the pictures could be as interesting and meaningful as the colorful images themselves. During this time I also discovered how certain words rhymed with each other—"fountain" sounded like "mountain" and "book" like "look." I started writing poems in my head after going to bed, but since I couldn't yet write, I would call out for Mom, and she would kindly pad into my room in her nightgown and write down my brilliant stanzas.

During my early years, I was continuously wrapped in a warm cocoon of stories read to me, movies that unveiled their strange worlds, and radio programs that shot adrenaline directly into my developing brain. In many ways, the real world was mundane and colorless compared to the fantastic realms in which I was often immersed.

I enjoyed playing alone because then I could invent my own universes without being interrupted by the intrusive fantasies of playmates. My imagined stories occasionally spilled over into my dreamtime in which my subconscious failed to recognize wakeful logic, defiantly twisting and molding the story elements into bizarre new fabrications.

As I grew older, I learned to problem-solve and foster creativity by lying down in a dark space, closing my eyes, and simply shutting down my conscious thoughts to unlock this secret inner playground. In that twilight zone, that creative sweet spot between awake and asleep called hypnagogia, I discovered that the subconscious ignores the usual boundaries we impose upon it and roams more freely. Some of my best ideas and solutions have thus surfaced when I was least conscious. The trick is to remember the fruits of the endeavor.

* * *

The scary movies I was constantly absorbing also bled into my dreams, sometimes morphing into horrifying scenarios that terrified me in the middle of the night. Even the nightly prayer my mother taught me caused great anxiety.

"Now I lay me down to sleep, I pray the Lord my soul to keep. If I should die before I wake, I pray the Lord my soul to take."

Who could calmly go to sleep after acknowledging the possibility of dying while asleep? And how would God take my soul if I died? Would it be ripped out of my chest? Or sucked out through my mouth? These are not comforting thoughts that foster relaxation.

My intense fear of nightmares escalated when one of them came true. I must have been around five because I was in kindergarten, which had started when I was almost five. The vivid nightmare was of an apartment building across the street catching on fire and people screaming to get out. In reality, there was no apartment building there, but the day after my dream, a house across the street burst into flames, and two fire trucks quickly quenched the blaze. For weeks, I felt responsible for that fire, as if I had conjured it into reality through my dream.

Desperate to put an end to my nightmares, I finally devised a surefire plan to protect against these nightly invasions. The idea was born during one of my subconscious play sessions. It merged prayer with my tendency toward compulsive behavior. Every night, I performed this same ritual, and over time my nightmares faded. I liked that the ritual was so simple. Lying in bed, I would close my eyes and say an identical sequence of words exactly three times. "Please, God, make it so that I won't dream tonight. Please, God, make it so that I won't dream tonight. Please, God, make it so that I won't dream tonight." The repetition was to make sure that God would hear me and know I was serious. Looking back on that incantation, I now think the repetition was a harmless manifestation of my compulsive nature, but it made me feel hopeful.

Father

Russell Harry Lindberg was the firstborn child of Harry and Victoria. Grandpa Harry, whose parents had immigrated to Minnesota from Sweden, had served in World War I and worked as a boiler engineer for the railroad. I have no doubt that Harry loved his son, but his Scandinavian stoicism made it difficult for him to express feelings, a trait passed down through his son to me, his firstborn grandson.

Grandpa Harry Lindberg and Grandma with me and my sister, Bonnie.

My father told me little about his growing up years, but one story he shared revealed an unfulfilled and often painful relationship with his own father. In high school, Dad was a gifted athlete excelling in track and field, a sport for which his body was perfectly constructed—a willowy five-foot-eleven with legs like titanium springs. When he set a high school record for the long jump, however, his father was not in attendance. Dad told me that Grandpa Lindberg had never seen him practice or compete.

The school's field was on Grandpa Lindberg's walking route home from work. Dad said that when he was training outdoors after school, he would see his father march by but never saw him wave or even turn his head for a glimpse of his son. "I think he wanted me to become self-sufficient—you know, not dependent on his attention or approval," Dad told me unconvincingly. I never saw the two of them share a tender moment, and I promised myself I would not make that same mistake with my children, unfortunately a promise I often broke.

I found this photo of Dad in an old album after he died. Since his father was the only family member with a camera at the time, I suspect that Grandpa Lindberg came to at least one of Dad's practices or meets and took this photo.

Other than track and field, my father had two significant obsessions, which matched well with his compulsiveness. The first was music. Dad was a gifted musician and mastered the guitar at an early age. Two famous guitarists had helped bring the guitar out of the rhythm section and into its future role as a solo instrument long before the reign of guitar gods in rock 'n roll.

Charlie Christian, an African American swing and jazz guitarist, developed a single-string technique for soloing and put electric pick-ups on the guitar so its sound could be amplified. In 1939, he became a featured artist in the Benny Goodman Sextet. Dad studied Charlie's technique by listening to recordings but was more infatuated by the musicianship of another guitarist of the era.

Django Reinhardt, a Romani-Belgian jazz guitarist who helped pioneer gypsy jazz, used complex, rapid-fire chord progressions and intricate guitar fills to create unique musical textures. Amazingly, when Django was just eighteen, he suffered burns over half his body when his family's wagon in a gypsy caravan burst into flames. His little finger and ring finger were severely injured, and doctors believed he would never play guitar again. But he adjusted by developing new fingerings. He and jazz violinist Stephane Grappelli formed the Paris-based Quintette du Hot Club de France, certainly the most innovative and influential European jazz group of the period and an inspiration for my father.

Dad was mesmerized by the gypsy guitarist's melodic inventions and harmonically complex rhythm patterns, which roamed up and down the fretboard. He set out to mimic and possibly surpass Django. After listening to recordings of both Django and my father, I believe they were neck and neck in their technical and artistic mastery. Dad also developed the ability to instantly improvise chord progressions for any song he had heard. He also possessed an uncanny ability to anticipate where the melody of a previously unheard song was going so he could create intricate musical accompaniments on the fly.

Dad formed a jazz group called The Four Downbeats, which played in nightclubs around the Twin Cities to the consternation of Dad's parents. They emulated the style of Quintette du Hot Club de France.

Dad's musical instincts eventually led him to write songs. One of his attempts at popular music earned a first-place award on a local TV talent show hosted by Cedric Adams, a popular figure in the Twin Cities. The prize was a box of floor tiles we installed in the kitchen. After Mom and Dad became born-again Christians, Dad turned to writing sacred songs with the sensibilities of pop music. Christian recording artists soon discovered these songs and started to record them, which made Dad extremely proud. When these artists learned about Dad's guitar artistry, they wanted him to provide accompaniment, and he became an in-demand studio guitarist. I designed the covers of his sheet music and his folios.

My father's other obsession was magic. He had been inspired by the performances of Erich Weisz, better known as Harry Houdini, an American-Hungarian escape artist, illusionist and stunt performer. He was also captivated by other sleight of hand artists such as Harry Blackstone, Okito and David Devant. Blackstone had published several how-to books, which Dad devoured, practicing the techniques for hours.

Sleight of hand, also known as prestidigitation, is the development of fine motor skills and extreme dexterity, which is then combined with misdirection and psychology to perform seemingly miraculous illusions that defy explanation. My father could make billiard balls appear and disappear in his hands, make a playing card rise from a fanned deck and turn goldfish into white doves. The goldfish, of course, had been purchased at a local dime store. Today we call them dollar stores.

Dad also had sources for rabbits and doves. These common creatures were the livestock that our household maintained so that audiences could be astonished when the animals appeared or vanished unexpectedly. We had our share of animal funerals, of course. After we moved to the suburbs, lightning struck a weeping willow in the backyard. Beneath the tree was a cage with one rabbit, which did not survive. For several weeks, I had nightmares about that rabbit coming back to life and haunting the family.

Russell Harry Lindberg, then, was a talented musician, songwriter and magician, but through genes or example had inherited an inability to connect emotionally with a son. I have no doubt he loved me, and I am sure he was aware of my love for him, but we seldom expressed those sentiments out loud to each other. Instead, I became an active participant in his passions so we would have a reason to spend time together.

For most of my eighty years, I have often lamented that Dad always seemed to favor my sister. From the beginning, they were emotionally close unlike my father and me. I always felt that Bonnie simply was his favorite. Dad changed her diapers, not Mom. Dad rocked her to sleep but never rocked me. Dad got up in the middle of the night when she was crying. On the other hand, when I had nightmares, it was Mom who rescued me. When I had written a poem in my head, Mom was the parent who wrote it down for posterity.

As my sister was previewing this chapter for accuracy, she approached me with something I had never known. "Mom told me more than once," Bonnie said, "that before Dad left for the South Pacific, he told Mom he wanted to have another child, maybe a girl. Mom told him, 'Not unless you're the one to take care of her.' So that's why Dad was always there for me—it was a bargain he struck with Mom. He promised to be the one to take care of me, just as Mom always took care of you."

This made so much sense. It was why Dad looked after Bonnie the way Mom looked after me. Knowing this simple fact helped me release a residue of stubborn resentment over Bonnie being Dad's favorite child and appreciate how my father had continued to honor his long-ago pledge to Mom. He was really a good guy.

* * *

Music and magic couldn't sustain a family financially, so after Dad returned to Minneapolis from the War, he took a job as a driver/salesperson for Leo Singer Candy and Tobacco, a local wholesaler. He drove a panel truck packed with an assortment of edibles and smokeables, working about sixty hours per week to make as much money as possible. After making rounds, he would park the truck at our house on Garfield Avenue. I loved going into that truck. The pungent blend of aromas was like no other sensory experience in my life, and I dreamed of having a wonderful job like Dad's, in which I was surrounded all day by delicious smells.

I had no idea that Dad hated this foul-smelling job and filled his days thinking about how music and magic could somehow save him from it. Every day he would eat a bag lunch in his truck and scribble, sometimes on the brown bag itself, musical notations of new songs that were whizzing through his brain. Much later in life, he would tell me, "That kept me sane."

Before I went into first grade, my parents sold their duplex on Garfield and moved to a new little cracker-box home at 2940 Hampshire Avenue South in the suburb of St. Louis Park. My father started his own business, Taylor & Lindberg Painting and Papering, with a Bible College student name Dave Taylor. About a year later, Dave's wife died of Hodgkin's Disease and Dave plummeted into alcoholism.

The ugly truck that Dad was so proud of.

Dad was proud of his truck and during cold, winter mornings, would drive me to school in it. But I was embarrassed by riding in an ugly truck with our name on it, so I always insisted that he drop me off a block away from the school. Looking back on this, I am sure my attitude about Dad's cherished truck deeply hurt his pride, but he never let on. How I wish I could go back and change my adolescent surliness. He deserved kinder treatment from his son.

After Dave left the business, Dad continued his work as a house painter and wallpaper hanger with Mom sometimes assisting. To these mundane jobs he brought his native compulsiveness and artistic awareness. To him, every job, no matter how ordinary, was showtime. He needed to be appreciated, to perform better than others in his profession—to be the Django Reinhardt of house painting. He bought the finest grade of paints and accomplished every step from preparation to clean-up with the greatest care and attention to detail.

***

When I turned thirteen, I asked my parents for a guitar so I could play music with Dad. Mom found an electric guitar for under fifty dollars in the Montgomery Ward catalog, and my father taught me how to play it. The cheap guitar had strings set too high above the fretboard, which made them hard to press down, but after my tender fingertips developed the necessary armor, I learned how to play anyway. Having been taught by a master, I excelled at improvising single string solos but could never fully comprehend the chording techniques and progressions improvised by Dad. His guitar work always seemed like a blend of his music and his magic.

Before long, the Christian artists recording Dad's music learned about my guitar proficiency. My plan to spend more time with Dad was paying off as we frequently recorded as a team, often at Kay Bank Studio in south Minneapolis.

As demand for my father's magic performances expanded from birthday parties to company sales meetings, boy scout troop events and charity fundraisers, my mother grew increasingly resistant to being Dad's pretty stage assistant and prevailed upon me to replace her—or at least be her back-up. Consequently, I commonly found myself escaping from a locked and bound steamer trunk, one of Dad's best illusions.

After locking me inside the trunk, volunteers from the audience would hoist a black drape to temporarily block the audience's view of the trunk. My father would then walk behind the drape. Almost immediately, hands would appear above the drape and pull it down, revealing that the hands belonged not to my father but to me. Magically, I was standing outside the locked trunk, and Dad had vanished. It would take a minute or two for the volunteers to unstrap, untie and unlock the truck, but when they opened it, to the astonishment of the audience, my father had somehow replaced me inside. It seemed odd to me that Dad always got the applause when it was me who had escaped, but I never complained.

I also spent time levitating in mid-air and bursting through the roof of a tiny dollhouse that had been pierced by multiple swords. The doll house illusion was normally performed by my mother and father. Mom would hide behind a false rear wall in the dollhouse, her legs extended into the building's base-on-wheels. Dad would open the windows and the front door of the house so the audience could see that it was empty. Then he would stab swords through the windows and down the chimney, once again opening the front door so everyone could see the blades crisscrossing through the empty interior. The swords were pointed and made of solid metal, so they could cause damage, but the edges were dull for safety reasons. After Dad dramatically removed the swords, the roof would burst open and Mom would suddenly stand up, dwarfing the doll house. Amazed by the clever illusion, the audience would always stand and applaud.

On one occasion, however—at a sales meeting for a regional grocery store chain—Dad incorrectly aligned the components of the dollhouse so the holes for the rear swords were behind the black wall that hid Mom. I was watching the show from the back row, delighted that I was not assisting. As my father started pushing one of the rear swords into the dollhouse, it passed right in front of Mom's nose.

My mother, who was known for occasional outbursts of anger, was incensed at this assault on her person. She grabbed the sword and with great force shoved it out. From my seat, I watched that sword fly out of the house and across the stage. The audience gasped. My father, startled, appeared confused at first, but quickly gathered his wits and said to the audience, "Must be poltergeists!" The audience laughed.

Then Dad did something that really provoked his wife. Proving to her that he did not understand the nature of the problem, he walked to the other side of the doll house and plunged the second rear sword through the misaligned hole. After a muffled scream, that sword also flew out of the dollhouse. The audience erupted in laughter this time, assuming this was part of the act.

Afraid of putting in more swords, Dad recovered and said to the doll house, "Is anyone in there?" Suddenly Mom burst through the roof to abundant applause. But this time she was not smiling. My recollection is that Mom and Dad did not speak to each other for about a week.

* * *

Earning enough money to support the family, which had expanded to four counting my sister who was born in July of 1949, put a lot of pressure on Dad. Though he had left Leo Singer's wholesale candy and tobacco business, Leo had helped Dad get started in house painting by referring him to numerous Jewish friends. And since we lived in a largely Jewish neighborhood in "Saint Jewish Park," as it was often called, referrals from one happy Jewish client to another provided a loyal base of revenue. My father became the recommended source in the Jewish community for high-quality home decorating services, and those who used him bragged about it.

I inadvertently assisted in burnishing Dad's reputation by becoming the local *shabbos goy*, a non-Jew who performed tasks that were religiously forbidden to be performed by Jews on Shabbat, the Jewish holy day. I became good friends with our Jewish neighbors by making the rounds every Saturday to turn on and off gas ranges, start lawn sprinklers and perform other tasks that were prohibited for reasons no one could remember.

I was often offered money for my services, which I always refused because Dad told me personal favors should be done for friendship. As a pale, blue-eyed blonde in a Jewish enclave, some of the neighbors started good-naturedly teasing that I must be an albino Jew. In truth, I attended numerous bar and bat mitzvahs—Jewish coming-of-age celebrations—before ever attending a Christian baptism or confirmation service. I felt accepted and comfortable with my many Jewish friends. When I first learned about anti-semitism, I took it personally.

Dad never showed prejudice for any race or ethnicity, but he sometimes used language common to the 1940s and '50s that today is considered politically incorrect. There were few African Americans in Minneapolis in those days, so he'd had no opportunity to learn that some terms could be hurtful. As a peanut lover, he often called Brazil nuts "nigger toes," as did just about everyone else. When searching for something in the house or in his cluttered truck, I heard him say a few times that it was "like finding a nigger in a woodpile." I am sure that he did not consider the "n" word to be derogatory—just a silly cliché. Sometimes he would refer to close friends of distinct ethnic origins as "the Greeks" or "the Italians." For Dad, this was simply shorthand, and we all knew who he meant without assigning negative meaning to his designations. After all, we were sometimes called "the Swedes" and never took offense. Much later in life, Dad told me that he recalled using some of these common racial epithets and regretted it, though he had never imagined they might have caused pain to anyone.

The open-mindedness and lack of judgment of both my parents was astonishing for an era in which prejudice was largely invisible to most people. It must have been around 1954 when Mom and Dad told my five-year-old sister and me that they had invited a new friend to dinner, and we should be especially nice to this guest because she had been through some serious trauma. They told us that Pat had been born a boy but had always believed a mistake of birth had occurred and she was really a girl. Eventually, surgery helped Pat become the woman she was supposed to be.

Pat's decision was inspired by the story of George William Jorgensen who had suffered from similar gender identity confusion until finally and boldly traveling to Denmark. There she met endocrinologist Dr. Christian Hamburger, the first medical professional to diagnose George as transexual and not homosexual. After two years of hormone therapy and psychiatric evaluations, George underwent surgery to remove her male genitalia and then changed her name to Christine.

I recalled the story of Christine Jorgensen when news of her sex change had first appeared. Kids at school joked about the "Dr. Frankenstein's monster" that had been created. Frankly, I was horrified at the notion of cutting off a man's genitals and possibly replacing them with a vagina. What kind of person would be the result of this disfigurement? And now Mom and Dad were bringing home one of these creatures!

I don't know how Dad had met Pat, or how Mom had first reacted when he introduced her to the trans woman. But the calmness with which Dad told us about our dinner guest, and the genuine smile on my mother's face—so unlike her artificial smile, which I knew well—eased my discomfort. I remained nervous, though, until Dad fetched Pat in the family car and brought her to our home. As Pat walked through the front door, Mom gave her a big hug, then turned to Dad and asked him to introduce Pat to Bonnie and me.

Pat didn't look like a monster. Her voice was a bit lower than most female voices I knew, and she wore heavy makeup, but she looked more like a woman than a man. I looked for signs of whiskers but saw none. Mom served the one meal she was proficient at— roast beef, mashed potatoes and gravy, and whole kernel corn. Within minutes, I felt comfortable with Pat and even stopped thinking about her unusual surgery, which we never discussed. What would be the point? Patrick had become Patricia. A mistake had been corrected. Clearly, this was no big deal in the Lindberg household—except that today, in the twenty-first century, it is still a big deal to many people. If not for Mom and Dad, it might be a big deal for Bonnie and me too.

An Improbable Series of Risky Events

* * *

In the '50s, once you had encountered your first trans person, not much else could be surprising. A year later, though, I was shaken to the core when Dad did something that threatened the entire family.

At eleven and twelve, I admired my father and his artistic genius. I didn't see him as a housepainter, but as an artist who was trapped into painting homes to support his family. He was always just a bit distant, as if lost in melodic dreams or the invention of new illusions, but his father had also been emotionally remote with his son. That's why I was so surprised when Dad had an affair with another woman. My first instinct was not to question how Mom had failed to satisfy him emotionally, but how I had failed. It must have been my fault.

That scene is indelibly implanted into my memory. Bonnie and I were seated in the front room. Mom and her parents—Velma and Les Averill—were in the dining room having coffee. I don't remember Mom explaining what was going on, but I knew somehow that Dad had "fallen in love" with someone else, whatever that meant, and this was the evening when he would decide to leave his family for that other woman or come home to us.

Mom and Dad had mercifully kept their relationship issues from us kids, which meant that I felt blindsided and betrayed. All I knew was that Mom sometimes expressed dismay at Dad's obsession with his magic and music, and sometimes this dismay boiled over into arguments. Mom could be a verbal gunslinger when provoked. Maybe Dad had just grown weary of defending his artistic pursuits and sought solace somewhere else.

The agonizing wait for Dad's decision reminded me of the suspenseful showdown in the western film *High Noon*, which I had watched with Mom and Dad. In the movie, one of the first to take place in real time, the sense of duty of a town marshal, played by Gary Cooper, is tested when he must decide to either face a gang of killers alone or leave town with his new wife. The excruciating tension of waiting for that marshal's decision and the inevitable consequences, however, was nothing compared to waiting for Dad to make up his mind.

Startling all of us, the phone suddenly rang and everyone turned toward Mom. She looked at Bonnie and me. "Probably your dad," she said flatly. She picked up the call. "Hello?" There was a pause, then she said, "I didn't know if you would call. Someone here wants to talk to you."

Mom set the receiver on the table and walked over to my little sister and said, "You need to speak with your daddy and tell him you want him to come home. Can you do that?"

Bonnie started crying, but she walked with Mom back to the phone and picked up the receiver. All I can remember her saying is, "Daddy? When are you coming back?" Then she sobbed into the phone.

Mom took the phone away from Bonnie and said to Dad, "What are you going to do?" She stood there motionless for a moment before nodding and hanging up. I was sure the shootout had occurred, but I still didn't know the outcome.

At last Mom said, "He's coming home," and then walked into the bedroom. She closed the door behind her, but we could all hear her crying. *Must be tears of joy*, I thought, ignorant of the complexities of adult relationships.

I ran over to Grandma Averill, who had always shown me great affection, and she wrapped her arms around me. "Forgive your dad," she whispered to me. "We all make mistakes." Frankly, I was amazed at her forgiveness of the man who had betrayed her daughter. My relief was instant. Now, everything was going to return to normal.

I have often thought about the impact of this event on my life. I was too young then to have any life-changing epiphanies, but upon later reflection I could see that infidelity predictably produced a lot of collateral damage, so I pledged that I would never betray my wife if I got married. In subsequent years, I sometimes found this decision hard to honor. But remembering the pain of my eleven-year-old self on that desperate evening in St. Louis Park always helped pull me through. The truth is, though, that I would make plenty of other mistakes.

Mother

My mother, Elaine Verna Averill, was born in 1923 in Little Sauk, Minnesota, the second child of Velma Gladys (Breithaupt) and Leslie Loyd Averill. Mom's brother, Romain Darwin Averill, was older than Mom by a year and died at twenty shortly after marrying Doris Mae and fathering a son. Family lore stated that, while still in school, Romain had endured a head injury by a stone flung from a buddy's slingshot. Apparently, a blood clot from the injury later caused a brain embolism, and he died. This family tragedy created a string of consequences that affected many lives.

Romain's wedding to Doris Mae with Mom on the far right. Until I found this photograph, I had not known that Dad (far left) was also in the wedding party.

Shortly after Romain's death, a financial dispute caused a rift between the Averills and Romain's wife, who angrily broke off all future communication. Mom would see her only nephew just once in her lifetime when he was about eighteen, and then for only a few minutes. That occurred around 1960 after I pushed Mom to find her nephew because he was the one first cousin I had never met. I could not imagine that he would not want to meet his lost aunt and cousin. I also knew that this nephew was the closest blood link Mom had to her beloved brother except for her parents.

Mom demonstrated her sleuthing capability by learning that her nephew, David, who was a senior in high school, was an amateur herpetologist and would be attending a school scientific event in St. Paul. Since I had prompted Mom to find her nephew, she asked me to accompany her.

My long-lost cousin, David, shows me one of his reptiles at a science exhibit. I don't remember who took this photo, but it was probably my mother after convincing David's mother to allow one picture.

I'm sure that David and his mother, Doris, felt ambushed when we approached them. The encounter did not go well. Though Romain had died nearly two decades earlier, Doris Mae showed that her grudge against the Averills was as strong as ever. Angrily, Doris told us never to approach her or her son again.

While Doris and Mom were sharing a combustible minute, I quietly offered my hand to my cousin and introduced myself, telling him that I also had an interest in reptiles and amphibians—which I did, in the most general of terms. I asked how he had become interested in herpetology. His face brightened, but as he started to explain, his mother dragged him away.

I never saw him again, nor did Mom. And neither of us ever learned the details behind the divisive family feud. The consequences of this conflict were less hurtful for Mom than for Grandma and Grandpa Averill, though, because their small family contained only three grandchildren, one of whom they were not allowed to see.

During his brief life, Romain had been a talented and popular student. His father, Les, was a self-taught auto mechanic who eked out a living in small-town Minnesota, but Romain showed promise. He was athletic, he played the trombone in the band, and he was chased by pretty co-eds. He had a grand future ahead of him, and his father was particularly proud of him. On the other hand, Mom was, well... a girl. Enough said.

When Romain suddenly died, his father was devastated, Mom told me many times. The tragic death of his "favorite child," which Mom believed was Romain, turned a normally dour man into an angry one. Mom's accomplishments were overlooked or criticized, wounding her deeply. Grandpa's increasing bitterness likely began when something happened that caused Grandpa and Grandma to drift apart.

Family relationships can be hard to decipher because of secrets, lies, betrayals and family folklore. In the small Averill household, according to my mom, something had switched in Grandpa when Romain died. Mom assumed it was because his favorite child had died, and he was angry that Mom had not. But Grandpa's anger continued to deepen with time rather than diminish. And his anger became increasingly aimed at his wife, Velma. Clearly, something had happened in their relationship.

My Grandma (Velma) and Grandpa (Les) Averill.

Most of my memories of Grandpa Averill were of a grumpy old man who didn't like talking to anyone but was downright gruff and rude to his wife. At a family event, he would sit for a while scowling at everyone, then wordlessly walk out to his car and honk the horn, letting Grandma know it was time to leave. I remember his cutting remarks about Grandma at parties and his refusal to sit by her during their visits.

After riding my bike to their home in Hopkins, Minnesota, for a visit, I would sometimes spend time in their cave-like basement where Grandpa Averill had a cluttered workshop. Whenever we were alone down there, he could be friendly, showing me how he was inventing some mechanical device or fixing one of the neighbor's tools. But once we went upstairs where Grandma ruled, he clammed up and bitterness overtook him.

Sifting through the abundance of clues retrieved from our memories, my sister and I finally decided the best explanation for Grandpa's behavior was that Grandma had betrayed him. Perhaps, having grown weary of his unrelieved petulance after Romain's death, she had sought relief in the company of another man. Perhaps the reason why Grandma had been so forgiving of Dad's indiscretion a few years earlier was because she had made the same mistake. The punishment administered by Grandpa for his wife's betrayal may have been his unrelenting, passive-aggressive anger. He had sentenced her to an unforgiven life.

If this is true, Mom failed to learn from her father's confused and counterproductive response to Grandma's offense. After suffering the humiliation of Dad's affair, Mom accepted him home but adopted the same approach to retribution as her father had used with her mother. She was far more subtle than Grandpa, however, as for many years she delicately manipulated Dad's guilt to her advantage. The sad effect of the power she wielded was that Dad spent over a decade serving out his sentence just as Grandma was serving hers.

* * *

After Mom's brother died, Grandpa and Grandma Averill fell on hard times and moved to the big city of Minneapolis where they hoped Les could earn more money. They found a small apartment at 206 E. 26th St., and he took a job as an assembler at Northern Pump Company. To help out financially, Grandma took a part-time job as a cashier in a small neighborhood grocery store within walking distance from the home where Mom rented a room.

Mom also looked for work, but her first menial jobs were ill-suited to her active mind. Smarter than most of her supervisors, she had failed at a job as a file clerk for an insurance company when she disagreed too often with the inefficient filing process. At her next job, after several weeks assembling greeting cards at Paper Masters, she was terminated for making too many mistakes. "Pure boredom," she told me.

The litany of failures began to affect her self-esteem. "Why couldn't she succeed at even the simplest of jobs?" her father wanted to know. After all, he was earning money assembling parts for pumps, which certainly didn't tax his inventive abilities.

When Mom told me how she had met Dad, she couldn't remember which job she was failing at, but she remembered one day walking into the store where her mother worked to say hello. My dad, a slender, blue-eyed blonde was delivering boxes of candy and tobacco out of a panel truck. My personal reconstruction of this momentous meeting, which eventually resulted in my conception, is that Mom was immediately infatuated with my father, who was instantly smitten by the woman who would become my mother. But like his future son, Dad was too timid to take advantage of the situation.

"This is my daughter, Elaine," Grandma must have said, sensing the mutual attraction as mothers usually do.

"Hi," my dad said, unsure of what do next. "You live around here?"

"With my mom and dad. A couple blocks away on 26th."

"Okay, well nice to meet you," Dad said, or something like it. "I live with my folks too, over on Franklin and Elliott."

"Pretty close."

"Yeah—well, got other stops to make. Good to see you, Velma. Nice meeting you, Elaine."

"Likewise."

Based on that timid encounter, if Grandma hadn't been so observant and approving of this candy salesman, I wouldn't be here. Fortunately, she sensed that Russ wanted to see Elaine again but would never figure out how to pull that off. Then, one day, Dad showed my future grandmother a dazzling card trick in the store.

"You're good with cards," Velma said. "Do you ever play cards?"

"Sure," Dad said. "I play a little pinochle and some poker."

"How about canasta?"

"Don't know how," Dad confessed.

I'm sure he was starting to see a path to another rendezvous with Elaine—one that Grandma was paving. Within a week, at a kitchen table in the small Averill apartment with my future mother and her parents, Dad was learning how to play the rummy-like card game. On some occasions, to his delight, it would be just him and Elaine.

Eventually, I'm sure, Dad would have performed a few card tricks, and Elaine would have been suitably impressed. When Dad brought his guitar over for the first time and played a pop song or two, singing in his beautiful tenor, I think Mom was a goner. And Dad too.

But my father's parents, who were devout, born-again Christians, were not enchanted by the new girlfriend. They were already dismayed at Dad's desire to play jazz at local night clubs with his new group, the Four Downbeats, which could have a corrupting influence on their only son. And now he was falling in love with a woman who had no discernible religious foundation and had probably lured him with her bedroom eyes and ample bosom. Dad's two younger sisters, both single at the time, were also dubious about the suitability of this woman of the world for their precious brother.

Sensitive to a fault, Mom immediately detected the "lack of enthusiasm" Dad's family showed when first meeting her. Much later, she told me that over the first years of her marriage, she always felt it would be impossible to meet their expectations. For that reason, our immediate family spent much more time with Grandma and Grandpa Averill despite Grandpa's persistent surliness.

***

Until much later, I don't remember picking up on one of Mom's primary traits—a tendency to swing from gregarious and affable to sullen and depressed. During most of my growing-up years, that was just Mom being Mom, or as Dad would say, "just being a woman." Mom overdid everything to a degree. When she was ill, if the doctor prescribed a pill twice a day, she would take two at a time. "Helps me get better faster," she would tell Dad. She could be the life of the party—Mom and Dad threw quite a few good ones—but when everyone was gone, she could become gloomy without provocation.

It wasn't until 1980 that the criteria for diagnosing manic depression became clear, and its official name was changed to bipolar disorder. I will never know for sure if Mom had it, but she had all the signs. Few friends and family saw her depressions, but when she was upbeat, my God, she was a Roman candle, and everyone loved her.

Mom's best friend was also her first cousin, Leona Glidden, the daughter of Grandma Averill's sister, Hazel. Leona and Mom shared all their secrets and were more like sisters than cousins. Leona's oldest daughter, Verna Lee, was only a few months older than me and quickly became my best friend, though we saw each other infrequently at family gatherings.

Leona was an emotionally troubled young woman, extremely fearful of almost everything in life, including her children's well-being. Her solution was to keep her children virtually imprisoned in their home when not in school. I was not aware of Leona's severe paranoia, because she was always happy and having a good time when she was with Mom. Only late in my life did Verna Lee confide that her perpetual confinement in her home made visits to Lindberg family events seem like a jail break.

Leona, Mom's cousin and best friend, is top center in this photo.

Mom was always riding a manic crest when she was with Leona, whose presence managed to dampen any anger and depression Mom may have been experiencing. And Leona always seemed sane and unconcerned about her kids when with Mom, which allowed Verna Lee and me the freedom to run off and play cowboys together—sometimes in matching western outfits Grandma Lindberg had made for us. Verna Lee was the only friend I could trust with my feelings—except for one secret. I dreamed that one day Verna Lee and I would marry and live happily ever after. We didn't, of course. But Leona and Mom continued their close friendship until Leona died. Verna Lee and I remain confidantes to this day.

Playing with my cousin Verna Lee. In the early '50s, no one thought twice about kids playing with guns. My toy machine gun fired sparks into the air.

* * *

Shortly after becoming pregnant with me, Mom pledged that she would be a full-time mother and homemaker until her children—she expected more than one—were educated and moved out of the household. This may have been due to her fear of more failures in the job market, but I think it was more likely an altruistic desire to create the happiest possible home life. She was truly in love with Dad and fascinated by the idea of being a mother. Most of all, she didn't want her husband to become an angry old sod like her father. That was unthinkable.

Because of the family dispute with Romain's wife and son, I was the only grandchild my Grandpa and Grandma Averill could see, and the first grandchild for Dad's parents too, so I was not lacking attention. My birth helped reconcile some hurt feelings between Mom and Grandma and Grandpa Lindberg, who appreciated what a dedicated mother their daughter-in-law had turned out to be after all.

I had quite a handmade wardrobe, all sewn by Grandma Lindberg for my photo sessions with Grandpa. But instead of finding a career in front of the camera, I would spend forty-five years behind the camera as a filmmaker.

I think that no child on the planet has ever had as many photos taken of him than me. Well, maybe Queen Elizabeth's children, but their pictures were not taken by their grandfather. Grandpa Lindberg's hobby was photography, and his new son-in-law, Lloyd Falck, had a darkroom, which made developing and printing pictures inexpensive. Consequently, almost every moment of my early years was documented in photos. Grandma Lindberg—"Vic," as Grandpa called her, short for Victoria—would sew precious little outfits for me to model. Grandpa would then dress me up in caps and suits and coach me through different expressions. I loved the attention, and Mom loved that the whole family was so obsessed with me, the first son-grandson-nephew in the Lindberg clan. At family gatherings, Mom told me, I was continually passed from lap to lap.

* * *

I was literally in love with Mom and her mom. After the war, when Dad reentered our lives, I would kiss him out of habit but kiss the two women in my life out of love.

I remember entering kindergarten when I was four—my late October birthday would have delayed the start of schooling for another year had my mother not intervened for an exception. She was anxious for my education to begin, probably because I was an inquisitive and demanding child, and she needed some personal time.

My kindergarten memories are faded except for one, which is vivid because of the emotion still attached to it. We kindergarten students had been asked to create a Valentine's Day card for our mothers. I wanted my card to be beautiful and special like my mother, so I cut out flowers and birds from colored construction paper and tried to glue them to the base of the card, but my clumsy fingers resisted every attempt to do the job properly, and the finished card, in my opinion, was an abomination. I couldn't give such a disastrous gift to Mom. When I imagined her inevitable disappointment, I started to cry in front of everyone. And after starting, I couldn't stop. I felt foolish—the other kids were all laughing at me—but I couldn't help it.

The teacher called my mother, who picked me up at school and brought me home. That's when I found out the teacher had given Mom my ugly Valentine's card. My failure had now been exposed. With horror, I watched Mom take the atrocity out of a little envelope and look at it. Her eyes grew moist with tears, and she said to me, "Thank you dear. I love it."

I liked hearing those tender words, but I knew she was lying. No one could love my disastrous craft project. I could see it was amateurish—nothing like the cards you could buy. If a kindergartener could tell the difference, certainly Mom could see it too. I knew she was trying to make me feel better by masking her disappointment. I think this was when Mom's attempts at encouragement lost their impact and started to have an unintended effect. Starting then, encouragement always seemed like I was failing and needed extra motivation. The more praise and encouragement I received, the more I felt that I could never live up to Mom's expectations.

* * *

Over the years, my stay-at-home mom became an activist in motherhood, at least in the 1950s sense. Rather than being neglected by their parents, as many of my friends were, my mom insisted on our home being the center of activity of all the neighborhood kids. As in the movie *Casablanca*, where "everybody comes to Rick's," the Lindberg house was where everyone went to have fun.

When my friends and I appeared bored, Mom suggested we start a bicycle club—headquartered, of course, at our Hampshire Avenue house. We boys took it from there and decided to have uniforms comprised of button-front, collared shirts and our fathers' ugliest neckties. Mom taught us all how to tie half Windsor knots, which served me well in my adulthood.

This boys' club took a strange turn, however, when Judy Anderson, a tomboy who lived across the street with her mother and occasionally her father or some other male adult, wanted to join the club. But being boys, my friends and I rejected her plea—until Mom intervened. Judy joined because, when confronted by my mother's relentless insistence on analyzing our thinking, we couldn't think of a good reason for her *not* to join.

When my friends were unavailable and I was tired of reading or drawing, Mom suggested I take up archery. Dad turned our backyard into an archery range by hanging a large carpet behind two hay bales to keep errant arrows from flying into the neighbors' yards. This attracted my friends, naturally, who all bought bows and arrows to make use of the new archery range. This led to a desire to apply our skills to bowhunting in the local woods. So, we started the Buckskinner's Bowhunting Club and started buying all our equipment by mail order from Herter's, a hunting supply company in Waseca, Minnesota, which Mom had sought out for us. Before long, she was driving us before sun-up to a more distant forest for hunting daytrips and then picking us up at dusk.

There were many other clubs too. Looking back on them, I see Mom's hand in getting them going. And I remember that I was the elected "president" of each one. Was this Mom's way of helping me acquire leadership skills? I think it most likely was the result of my friends deferring to my mother's dominance by electing me their leader.

On numerous occasions, I would come home from some activity and find a friend or two or three at my house with Mom holding court, paying attention to them, suggesting things to do, supervising activities.

One group I started by myself was a band like the Four Downbeats, my dad's former jazz group. But I could only find two other musician friends, so instead of a quartet we had a trio—my friend Wayne Selness, who could only play "Lady of Spain" on accordion; Jimmy Jones on sax; and me on guitar. We had no arrangements, no repertoire and frankly little talent, but we had fun. All rehearsals, of course, were at my house with Mom serving us lemonade.

Jimmy Jones (left), Wayne Selness (center) and me. We never advanced to naming our group.

In hindsight, I understand that my childhood friends mostly had absentee or highly dysfunctional parents and craved the attention of an adult who seemed to care for their well-being. At the time, though, I felt some resentment that Mom could so easily "adopt" these neglected children when she had two kids of her own. I also decided the main reason my friends spent time with me was to spend time with Mom. In a twisted way, then, I felt competitive with Mom. This didn't feel so good. Just as with my dad's magic tricks, though, the truth about Mom's motivation was much simpler than it appeared. When all the kids and friends were playing at our house, she knew what everyone was getting into.

* * *

My interest in bowhunting, which Mom had sparked, eventually became an obsession. I bought books on animal tracks and tracking. I practiced shooting arrows at cardboard disks flung into the air, which simulated pheasants spooked from tall grass. For this, my friends and I learned how to glue on huge, untrimmed feathers near each arrow's plastic nock. When the arrow was shot into the sky, the "flu-flu" feathers would quickly catch the air, halt the expensive arrow's flight and allow it to parachute back to earth so it could be retrieved.

Flu-flu fletching on a hunting arrow.

My interest in wildlife soon evolved from wanting to kill animals to a desire to preserve their beauty after they died. I sent away for a mail-order taxidermy course, which taught me how to stuff and mount small animals like squirrels and rabbits. Unfortunately, the instructions were hard to follow, plus I had a limited supply of dead squirrels and rabbits. Exactly zero, to be precise. So, my attentive mother found a museum-certified taxidermist, Harold Cecchi, in St. Paul and talked him into taking me on as a weekend apprentice.

I discovered that taxidermy was a respectful art, and not at all disgusting. We skinned the specimens but never cut into the bodies. One Saturday I arrived at Harold's workshop and found a still-frozen polar bear lying on a worktable. After it thawed, the two of us spent a day skinning it. Harold usually purchased glass eyes and forms in many sizes for mounting deer, elk and moose heads. For the polar bear, though, we were on our own.

Before I could work on customer specimens alone, Harold insisted that I bring in an animal of my choosing and successfully mount it solo. It was not hunting season, so Mom drove me to Armstrong's Game and Hunting Ranch where we bought a live pheasant and took it home flapping in a bag. I called Harold and asked him what to do next. He told me I had to kill it.

I didn't want to injure the skin and feathers, so I asked for a humane way to terminate the large bird's life. He told me to press hard on the breastbone until the heart stopped beating. Well, I tried, but the frightened bird's heart started beating faster and harder. I was starting to feel sorry for the poor critter.

I called Harold back, and he told me that I could buy a bottle of chloroform at the drug store. Then, when I got home, I should make a newspaper cone, stuff a big wad of cotton down into the cone and pour some chloroform on it. Finally, I should stuff the pheasant's head into the cone until it died a painless death.

Well, I tried, but pheasants are big birds and tough to keep restrained. In the basement of the small Hampshire house, I prepared the newspaper cone, poured in the chloroform—which I had no trouble purchasing, even as a teen—then grabbed the pheasant as firmly as I could and stuffed its head into the cone. The bird made it clear that it didn't want me to do that. It flapped and squawked, just as I would have done, but eventually I prevailed. With its final breath, the pheasant inhaled the fumes until I thought it might burst, then suddenly let it all out and went limp.

Exhausted, I climbed the stairs to the main floor and switched on the TV. After a half hour of recovering, I went back downstairs to figure out what to do with the dead pheasant. The newspaper cone was still there, but the bird was not. Apparently, the chloroform had merely put the bird to sleep. Hearing scurrying sounds at the other end of the basement, I quietly walked over to inspect. The pheasant saw me and darted away. For a few minutes, I chased that bird all over the basement. Finally, I had to recruit Mom and Dad to help corner the pheasant behind Dad's wet bar.

This time, I tied the pheasant's feet so it couldn't run and went through the cone-and-chloroform routine too, then waited for about thirty minutes. When the bird showed no signs of life, I carried it out to the garage where the Minnesota winter froze it solid. I did a good job mounting it, Harold said, and the pheasant accompanied me to all my residences for the next twenty-five years. I lost track of it at some point. Maybe it came back to life and just wandered away.

A memorial to my great pheasant stand-off.

By the time I was in junior and senior high, Mom had acquired a reputation as a kind of psychic or sorceress. She always knew where I was and what I was doing. My friends' parents would get calls checking up on me even when there was no discernible way for her to know where I was. It was downright spooky. She seemed to have eyes and spies everywhere.

One day, during my senior year, I coaxed several friends into skipping school—which we considered an obligatory senior prank. We decided to go to a movie downtown. As we were standing at a bus stop, Mom coincidentally drove by with my sister in the front seat. When she saw me on the corner, she slammed on the brakes, rolled down the window and shouted for me to get in the car. My friends dove into some bushes to hide. Like a bounty hunter, Mom turned me in to the principal, who sentenced me to detention with these words: "You should know better than to cross your mom." I learned that if I was going to get away with anything, I had to be cleverer than my mother, and this became one of the chief goals of my life.

* * *

After her children were out of the house, Mom leaped out of housewife/mother mode and sprinted into a whirlwind of personal discovery and accomplishment. This was more than just latent feminism breaking the bonds of society's constraints. She had chosen to be a housewife, and now she chose to expand her horizons—with my father's full support.

Having become interested in handwriting analysis, she quickly learned the craft and became a certified Graphoanalyst. Soon, she was not only analyzing questioned documents for the FBI and local police departments but also had a weekly radio show on which she analyzed personality traits for listeners' handwriting samples that had been previously submitted by mail. She, my father and I collaborated on a book called *The Power of Positive Handwriting* in which Mom showed readers how they could alter their personality traits by changing their handwriting.

Her work with lawyers and police led her to take a job in security at the large Dayton's department store in Minneapolis. Suddenly, my petite, five-foot-one mother was arresting extra-large shoplifters and coaxing them into a fifth floor holding room for interrogation. She told me that the excitement she felt before "making a bust" must have been like the excitement I felt when hunting deer and seeing a big buck twenty yards away.

In 1969, just after I was drafted into the army, Mom decided to open an art gallery. She and Dad had been importing oil paintings from overseas and selling them to Dad's decorating clients for about a year, and my ambitious mother wanted to make a business out of it. I'm sure I got my entrepreneurial drive from her. My parents rented space near Miracle Mile, a strip shopping center in St. Louis Park, and she named it Elayne Galleries, changing the spelling of her first name to make it appear more elegant.

The gallery's surprising success soon caused Mom to find a larger building four blocks away on a main thoroughfare. Before long, my sister, Bonnie, left her job and joined the gallery as part owner. Dad finally abandoned his house painting business to work at the gallery full-time in charge of framing. Later, my son Brendan went to work for the gallery and then my adopted daughter, Jennifer, joined the family business.

Mom was smart, creative, compassionate, sometimes volatile and always a force to be reckoned with. From her, I learned loyalty to family and friends, how to skirt the rules without causing harm, how to verbally brawl and nearly always win, and how to love. She was my North Star, for better or worse. But most often for the better.

Sister

The relationship with my sister, Bonnie, got off to a rough start. I had been the pride and joy of the Lindberg and Averill clans for years and was so accustomed to being the focus of attention that my sister's arrival five years and nine months later threw my world into chaos. Suddenly, I vanished from the stage, and Bonnie now occupied the throne of glory. I sensed my humiliating demotion the moment my sister was brought home.

Mom and Dad introduced me to the new family member, but I would have none of it. To make things worse, they placed her crib in my room. It took several days of sulking to develop a plan for regaining my rightful position in the family. Bonnie would have to go. So, I plotted a murder based on a mystery movie I had seen. I don't remember which one. I would snatch the whiny infant from her crib, then toss her into the air and let her fall to the ground. Everyone would think she had just fallen out of her crib. I would not only regain the family's attention, but also gain their sympathy for having lost my dear sister. It would be the perfect crime.

One afternoon, while Bonnie was sleeping, I put the plan into motion. I plucked Bonnie out of her crib—she was much heavier than I had thought—and prepared to toss her high into the air, which would not have been very high for a six-year-old. Fortunately, just then—like in the movies—my mother walked in. I must have flushed with guilt at being caught in the act, but to Mom it probably looked like I was holding my sister lovingly in my arms.

I don't remember what Mom said, but it would have been something like, "Oh, that's so sweet! I know you love your sister so much. Was she crying? Here, let me put her back."

I distinctly remember Mother taking Bonnie from my arms and placing her in the crib, then sitting down on a chair and lifting me onto her lap. Her exact words escape me, but as she stroked my blonde hair, she let me know that she understood how neglected I must be feeling with everyone fussing over the new baby.

How had Mom known my feelings? Had she also known what I had intended to do and what I needed from her? Somehow, Mom had found a way to let me know I had a new job now. I had to watch over my baby sister. I was the big brother.

I never tried to kill Bonnie again.

* * *

Having a younger sister still proved challenging, however. Bonnie was very sensitive, intensely inquisitive and highly intelligent. She learned things quickly and wanted to be involved in all the activities that my friends and I enjoyed. I didn't want her dead, but I also didn't want her nosing into my business. When my courteous attempts to establish boundaries failed, I would sometimes simply drag her into another room and yell at her. I thought she was a brat.

One of my favorite pastimes was playing with little plastic figures of cowboys and Indians or sometimes soldiers. Mom and Dad indulged me with hundreds of these "little men," as I called them, and I would spend hours creating elaborate tableaux on tabletops and the carpets. To me, each diorama was a scene in a story that I was creating in my head. The western figures had horses and wagons, fences to build corrals, little settler houses. The military scenes contained soldiers in many fighting positions with accompanying tanks, jeeps and sandbag bunkers. The little men ignited my imagination as I looked down on each scene with god-like vision.

Gary Lindberg

One of my western tableaux. More sophisticated versions could take up the floor of an entire room.

One evening, after spending hours creating my best western scene ever, three-year-old Bonnie stormed into the living room like a giant troll and defiantly kicked down the whole thing. My entire story had been deleted, and I was furious. It felt like she was insulting the fruits of my effort. I screamed at her, knowing it would make her cry. She cried, knowing that would summon Mom.

It was clear that both my sister and I had misbehaved, though the emotion of the moment temporarily mucked up the facts. Bonnie had destroyed my creative work of imagination, and I had threatened the little sister I had agreed to protect.

Mom sat us both down and demanded an explanation, though damage all around us told the story. At three, Bonnie could not have anticipated a formal inquiry, so she just cried, and Mom gave her a hug with some kind of gentle admonition. I tried to explain how hard I had worked on my project only to have my brat sister kick it all down, and Mom gave me a hug too, expressing her sympathy.

Without recalling the language Mom used, I remember that she offered a novel solution. Bonnie would have to help me rebuild the scene. At first, I resisted—I didn't want anything to do with my sister at that point—but, eventually, I relented. Bonnie and I called a truce, and for the first time in my recollection, we played together. It seemed fair that our joint activity was to rebuild my special project because, after all, I was the injured party. All these years later, my lingering impression is that Bonnie had just wanted to spend time with her big brother who was so caught up in his own world that he couldn't recognize that simple fact.

There were other sibling dust-ups, of course, but none like this one. The age gap between us interfered with creating a bond, because our interests were so different. I could not have appreciated then how important my sister would become to me in later years.

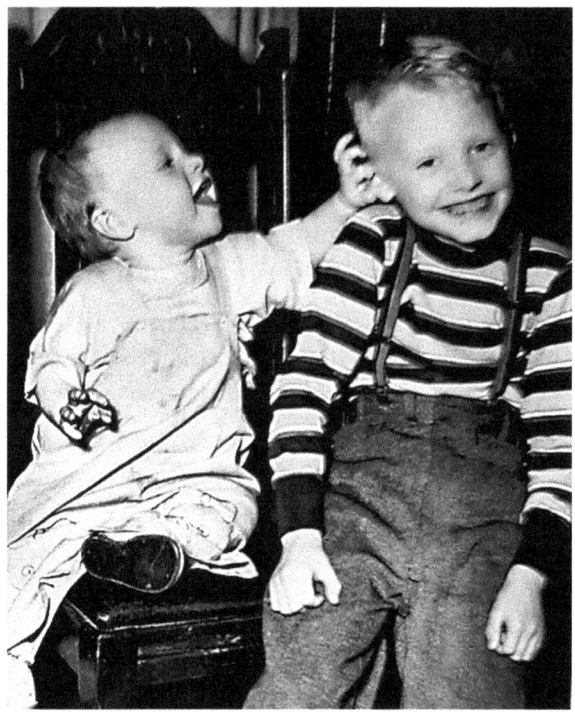

My sister and me during a truce. Clearly, I had learned to tolerate her.

During my junior and senior high years, my most memorable interactions with Bonnie were during family vacations, which were relatively rare. We usually didn't have the money to travel internationally, except for Canada, and neither Mom nor Dad were outdoor lovers, so vacations usually revolved around road trips, which gave Bonnie and me a lot of time together. Even then, Bonnie spent more time with Dad, and I spent more time with Mom.

I think I was about twelve and Bonnie six when we drove to a Canadian resort to go fishing on Lake of the Woods, which spills over from Canada into the Northwest Angle, that "chimney stack" on the northern Minnesota border. The lake is the largest freshwater lake in the US after the five Great Lakes and has 14,552 islands and 65,000 miles of shoreline. Get lost there and you may never find your way home.

My outdoor interests were at their peak at this time, so being in such a wilderness was exciting, though less thrilling to my other family members. Dad, though a Navy man, couldn't swim and was afraid of water. He had little interest in fishing and my mother even less so. Bonnie didn't care so long as there were kiddie activities. I must have lobbied hard for the Red Indian Lodge, as it was an odd choice for the Lindberg family.

On the second day at the resort, we bought Canadian fishing licenses and hired an Indian guide and a boat to go fishing. After a few minutes, I realized that as we motored away from the resort the many nearby islands started to close in and surround the boat so you couldn't tell where we had come from. Everything just merged into an ever-changing shoreline. I was already totally lost, but the guide said he knew where we were.

After an hour of motoring, we finally arrived at the guide's selected fishing hole where he expected we could catch walleyes. Mom, Dad and Bonnie wouldn't touch the live bait, so the guide set up their rods and reels. I did my own. To my recollection, we only caught a few walleyes, and only one was over two pounds. Bonnie caught most of them, to her delight. My competitive spirit, which normally would have left me feeling dispirited after catching only one puny northern pike, had evaporated into the clear air. I recall the pleasure I felt watching my little sister joyously howl each time she reeled in another fish, no matter how big.

The guide made a wonderful shore lunch of campfire-fried, fresh-caught fish and potatoes, which I think was Dad's favorite part of the excursion. I don't remember much more about the trip, but images of that day like colorful postcards are stamped into my memory. I hope I never lose them. I can still smell the fish frying in the skillet and hear my family laughing and chattering.

Another memorable family vacation to the South Dakota Badlands and Black Hills with Grandma and Grandpa Lindberg. Grandpa took the photo.

* * *

As my sister and I grew up, Mom's emotional volatility became more noticeable. While Mom and I were very close, I was constantly testing her to see how much I could get away with. Neither Bonnie nor Dad would do anything to provoke her because the consequences could be an unexpected outburst.

Mom and I, however, had frequent fights—verbal brawls that would grow in intensity, because neither of us liked to lose an argument. I learned from Mom how to fight dirty, how to push the opponent's emotional buttons to gain an advantage and how to use fake facts to support my arguments. Sometimes, these battles would grow heated with yelling and screaming. Often, the emotions released were real. But when we were done scratching and clawing, we would both sigh with relief and make up, hugging and kissing as if no tempers had been lost. I found these skirmishes oddly exhilarating and the final peacemaking cathartic. Neither Mom nor I ever held a grudge after sparring like this. We usually felt closer than ever.

Bonnie hated these fights and became the family peacemaker, adeptly helping her mother and brother calm down before things got out of hand. But sometimes she couldn't negotiate a settlement and the battle would begin. When this happened, she and Dad would leave the house, climb into the family Chevy or Dad's truck and drive around until they hoped the war would be over. When they came back, they often found Mom and me, the two lunatics, seated next to each other on the sofa, arms around each other, laughing and chatting happily.

I think music helped Bonnie endure her childhood. She had started piano lessons from Mom at age six, and two years later earned her way to professional lessons. By the sixth grade, she was accompanying the junior choir at church. Obviously, she was blessed with the Lindberg music gene. When she was fourteen, she made it to the state piano finals. We were all so excited for her. Unfortunately, the date of the finals conflicted with my first wedding, so she had to withdraw, put on a gown and stand up for my marriage partner. Afterward, Bonnie jokingly accused me of finally getting my revenge for kicking down my little men.

* * *

After I left home and Bonnie remained, things got harder for my sister as Mom's episodes of rage escalated, and I was not there to be the willing adversary. I have always been amazed that few people outside of our immediate family ever noticed Mom's struggles with these emotional riptides. She never endangered Dad or her children, never threatened any of us physically, and most of the time was kind and caring. When these jarring episodes occurred, usually with no warning, we barely took notice. It was just part of normal daily life for us. Just Mom's personality. Bonnie and Dad learned to tread lightly around her, though, for fear they might do or say something to set her off. Sometimes, I confess, I triggered her on purpose, usually because I wanted her attention or because I needed the intense feeling of cathartic release and closeness that always came after a sparring match.

Mom's episodes of anger and depression seemed to decline after Bonnie finally left and Mom, relieved of her commitment to stay home until the kids were raised, finally stepped into the world to claim her destiny and set in motion a series of family adventures.

After high school, Bonnie leaped onto the broader stage with incredible confidence. She landed a job with a fledgling ad agency, Carmichael Lynch, which would soon become a major force in national marketing. Surprisingly to me, a few years later, after Mom had launched an art gallery, Bonnie joined Mom and Dad in the new family business. Elayne Galleries grew into the largest and most influential gallery in Minnesota.

At first, my sister had some apprehension about Mom's ability to control her instability and coherently manage a growing business. Astonishingly, she witnessed firsthand a simple homemaker unexpectedly blossom and flourish with a set of new and unique skills. Bonnie and I would have a respectful on-again, off-again relationship for decades until fate and a series of adventures would reunite our hearts at a time when we greatly needed each other.

Neighborhood

Childhood amnesia has robbed me of all but a handful of early recollections, but after our family sold the Garfield duplex and moved into a new cracker-box house in St. Louis Park, my memories are numerous and have far greater fidelity. We were one house down from the main street, Minnetonka Boulevard, on Hampshire Ave. I started second grade at Lenox Elementary, which conveniently was kitty-corner from our new home. A big church that we never attended, the Evangelical Free Church of St. Louis Park, was directly across Hampshire Ave. from the school. Shari, a pretty second-grader at the school, became one of my first friends along with Randy Mueller, who would become my first business partner.

While our new house was being constructed, Mom and Dad would often drive me and my baby sister to the site to check the progress. I can remember my enthusiasm on one trip when the new house looked like a real home except for the absent lawn.

To save money, my parents had decided to do all the painting and decorating themselves. As we walked through the half-finished rooms, Mom and Dad chatted amiably about wallpaper patterns and paint colors. Next door, the foundation had just been dug for another house. The pit looked like a great place to play soldiers.

After moving in, I was immediately disappointed that I would still be sharing a bedroom with my sister, who was too young to have a complaint. My disappointment was soon assuaged, however, when I walked out one day to watch construction on the house next door.

The neighbors-to-be, a Jewish family named Orenstein, were there talking to the project manager. Standing next to them and looking very bored was a dazzlingly beautiful girl about two years older than me. I fell instantly in love. Her dark hair, tan skin and smoldering eyes (yes, I am embellishing slightly) captivated me, but I was too timid to approach.

Suddenly, the girl's father turned and motioned me over. "Do you live there?" he asked, gesturing toward my house.

I nodded.

"This is my daughter, Sheila," he said.

Sheila was even prettier than Alice, my first love in the old neighborhood. Sheila smiled and extended her hand, which I grasped. We shook hands like adults. Her touch sent sparks through my body. I hoped she wouldn't notice.

My memory ends there, but even today I wonder why a six-year-old boy would be so excited by an eight-year-old girl, but I was. So be it. Watching Sheila grow up was one of the great delights of living on Hampshire Avenue.

Two doors down from the Orenstein place was the Jones family. Well, part of the family, anyway. Jimmy was my age but taller and stouter. No mental giant, he was nevertheless a good-natured and loyal friend, eagerly joining every neighborhood club I started. Jimmy's father had either left or died. Jimmy was always vague about the details. His mother rarely showed herself, and I don't remember ever knowing her name. Whenever I would go to Jimmy's house, she would be asleep on the living room sofa or in a recliner. I learned later that she was addicted to cough medicine laced with codeine, which was available over the counter in those days.

Directly across the street from Jimmy lived Mr. and Mrs. Selness and a daughter who was several years older than her brother, Wayne. In the neighborhood, Wayne was my best friend. He was short and wiry, athletic, smart and always wore a baseball cap. When he was old enough, he made it onto the Little League baseball team as a shortstop.

When Wayne and I were about fourteen, his sister—who was beautiful, I thought—suddenly disappeared. I had always watched her leave for high school in the morning, so I noticed when she was no longer in the house. No one ever mentioned what had happened, so I casually asked Wayne, who gave me an embarrassed smile and said, "No one is supposed to know, but Dad sent her to live with relatives in California because she got pregnant."

These were the days when "living in sin" was condemned by society. Having a child out of wedlock was shocking evidence of fornication—if not a mortal sin, certainly one worthy of dishonoring and dividing a family.

I never saw Wayne's sister again. I hope she and her child thrived.

The Johnsons—Dee and her husband Hal—lived directly across the street from us. I lived in the neighborhood for a few years before I learned why police cars frequently showed up at the Johnsons but nowhere else. Hal had an irrepressible urge to expose his genitals to girls in public. Whenever a sexual crime occurred in the vicinity, Hal was one of the first offenders to be interviewed.

To me, Hal's rude behavior was irrational. He was on the cop list of sex offenders. He would never get away with doing such a thing. The irrationality became even more obvious one night when he exposed himself to a teenage girl who was babysitting next door to his own house.

Hal's wife, Dee, had few friends. The neighbors all knew about her husband's problem and couldn't understand why she stayed with him. The only neighbors who would speak to her were my parents, who remained kind even though they told Bonnie and me that they didn't understand the situation either—it just didn't seem fair that Dee should be punished for her husband's offenses.

Directly across the street from Lenox Elementary was my friend Judy Anderson, the tomboy, who lived with her mother and a revolving assortment of her mom's boyfriends. Looking back on my neighborhood, which I had always considered a safe and wholesome place to grow up, I realize it more closely resembled Peyton Place.

Peyton Place, a novel by Grace Metalious, was released in 1956 just before I turned thirteen. Instantly, the book was condemned by many for its salacious themes and blunt language. Predictably, as a hormone-charged teenager and devout reader of fiction, I managed to get a copy of it and surreptitiously read every word. For the 1950s, it was shocking indeed. And titillating. I couldn't believe it was legal.

The novel is the story of three women in a conservative, gossipy town who are forced to deal with their identities as women and sexual beings. While the book admirably attacks hypocrisy and social inequities, what caused a public outcry were graphic scenes of incest, abortion, adultery, lust, rape and murder—all of which made it an instant bestseller even as many readers clucked their tongues in feigned dismay. "Peyton Place" entered the American lexicon as a description of any small town, neighborhood or group that holds scandalous secrets—including, apparently, my beloved suburban neighborhood.

During the summer before I entered fifth grade, I wanted to be a journalist. The perfect place to start was in my neighborhood, so I delivered a note to the neighbors and persuaded them to pay me ten cents per copy for a weekly newspaper about neighborly happenings—anniversaries, visits from relatives, vacations, et cetera. There were no copy machines in those days, so I used my father's guilt of parental negligence to obtain his help.

Using typing skills he had learned as a Navy bursar, meaning he handled the money on board ship and made payments to the sailors, Dad typed my little newsletters. He made copies with carbon paper—thin sheets coated on one side with carbon that produced copies when inscribed by a typewriter. He could make about three legible copies at a time. I only published three editions of the local rag but had a great time gathering information and writing stories with no idea that I would eventually get a college degree in journalism.

* * *

As my view of the neighborhood was evolving, so was my body—unfortunately, not as unimpaired nature had intended. The problem was with my dentition, as the dentist called it. In my defective body, the roots of my baby teeth had all refused to dissolve as they were supposed to when permanent teeth pushed their way into my mouth. Having no vacancies to occupy, the adult teeth erupted alongside the baby teeth or in rows behind them. My mouth soon looked like someone had clutched a handful of random teeth and thrown them in.

I couldn't bear to look at my freakish self in a mirror. I had literally become a monster to look at. In school, I refused to smile, even for class pictures. I became more reclusive, refusing to talk for fear of exposing my ugly mess of teeth. Some kids laughed at me, others simply stared rudely. I felt like an outcast, and I'm certain my malformed mouth adversely affected my social development. But it also helped me understand the plight of others who had disfigurement issues like cleft palates and deformed limbs. I also learned to appreciate the indignities that Pat, the family's transgender friend, must have endured after becoming a woman.

Mom and Dad sought a remedy, but until all my permanent teeth had come in, the dentist would not start braces to straighten my teeth. Unfortunately, the last of my adult teeth were slow to appear, and so we waited… and waited. Finally, I declared that I would wait no longer, and Mom found a dentist to apply my first set of stainless-steel braces. I remember Dr. Quamme's expression when he first looked at the tangle of teeth in my mouth. Obviously, he had not been trained to hide his panic from patients. Since I was the first patient he had put braces on, he learned on the job.

For five years, I lived with a mouth full of misaligned teeth and metal bands with sharp wires sticking into my cheeks and tongue. Twice a week, I took my chrome plated mouth to Dr. Quamme for an "adjustment," meaning he tightened individual wires that gradually twisted each tooth in the desired direction. Between visits, my teeth and gums ached from the manipulation, which also made biting and chewing painful. The almost unnoticeable progression of results was discouraging.

Five years from the start of this torture, I insisted on having the braces removed. My teeth were not perfect, but they were straight enough for me. My tongue was surprised at the exotic feel of smooth teeth. It took a long time, though, to regain my dignity and self-esteem, which had been damaged by my grotesque appearance. To this day, I still instinctively smile with my lips closed and turn away when cameras are clicking.

* * *

Around the time I entered junior high, the family made a major decision. To be fair, Dad made the decision, then persuaded Mom to agree before they announced it to Bonnie and me.

My parents had become "born again" Christians, and from now on, they told us, we would all be going to the Evangelical Free Church across the street, which was the same denomination as the church Dad's family members all belonged to in Minneapolis. I never understood the motivation for my parents' decision, but I'm certain that Grandma and Grandpa Lindberg and Dad's sisters were delighted to know Mom and Dad were no longer bound for hell. Our evangelical sect interpreted the Bible literally and expected members to abide by strict rules of conduct common in the 1950s such as:

> No dancing (which promoted promiscuity). This would be a sacrifice for Mom and Dad, who both loved ballroom dancing.
>
> No playing or listening to rock 'n roll music. This also promoted promiscuity.
>
> No drinking or smoking. This meant Dad had to throw away all his magic tricks that involved cigarettes, which could promote tobacco use, and unstock his seldom-used basement wet bar.
>
> No swearing. "Goddamn" would be replaced with "gol darn," and "hell" would be replaced with "h-e-double toothpicks," unless one was reading from the Scriptures. "Shit" was forbidden and "crap" was discouraged, so everybody had to find a workaround for those useful words.

No going to movies. Theaters were dens of iniquity. We could not even go to Christian movies released by the Billy Graham Evangelistic Association if they were shown in movie houses, as most were.

No petting, necking or sexual activity outside of marriage. Sex was not for personal pleasure but for procreation. (I always wondered what this meant for elderly couples.)

Every Sunday, starting with Dad's proclamation, we went to church as a family. I was enrolled by my parents in FCYF, the Free Church Youth Fellowship. Since this was a lot like the neighborhood clubs I had started, I quickly became the president of the youth group. Dad was soon appointed as a church Deacon, which governed matters related to spiritual issues and member conduct, and Mom became a Deaconess, which mainly supervised social activities and had no authority.

I became educated in the wages of sin—hellfire and eternal damnation—which caused me to start having nightmares again. I was taught that only the blood of Jesus could take away my sins, which I had inherited from my father and mother and all their ancestors. I didn't understand how I could be blamed for my forebearers' wrongdoing, and no one could explain how that was fair, but I wasn't an authority like the church fathers who knew better than me. I learned that unless I personally asked Jesus to come into my heart and save me, I would die and burn forever in hell. But I had to be sincere when I did this or it wouldn't work, and one day I would wake up on a bed of hot coals.

Periodically, "revivalists" would travel through and set up tent meetings. All the local people would be invited to attend. I came to think of these revival meetings as horror shows intended to scare unbelievers into becoming believers with tales of unimaginable pain and suffering for all unrepentant individuals. Every show—that is, *meeting*—ended with an altar call, at which time the truly frightened attendees would march toward the preacher's altar to become "born again" as a redeemed Christian.

Because I was never entirely sure that I had been sincere in my earlier requests for salvation, I always answered the altar call just to make sure I was guaranteed a mansion in heaven as had been promised. My memory suggests I was "saved" over thirty times, thus my ticket to paradise was guaranteed and could never be revoked.

Some of the fun we had as young Christians involved participating on Bible Quiz Teams, an inter-church competition that pitted teams of youth against each other. Four of us would study specific books of the Bible and take a seat on a chair wired with a pressure sensor that would sound an alarm when we stood up. A moderator would start to ask a question, and the first contestant to figure out the completed question and know the answer would rise, the alarm would sound, and the contestant would finish the question, give the answer and quote from memory the Bible verse on which the answer was based. Usually, the moderator would only get out a few words of the question before someone would jump up.

I can remember memorizing the book of James in the New Testament and winning every question in a competition. My parents were so proud of me they would ask me to perform at family gatherings. Guests would name a book of the Bible with a chapter and verse citation to see if I could quote it, which I usually could, at least for the four Gospels and the books of Romans and James. Except for these events, I never had an opportunity to use this skill.

Many of my school friends were also members of the church. We were all encouraged to "witness" to unbelievers our personal belief in Jesus. One way to do this, we were told, was to carry a Bible to all school activities. When friends would ask what it was, we were instructed to say, "It's a Bible." When they asked why we carried it, we could then give our "testimony" about being saved by the blood of Jesus as described in the Bible. Because we were well-read Christians, we could turn the onionskin pages and show them the Bible's instructions, which could save their souls.

Mostly, though, when we carried our Bibles to school, we were ridiculed and considered weirdos or cultists. For a kid who self-consciously wore braces to school and already felt like a freak, this practice almost destroyed my self-esteem. I just wanted to feel like a normal kid, to be accepted by others, not labelled as an outsider. Still, for a year, I carried a Bible to school and got laughed at. I gave it a fair shot, and when no one ever asked me what I was carrying or why I carried it, I finally started leaving the Bible at home and started feeling normal again.

* * *

About this time, my parents, who were now doing well financially, decided to sell the tiny Hampshire house, buy a Minneapolis duplex as rental property, and live on the main floor while building a larger home in St. Louis Park. I helped Dad decorate both floors of the duplex, and we had fun working together on the family project.

Coincidentally, at sixteen, I also started my first of fifteen start-up companies with my grade school friend and church buddy, Randy Mueller. Our new company offered hand-painted paper banners for grocery and convenience stores to promote sale prices on various food items. The business took off and the income allowed me to buy a used 1952 Buick Roadmaster for three hundred dollars so I could drive to high school in St. Louis Park.

This is what my Buick Roadmaster looked like without the rust.

The Buick looked and rode like a Sherman Tank. It may have been indestructible—at least I drove as if it were. On my way home from school one day, I was driving on a residential side street and approaching an intersection when I saw a Talmud Torah school bus approach the same crossing. I was sure I could beat it, but my old Buick couldn't rev up fast enough and my car T-boned the bus. WHAM! (a word I had learned from my comics). Fortunately, none of the little Jewish kids on their way to Hebrew School were injured. Amazingly, my sturdy Buick drove away but the bus had to be towed. I became a hero to all the cheering kids on the bus for engineering an afternoon off.

As usual, Mom wanted Randy and I to have the sign business nearby, so she offered the attic of the duplex as a free workspace. Dad helped Randy and me build long tables for the big rolls of sign paper. Because of the upper-floor location of our business, we named it Penthouse Sign Company. Randy continued to operate it as Sign Center until his death in 2023.

As Randy and I entered our senior year, we decided to use our improved marketing capabilities in a unique way. Elections for senior class officers were coming up, so I suggested it might be fun to elect a fake candidate. Randy thought it was a great idea and suggested the name Sue Johnson. In Minnesota, who doesn't know a Sue Johnson?

We enrolled our friends in this senior prank, and Randy and I started creating marketing slogans and SUE JOHNSON FOR PRESIDENT signs. Soon, we had a small army of students putting up our materials all over the school. The administrators did not appreciate the joke, especially since SUE JOHNSON signs were appearing everywhere, even in the lavatories. A few of us sneaked into the office of our church and "borrowed" the mimeograph machine during prayer meetings to duplicate flyers. This early prototype of a copy machine used an alcohol-based ink to render printed copies. At times, we got high from the fumes, which made the task more pleasurable.

Somehow, the principal found out I was involved in the fraud and called me into the office. We negotiated a truce the day before the election. Randy helped convince our friends to take down the signs, but it was too late. Sue Johnson won by a landslide but was declared ineligible to take office because, well… she did not exist. Her legend, however, lives on.

* * *

I was increasingly fed up with school. I considered it a waste of time and had no interest in getting good grades. Most of the classes were terminally boring. Teachers moved us through the material at the speed of the slowest student in the class. Homework assignments were clearly designed to eliminate after-school free time, not teach us anything useful. The tests and pop quizzes were a joke—after a quiz or two, overworked teachers revealed their quiz-writing patterns and most of them simply imposed on us T/F or multiple-choice questions because they were easy to check. They understood that fill-in-the-blank and essay answers required a lot more time to grade.

Unless I was abnormally interested in a topic, I almost never did any serious studying or text prep. My report cards were filled with Bs and Cs—enough to get me into a local college. I had a lot of interests, but few of them lived in classrooms. I did enjoy assigned essays, though, which most of my classmates dreaded. In an essay, I could practice my vocabulary building—one of my interests—and sneak into the text my often-contrary opinions about the standardized content we were being fed.

My least favorite subject was social studies until I was assigned to a class taught by Mr. Ulrich. Most of the kids hated Ulrich because his unique instructional methodology forced them to think, which was a foreign concept to many. After delivering a lecture about some topic, he would assign independent reading, which a student couldn't ignore because the final stage was to write his or her "conclusions" about the topic.

It took me several weeks to figure out what Ulrich was asking for, but then it clicked. He wanted us to think hard about the topic, make up our own minds about the points covered, the decisions others had made and the quality of the arguments presented in the readings. Suddenly, social studies became interesting, and I was permitted—indeed, invited—to have personal opinions instead of just regurgitate what scholars had concluded. The textbook pablum had suddenly become crème brulée. Unfortunately, most of my classmates surrendered to failing grades because they never solved the mystery of what Ulrich was asking for. I, however, never forgot his innovation and put it to good use much later when I created a new methodology for online adult learning called HyperLearning.

    The Ulrichs went to my church. After a Sunday service that Mr. Ulrich did not attend, I drummed up the courage to approach his wife and express how much I liked her husband's methods and how he had ignited my interest in social studies. Her eyes moistened. She took my hand and led me away from the departing congregation to say she would convey her message to her husband. I learned in confidence that Mr. Ulrich was extremely shy and needed encouragement every morning to go to school and face the students he knew disliked him. But he was dedicated, she said, to helping us all develop our critical thinking skills because that was more important than the rote learning of content that plagued education.

Wife 1: Georgia

During my two years at St. Louis Park High School, I dated several girls from the church. One was Shari, an attractive and sassy girl I had known since second grade. I loved her wit and fearlessness in expressing opinions about everything. Despite a rough upbringing, standing up to her crusty, hard-drinking father had made her an independent spirit. And she was a good kisser.

I briefly dated the Keskitalo twins and a couple other girls from church, but the other one who truly fascinated me was Georgia. She was beautiful, and her mother was a former model who had turned to organizing fashion shows. From the beginning, Georgia and I had chemistry—actually, we had chemistry class together, which oddly had given me my first D+ grade. I may have been distracted.

Georgia's mother was divorced and remarried to a gas station operator who was eleven years her junior, making him only seven years older than Georgia. This unbalanced family constellation had led to certain awkward situations in which stepdad expressed more than stepfatherly interest in his stepdaughter. I worried, of course, that Georgia's interest in me might have been influenced by her need for a boyfriend to discourage these unwelcome advances.

When I graduated and attended Augsburg College in Minneapolis, a liberal Lutheran school, Georgia had a year of high school left. I wasn't a Lutheran, but the school was the first to accept my application, so I signed up with the agreement that my parents would pay the first year's tuition. I lived free at home and commuted to classes. Georgia and I continued to date, and after graduation she took training to become an electroencephalogram (EEG) technician.

Augsburg was too small for my tastes and the classes too much like high school remediation, so I transferred to the University for my sophomore year. With nearly 50,000 students at that time, the campus was as large as a medium-sized city. I chose to major in journalism because it was a practical choice with a known career path, and I was now paying my own way. My first class in news reporting required me to be able to type thirty-five words per minute and George Hagge, the instructor, threatened all quarter to test our skills, but he never did. Maybe learning that influential people often bluff was an important lesson for a fledgling journalist.

Since I had always relied on my father for typing, I learned to skip the outlining step favored by Mr. Hagge and combine the organizing and writing steps in my head so that my slow keyboarding would not penalize me during timed writing exercises. Before long, I decided that news reporting was not for me—it was too limited by facts and reality—so I switched to the school's advertising curriculum with a specialty in photojournalism.

The School of Journalism became my home away from home. Before long, I became art director of the *Gopher Yearbook*, was writing articles for the campus newspaper, *The Minnesota Daily*, and designing pages and covers alongside Garrison Keillor, editor of the University's literary magazine, *The Ivory Tower*. Everybody I hung out with was interested in communications!

The statute of limitations having now expired, I can now admit I made a major mistake that doomed my marriage to my first wife. Georgia and I were married on March 21, 1964, at the beginning of a week off between winter and spring quarters of my junior year. To save money, we moved into an apartment my parents had created in their basement.

This is the only picture I have of my wedding to Georgia, taken by a relative. A photographer friend from the Yearbook staff had taken our wedding pictures, but the photo lab lost the film, perhaps a sign of things to come.

Georgia and I were anticipating a romantic, weeklong honeymoon at a resort in northern Minnesota. Days before the wedding, however, I had been unexpectedly invited to a one-week internship at a local trade magazine to conduct interviews and write stories. The editor was trolling for future employees.

Anxious for validation that I was employable, I considered this to be an opportunity. Although *Hardware Trade Magazine* was not my dream employer, I was sure the internship would be invaluable work experience to put on my resumé. Somehow, I persuaded my disappointed wife-to-be that the work experience would be good for our collective future. I spent our honeymoon visiting hardware stores and writing about new merchandising techniques to sell power tools instead of walking trails, sipping wine and making love to my new wife.

Shortly before spring quarter ended, I was invited to a summer internship. John Deere, the country's dominant farm implement manufacturer, wanted me to work at its headquarters in Moline,

Illinois. Interestingly, though their survey of potential interns had come through the School of Journalism, I was invited to work in the art department. After dismissing my confusion, I accepted. Georgia and I rented an old, bat-infested apartment in Rock Island, Illinois, and I commuted every day to the company's new headquarters building, a dramatic, rusty-steel monument designed by famed architect Eero Saarinen in a pastoral, 1,600-acre wooded setting. I was enchanted. This felt like the big time.

Several weeks into my internship, which I loved, I was asked to accompany a film crew from Reid H. Ray Film Industries that was in Moline to produce a promotional film. The filmmakers were from my home base, the Twin Cities. At that time, I had no idea there was a motion picture industry in Minnesota.

The next day, I drove to a Moline farm where the crew was setting up to film a new manure spreader. I helped pull plastic sheeting over the cinematographer who was lying on the ground to get a POV shot of the liquified manure spitting out of the big, green machine. It was hot, humid, smelly work, definitely not glamorous, but I was hooked. Making Hollywood films seemed too impossible for a Minnesota kid to envision, but making industrial films, maybe even commercials, suddenly seemed within reach. When I previewed the final work before ending my internship, I saw how all my interests—writing, photography, art and even music—all came together in this one medium. At last, I had a unifying vision for my random skills.

Meanwhile, at our Rock Island home, Georgia was chasing bats out of the house with a tennis racket and researching methods for cooling the bedroom without air conditioning during the insufferable summer hot spells. I was so engaged with my new experiences that I never thought about her boring, uncomfortable summer away from family and friends. Following her lost honeymoon and long, hot summer, if she was still thinking her marriage might still work out, she must have been even more sorely disappointed by the next few months.

* * *

As my senior year began, I got a phone call from a friend, David L.C. Anderson, who was a singer and a Lutheran evangelist. I kidded him that the "L.C." in his name stood for "Lutheran Church." I had backed him on guitar in some concerts and recordings, and once I accepted the idea of a Lutheran also being an evangelist—such an unlikely combo!—we occasionally hung out together talking about interesting future projects.

On the call, David told me that he had begun visiting inmates at the state prison in Stillwater to help willing prisoners sort out their spiritual issues and possibly become Christians. One of them was unusually receptive, he thought—a prisoner named Ronald Steeves. David wanted me to attend his next meeting with this inmate, who he admitted was a bit creepy to be with alone.

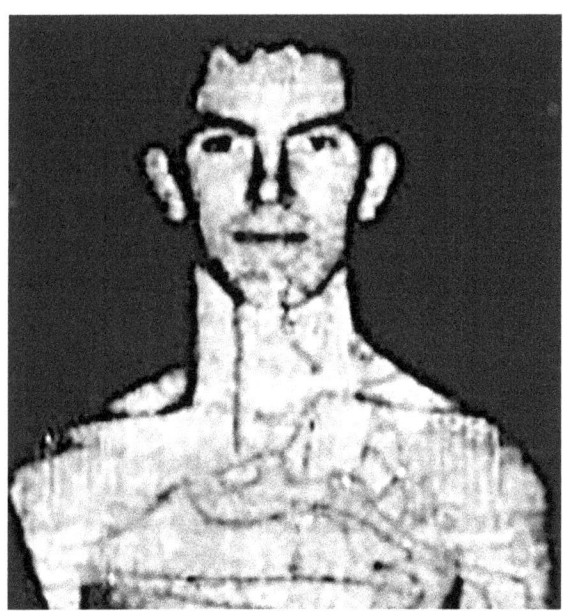

Ronald Steeves after his arrest.

At nineteen, while on parole, Steeves had confessed to brutally murdering Mary Bell, the pretty, fifteen-year-old sister of his girlfriend, and abandoning the body in a snowy woods in Minnehaha Park on February 27, 1963. He had lured Mary away from a babysitting job to discuss his fears that she would tell her parents he was still dating

Mary's older sister, Pat, who was sixteen. Steeves had been banned from dating Pat by her parents because they were Protestant and Steeves was Catholic, and because the couple had fled months earlier to South Dakota where they had unsuccessfully tried to get married.

As Steeves and Mary Bell were walking down a path in the park, Steeves grew agitated and impulsively stabbed Mary in the chest. Realizing what he had done, he tried to help her to his car. About halfway back, though, he decided that he had just perpetrated a violent crime and had better eliminate the only witness, so he killed Mary. It was a grotesque and brutal murder. He stabbed the girl over fifty times, slashed her throat and beat her with a tire iron just to make sure she was dead. A month after his conviction in May of 1963, he unsuccessfully attempted suicide in his prison cell by slashing his wrists with a razor.

I was nervous before meeting Ron for the first time but found him eerily calm and candid. He freely discussed his crime but showed no remorse. David, in full evangelist mode, tried to convince Steeves to acknowledge his sins, repent and ask God for forgiveness. I thought that Steeves, who seldom had a visitor, just wanted someone to relieve the boredom of serving a life sentence.

I accompanied David on a half-dozen visits before deciding to stop. On my last meeting with Steeves, however, he told us something that would stay with me for the rest of my life. He told us that he had hidden some important objects and documents that would help us understand his case better, then gave us directions for how to find the buried treasure in a metal box beneath a small railroad shanty along the tracks at a particular spot we could recognize from his clues. Perhaps he was putting us on, but I don't think so. He was dead serious when giving us directions. David and I debated what the hidden materials might be—evidence of other murders, a letter to his girlfriend Pat, *what*?

Several times we drove out to the section of tracks described by Steeves, but the shanty had obviously been moved and updated. We searched diligently but never found the metal box Steeves said he had hidden. That box still haunts me.

At that time, a person serving a life sentence in Minnesota was eligible for parole after twenty years of good behavior. Steeves was paroled on schedule but arrested a few years later for rape. He tried calling me when he was out of jail and left a message requesting help, claiming he had become a Christian and was not guilty of the most recent crime. I didn't return his call, but suddenly that mysterious box resurfaced in my mind, and I still can't get rid of the prospect of it.

Exactly fifty-seven years after Mary Bell had been murdered, a small wooden cross memorializing the teenager's death mysteriously appeared at the precise location where her body had been found. No one knows who put it there—another unsolved mystery.

This small wooden cross appeared where Mary Bell's mutilated body was found exactly fifty-seven years after her murder.

* * *

With everything going on in my life, I concluded that my marriage had been a mistake. Georgia and I were poorly matched and had few common interests. I was career-driven, and she wanted a settled home life. I craved exciting, new experiences, and she resisted them. I take responsibility for making almost no attempt to reconcile these differences. Instead, as I reengaged in my studies and work on campus publications, we drifted apart. My friends at the University shared my interests and were eager to follow my lead in trying new things in design and writing. I couldn't get enough of the attention and acclaim I was earning.

I never physically cheated on Georgia, but I remember two women during that time who captured my heart. The first was Judy, a photographer, who showed up in class one day clad in assassin garb—a black sweater, form-fit black pants and black boots. She was slender and beautiful with shiny, black hair and a mysterious, thread-thin scar on her cheek that I found absolutely tantalizing. We sometimes worked in the darkroom together, the red light bathing her presence with even more mystery. Her photographic work was stunning—intimidating, really. She used light and composition almost supernaturally to inject emotion into her pictures. For this, I hated her. About everything else, though, I was infatuated.

I never worked up the courage to explore a relationship. After all, I was a married man. Unless she reads this memoir, she will never know of my attraction to her. Eventually, she became a famous and well-respected photographer with several beautiful books of her published photographs.

A hazy recollection of Judy in the 1960s.

The second woman was a staffer on the yearbook. Cathy and I had worked alongside each other on the 1964-1965 edition and had slowly developed a relationship of respect that had grown into unrequited desire—so much, in fact, that I felt guilty about the lack of attention I was paying to my wife. To assuage my guilt, I asked my current best friend, Mike, an orphan who had grown up next door to my Grandma Averill, to spend some time with Georgia. I hoped his attention would make my frequent absences and inattention more tolerable for her.

Even as Georgia and I continued to live in my parents' basement, the distance between us grew wider and louder. Our frequent arguments disturbed my parents upstairs and eventually Mom asked me to move out. Georgia stayed. I thought this new geometry was odd, but at least the stress of an unfulfilling relationship evaporated.

Georgia ultimately decided that Mike was a far better catch than me and asked for a divorce, saving me from the same decision, which would make me the bad guy. Separated from the complication of marriage, even though I was not yet divorced, I moved into various apartments near the University and developed a deeper relationship with Cathy. We had the common bond of being writers and working on the yearbook.

After graduation, I couldn't bear leaving school and my chums behind, so I enrolled in graduate school. That way I could be named editor of the 1965-1966 Gopher Yearbook, which would prove to be the last edition. I spent most of my time with Cathy—more nights at her apartment than at my own place. She was intellectual, a world traveler, a sorority girl and a superb writer. She had spent time in Greece working for the Student Project for Amity among Nations (SPAN) doing independent research and immersing herself in Greek culture. Her stories of sleeping on the sparkling white beaches of Greek islands captivated me, provoking dreams of traveling with her to exotic destinations and sex on sandy beaches with the sounds of surf in our ears.

* * *

My pending divorce from Georgia, however, had consequences that would soon reshape my life in unforeseen ways. The Vietnam War was heating up, and while my marriage had earned me a marital deferment from military service, the divorce threw me back into the draft pool. The army's enormous appetite for cannon fodder put the US Army on my newly vulnerable scent trail. Fiercely against the war and afraid of being blown up in a steamy jungle, I learned to play the draft games, using numerous delay tactics. But I was sensing that the army was closing in. Desperation often provokes desperate measures, even unethical ones, and I succumbed to the pressure. In a deviously creative scheme, I planned a surefire ploy to evade the evil draft.

I would enter the seminary.

At the time, ordained ministers and seminary students also had a draft deferment, so I set about finding a protestant seminary that had a new semester starting soon. Bethel Seminary, a Baptist school, was starting a new semester within several weeks, so I applied. The answer came quickly. Somehow, the school had learned that I was in the process of divorcing my wife. For Baptists, divorce is unacceptable, particularly for clergy who must model the highest grade of behavior for their congregants. The notice of disqualification came as a shock. It was too late to find another seminary, so I took the only path available to me. I lied.

The fraud I perpetrated had several moving pieces and required another willing participant. I knew just the person—one of my yearbook staffers, a rebel at heart and a woman always willing to join an adventure. Her name was Heidi Carla Gretl von Heideman Hanover, or so she claimed. "Heidi" grinned broadly when I outlined my plan and became a willing co-conspirator.

Heidi was eccentric in many ways. She lived in a house near Seven Corners, a slummy neighborhood next to the University. The house was owned by her friend Keith, a University professor and slum lord. The exact nature of their relationship was never clear to me, but she lived in the house rent free and loved to throw parties. Often, she would put the word out and that evening students would pour to her house and party, including Bob Zimmerman, later known as Bob Dylan. I remember a couple of parties where "Bob" and I played guitars, and he sang original songs in a back bedroom of Heidi's rent-free digs.

My get-out-of-the-draft scheme was simple. I had learned that the dean of the seminary had a brother who was the lead pastor at a St. Paul Baptist Church. Pretending to be my wife, Heidi would accompany me to a meeting with the pastor and after receiving his wise counsel we would fake-reconcile in front of him, pledging to call off the divorce. The pastor would tell his brother, the dean, that I was now eligible to enter the seminary and all would be good again.

It worked. Heidi could have earned an Academy Award for her performance as Mrs. Georgia Lindberg. I entered the seminary on schedule and surprisingly enjoyed the experience from the first day, particularly my six-credit course on comparative religions. Everyone was kind and loving, the campus was beautiful and the Minnesota winter had not yet arrived. Briefly, I entertained thoughts about carrying on my studies and becoming ordained as a minister in the Baptist Convention. Had I found my true calling?

I felt some guilt about my actions, of course. I had lied to a preacher and deceived a seminary to gain admittance while in an intimate, unmarried relationship with Cathy. Yet, when feeling these uneasy spasms of remorse, I diverted my thinking to the purpose of all my machinations—staying out of the Vietnam War. I would never become a minister—certainly I did not deserve to be one—but I would stay alive and not be a party to an even more evil military endeavor.

For six weeks, I enjoyed my life as a ministerial candidate. But then, the thin-skinned balloon suddenly burst. Someone betrayed my deceit to the dean, and I was kicked back into the draft pool. Humiliated and again at risk, I returned to delay tactics to avoid the draft. If they got me, I knew I only had myself to blame.

During this time, I had also become convinced that Cathy was a more talented writer than me. I envied her craft. I knew how hard it would be to continue a relationship with someone I would eventually view as competition. Cathy shared my sense of adventure, but this too could become a problem. I recalled how many times I had let my impulses guide me into bad decisions because no one would simply say, "No, that's stupid. Settle down." I longed for a fellow adventurer, but I needed a counterbalance even more, or so I thought. Someone who could tame my more impulsive and devious nature.

When my cousin, Verna Lee, asked if I wanted to come for dinner and meet one of her woman friends, I was curious and said yes. I was responding to the kind of impulse that a responsible, rational person would have restrained, which would ultimately draw me into countless implausible adventures.

Wife 2: Karen

When I arrived, Karen Walterson was seated on the sofa of Verna Lee's apartment chatting with my cousin's husband, Gordon. I have no idea why I chose to wear a black leather jacket to that dinner—maybe I wanted to scare off my cousin's woman friend, or perhaps I wanted to test her spirit of adventure—but its effect was immediate. Karen was startled, but quickly covered it up, which I interpreted as a sign of her compassion. She didn't want to hurt my feelings.

We ate spaghetti and meatballs. Unlike past spaghetti misadventures, I didn't spill on my shirt. When Gordon pulled out a guitar and suggested I play something, I did.

Karen was a pretty and proper woman, and I liked her. She had just taken a job as office manager for the Upper Midwest Regional Educational Laboratory (UMREL). I still don't know what that organization did, but I joked that Karen must be the "girl from UMREL," a dumb reference to a current TV series about spies, *The Man from U.N.C.L.E.*, starring Robert Vaughn and David McCallum.

I think it was Karen's laugh that did it, the sound and sincerity of it. At that moment, my brain shifted into a higher gear, and I moved closer to her. I don't remember what Verna Lee and Gordon did after that, but I couldn't stop talking to Karen, an obviously willing fellow-adventurer who never smirked or rolled her eyes when I told her of my plans to start an ad agency or be a moviemaker. Instinctively, I knew that Karen was more practical than me or Cathy. I made a snap judgement that of all the women I had met, she could most likely keep me tethered to reality while letting me have my impractical dreams. I was too immature, of course, to consider how I might meet her needs.

Several months later, I took my first real job at Graco, a manufacturer of pumps and spray-painting equipment. My low-paying job as a sales promotion specialist was the definition of boring. I wrote and edited the firm's internal newsletter, covering such fascinating topics as new product introductions, employee achievements and anniversaries, and customer testimonials. My dream of a more stimulating job that would use my unique talents was fading, but my draft evasion tactics were working. I thought I could make it to age twenty-six, at which time I would be ineligible.

After painfully ending my relationship with Cathy, I was now happily spending most of my non-working time with Karen. On December 9, 1967, we were married at Hope Presbyterian in Richfield, Minnesota. I wore a tux, not a leather jacket. The marriage got off to a better start than my first one, perhaps because I didn't work during our honeymoon. But even a happy marriage and Karen's quirky Siamese cat couldn't cure my despondency over an unchallenging, dead-end job.

In this photo of my wedding to Karen are, from the left: my cousin Verna Lee; my sister Bonnie; Karen's sister Linda; my past sign painting partner Randy; Graco workmate and Somerset Limited co-founder Lowell Nielsen; and Verna Lee's husband Gordon.

I told Karen that I had to find other work even if it meant some financial uncertainty for a while, and she nodded supportively. She had no idea where that nod would lead us, but she never wavered in her support, even when things got scary.

One evening, after reflecting on my brief filmmaking adventure for John Deere and the lackluster film produced by Reid Ray, I decided that I could make a better movie than that. All I needed was a creative and technical staff, some start-up capital, a place to office, a bunch of film equipment and some paying customers. In other words, I would have to start a production company. How hard could that be? After all, I had started a sign painting company at sixteen.

Karen, bless her, never attempted to discourage me. In fact, her highly organized mind contributed mightily to our home-made business plan, which we both knew had less than a 1 percent chance of succeeding. I briefly wondered if Karen might not have been the practical woman I had thought she was, but over time I found she just wanted some excitement in her regimented life too. Plus, she had a well-paying job and could support us if everything fell apart.

I had started lots of neighborhood clubs, so I set out to assemble a team of friends who were talented in relevant areas but also crazy enough to adopt my crazy dream as their own. Greg Cummins, a photographer from my yearbook team, agreed to join as cinematographer and editor. Others I recruited from Graco workmates and their acquaintances. Five of us formed a filmmaking outfit called Somerset Limited, named after Somerset, Wisconsin, where three of our founders lived. I became president and CEO—nobody else wanted that responsibility. Everyone agreed to come on board once I raised enough money.

Ah, yes… the money.

I was realistic enough to know I couldn't raise the funding to start a movie company by myself. I knew a few people of means, but they were Board of Directors candidates, not qualified investors. Finally, I found a small investment company that liked our business plan and was intrigued with the idea of a movie production company in Minnesota. The principals of that firm agreed to approach their investors on our behalf, but only if we agreed to take the new venture public, which was a huge escalation in complexity and risk.

Naturally, I said yes. It was about time I started a public corporation. After all, at twenty-four, I was approaching middle age. The investment company taught me how to prepare a pitch for wealthy investors, how to answer their likely questions, and how to structure and write an offering memorandum. When we were ready and the offering was approved by the state, they lined up a series of investor presentations. All the potential investors were qualified, which means they had at least a million dollars in liquid assets to risk in speculative investments. As CEO and president, I repeated the same story and answered the same basic questions countless times.

To be honest, this was much harder than asking my St. Louis Park neighbors to subscribe to my local newsletter for a dime per week. But I found that my sincerity and honesty often cut through the formality that investors were expecting in these kinds of pitches. The money folks who invested at least $50,000—by law, the minimum—were usually the ones I was able to bond with.

We successfully closed the deal and became the first publicly held movie company in Minnesota. With the proceeds, we bought equipment and rented an old drugstore in St. Paul, converting it into a studio with surrounding office space. I convinced our new landlord, Tony D'Antonio, to join us as head of sales, because the final thing we needed was paying clients and Tony knew a lot of possible targets.

To retain as much control of the business as possible, I chose to take zero cash from the public offering and a very low initial salary, electing instead to take more shares of stock. This decision would prove to be very costly in the future.

Frankly, none of us knew what we were doing, and a lot of people had now invested in our ability to make a profit. What had I impulsively gotten us all into?

Karen came to work for us as office manager, the same position she had left at UMREL. I worried that if the company failed, both Karen and I would now be out of work, but she wanted to help us succeed.

Our first-ever paying contract was a fundraising film for Camp Courage, an outdoor facility for disabled kids run by the Minnesota Society for Crippled Children and Adults (MnSCCA.) I hired my former girlfriend, Cathy, to write the script. This sounds weird, I know, but neither she nor my new wife, Karen, knew that their relationships with me had overlapped, so it worked out. The successful production was well received by our client and their funders.

* * *

In the '60s, movie theaters often booked cartoons or "short subjects"—fifteen-minute entertainment films or documentaries—to accompany the main feature. I decided that producing these short films could be a lucrative business for Somerset. We could use some of our investment proceeds to finance these projects.

The first production was a short film showing snowmobiles—most brands like Polaris and Arctic Cat were built in Minnesota—doing exotic stunts and making choreographed designs in the snow. Due to this project, we gained some contracts to produce promotional films for the snowmobile companies.

The second short film became the first of my myriad great adventures. The idea for it came from a young man who simply walked in our front door with a wild story. Terry Mitchell was a few years older than me and had made a fortune by designing and then manufacturing a plush toy called a "Slurp." This adorable, foot-tall ball of fur had webbed feet and protruding, bloodshot eyes, and it came in an assortment of colors. For reasons known only to the gods of stuffed animals, this Borg fabric creature, patent no. D-202626, became a national craze.

Terry had formed a company called Spectacular Products in Cannon Falls, Minnesota, to manufacture the product. Originally, six employees hand-stitched the creatures for shipment. When demand suddenly exceeded supply, Terry asked his father to help build up the business. Terry's dad went a step further. Seeing the enormous profit potential for the Slurp, he had his son committed to a mental institution for schizophrenia and then, as named guardian for Terry's assets, took over the business.

Meet the Slurp.

Terry explained to me that he did indeed suffer from mild schizophrenia but considered it a gift responsible for his outlandish creativity. He had since been released from his "captivity," as he called it, but had lost everything to his father, whom he had not spoken to in over a year. The reason he had sought me out was to present a concept he thought could be a successful theatrical short subject.

Frankly, I have always been fascinated by eccentricities and people who thought differently than I did. I liked witnessing how different minds could see things I could not see because of my own limiting paradigms. I found that having my mind changed by an unexpected revelation was a pleasurable thing, an adventure, which often opened up new mental pathways to explore.

Terry's movie concept required a very open mind, as it offered an entirely new theory about the Loch Ness Monster. Certainly, this topic sparkled with marketing opportunities, so I sat back as Terry unzipped a portfolio and removed some visual materials to support his pitch.

"Most people think that 'Nessie' must be a kind of sea monster with an elongated, serpentine body," Terry said. "This notion has been put into the heads of people because of a few famous but fuzzy photos showing a creature with humps swimming in the Loch. But I am here to explain that these humps are an illusion."

Terry showed several "Nessie" photos showing the distinctive serpentine humps.

"Look carefully," he told me. "If these humps were those of a serpentine creature, it would have to be swimming from left to right or from right to left. But where is the trailing wake? When an object or a creature swims, it always leaves a wake behind."

I studied the photos. "I can't see a wake," I confessed.

"That's because the creature is swimming *toward the camera*, not across the horizon. The wake is on the opposite side of the creature where we cannot see it."

I nodded. This now seemed obvious. "So, what kind of creature shows three humps when swimming toward you?" I asked.

"Only one known to science," Terry said confidently. "A manta ray."

"I thought rays were basically flat, like saucers," I replied. "And that they lived in the sea. Loch Ness is fresh water."

"Yes, rays are flat—most of the time," Terry said. "But when they want to rise gently to the surface, they can inflate two air bladders—one above each eye—giving the appearance of humps when the creature is partially submerged."

He showed me another photo of a manta ray with these bladders inflated. They did look like the humps of a sea monster.

Terry continued. "Regarding your freshwater question, we know that manta rays live in saltwater, though their cousins, stingrays, can live in freshwater. Keep in mind, though, that Loch Ness is connected to the North Sea through many deep channels that let in saltwater from the sea and flush out freshwater from the loch. Who is to say that an unknown species of manta ray has not evolved to survive in both fresh and salt water? Perhaps these creatures often travel from loch to sea and then back again."

"Are rays big enough to be mistaken for a sea monster?"

Terry nodded. "The oceanic ray, which many call the giant manta ray, is huge. The distance between the tips of a giant manta ray's two pectoral fins can reach nearly the height of a three-story building. But I think that a family of unmolested rays in a big body of water like Loch Ness could evolve into even larger creatures. Loch Ness covers over twenty square miles and is more than 750 feet deep."

I studied Terry's photos more carefully. His evidence was impressive even if his theory was unorthodox.

"In addition," Terry continued, "manta rays are wickedly smart. They have one of the highest brain-to-body ratios of any fish. Like dolphins, they've shown high levels of intelligence and long-term memory."

"So, what do you propose, Terry?" I asked. "An expedition to find the monster? Lots of people have tried that. As you admitted, it's a big body of water to search."

"No, not that," Terry said. "It doesn't make sense to float around and wait for a sighting, I agree. What I propose is that we call Nessie to us, just as hunters attract ducks with a duck call."

I laughed. "I suppose you know what kind of sound would attract the Loch Ness Monster."

"Yes, I do," he said. And thus began an exercise in deductive logic that encircled the entirety of geographic Loch Ness. During construction of a new road around the loch in the 1930s, sightings of the monster reached an all-time high, Terry pointed out. He theorized that the dynamite explosions during this construction process excited the beast or beasts, causing them to show themselves more frequently. He believed that the sightings were due to the similarity of these explosive sounds to the natural sounds of manta rays leaping out of the air and thunderously belly flopping onto the water's surface.

A 1940's image of a section of completed road encircling Loch Ness.

Scientists are still uncertain about why manta rays leap into the air and land explosively on the water.

Terry showed me photographs of groups of rays appearing to "fly" over the sea. They had leaped up to seven feet above the water, all at the same approximate time, in some kind of frenzy or ritual, only to crash land into the sea with cringe-worthy volume. Scientists had conjectured that this could be an attempt to dislodge annoying parasites or a mating ritual in which the bigger and louder slaps attract prize female partners. Statistics seemed to confirm the connection between sightings and road construction. When the construction was completed, Nessie sightings had dropped to previous levels. I decided this would make an exciting documentary, but my wife, Karen, was dubious about the prospect of partnering with a diagnosed schizophrenic. In the end, our entire team found the concept too intriguing to pass up. I signed Terry to a contract that guaranteed he would lead an expedition to employ giant hydrophones to pump explosive sounds into Loch Ness, hoping to provoke Nessie into revealing itself. In my mind, the expedition did not need to succeed. The adventure would be in the attempt.

We did not lure Nessie into her maiden performance on film, unfortunately, but the short movie was popular among movie theater audiences and helped create a new film genre, the expedition documentary, which in many variations is now a staple of reality-based streaming services.

At the time, it didn't occur to me that this project, which had simply walked in the front door, was evidence that I had become a kind of lightning rod for unsolicited and sometimes unwanted adventures. The rest of my life would be distinguished by countless direct strikes.

Military Life

The next lightning strike should not have surprised me. This one, however, came in the mail. It was a draft notice matter-of-factly stating that I had been drafted and my physical exam had been scheduled. The government apparently did not consider my status as president of a publicly held corporation to be grounds for military deferment. I was just a month into my twenty-fifth year, so I came up eleven months shy of escaping the draft. I was told, though, that if I was employed before being drafted, government regulations entitled me to get my job back when my tour of duty was over.

It took Karen and I a couple of days to recover from this news. Many questions swarmed around us. What would happen to Somerset Limited and its employees? Could the company continue? What should we tell our investors? Few of them knew how young I was, and none had asked if I was eligible for the draft. What kind of hell now awaited Karen and me?

I was out of tricks. I thought of fleeing to Canada but dismissed that idea. I was born in the US, was an American citizen and would remain so. Somehow, Karen and I would make it through this terrible turn of events. I admit that the idea of going from the rank of president of a corporation to a US Army private seemed like a large demotion.

The perfunctory physical examination took about five minutes plus an hour of waiting in line. It was not designed to preserve one's privacy or dignity. If a draftee failed this exam, he was ineligible for military service. Unfortunately, I was fit for duty. My enlistment date was scheduled for February 17, 1969, at which time I would leave home early in the morning, travel to the Federal Building in downtown Minneapolis, then board a bus destined for Fort Campbell near Clarksville, Kentucky, to begin basic training.

Like most draftees and recruits, I overpacked. Upon arriving at Fort Campbell and being herded into a wooden barracks built for World War II soldiers, most of our possessions were taken from us. We were issued military clothing and boots in approximately correct sizes, all personal prohibited items such as pornographic magazines, weapons and drugs were seized, and we were given basic toiletries in return.

Newly minted soldiers arriving at Fort Campbell, Kentucky, in 1969, to begin boot camp.

During "zero week," we were indoctrinated into the military rules of conduct for basic trainees and introduced to our drill sergeants—mean-faced, non-commissioned officers whose job was to belittle and demean the recruits and whip the humanity out of us. Only then, the army believed, could we be rebuilt as efficient, lean, obedient fighting machines. Drill sergeants never slept or spoke in civil tones, always cussing or barking orders.

We also took written tests, the most important of which produced a GT (General Technical) score that measured skills in reading, language, reasoning and basic math. This was the military's version of an IQ test. The results were not shared with us, though a failing score could mean a recruit was ineligible for service. Following this transitional week, we faced eight weeks of intensive basic training in how to kill the enemy and stay alive.

My basic training company, called Charlie Company, had 230 young men stuffed into a barracks meant for no more than 150. Roughly 215 recruits were teenage enlistees who had volunteered for duty. Fifteen of us were "old men," as the younger ones called us, and I was the oldest of the lot. The "kids" could not get enough running through mud, stabbing dummies with bayonets, sleeping outdoors in the rain and competing in physical training drills. We old men looked for ways to avoid discomfort. I found an easy path when I discovered the company commander's clerk could not type. The paperwork in the office, all of which required typing with no errors, was stacking up. I let my drill sergeant know that I was an excellent typist, and he earned some gold stars by suggesting to his captain that I might be useful in the office. My typing duties often meant I was not available for less desirable activities such as PT and KP.

The cold, icy, Kentucky winter kept everyone "swapping spit" with coughs and sneezes due to upper respiratory infections and influenza. By the end of zero week, no one was healthy, but everyone was expected to pretend they were or suffer being recycled back to the beginning with no credit for the work they had already put in. As I was entering my fifth week, I suffered a serious but embarrassing injury—ruptured hemorrhoids. In terrible pain, I explained my condition to my drill sergeant who accused me of malingering until I took off one of my boots and poured out the blood that had been running down my leg. He told me the nearest infirmary was about a half mile away, but I would have to hoof it there on my own.

The medic in charge admitted me to the post hospital. For ten days, I was confined to absolute bed rest with compresses soaked in witch hazel applied to my affected parts. The only alternative treatment offered was a hemorrhoidectomy performed by an army surgeon. I chose bed rest and witch hazel. In the army, of course, prescribed bed rest had little meaning. Every morning at dawn, I was ordered to get out of bed and polish the ward's floors with a runaway power waxing machine. Somehow, I survived my stay in the hospital. But not until I learned one powerful lesson.

On the third night of my recovery, my sleep was disturbed at about three in the morning by a young man being brought by two nurses to an empty bed next to mine. It took about a half hour to suspend him above the mattress in a sling device and connect his multiple IV bags. I caught a glimpse of his nasty wounds. His entire backside looked like raw hamburger, which explained why he couldn't lie on it. Numerous smaller wounds were bleeding through dressings on his torso and the fronts of his thighs.

After the nurses left, he glanced over at me. In speech slurred by morphine, he said, "Sorry for that. I'm Robert."

"I'm Gary," I said. "You look pretty beat up."

"Mortar. Actually, I'm lucky, I guess. The guys who were next to me are dead."

Robert, it turns out, was in the same basic training company as me two cycles ago. He had gone through AIT and was shipped out immediately to Vietnam. In his first week there, he was blown up.

"Didn't think I'd make it back to the states this quick," he said. "I got just one piece of advice to give you." He paused so long I thought he had fallen asleep, but then he coughed and said, "Pay attention to your training. It can save your life over there."

Right then I made two important decisions. The first was to make sure I didn't end up in Vietnam, no matter what. And the second was to pay attention to all the survival training. This was not kid stuff.

When I returned to Charlie Company, the commander, a captain, said he was going to recycle me back to zero week because I had missed too much training. He didn't have time to discuss the decision because all the basic training companies were preparing for a competition in which the commanders of the best maintained and most interestingly decorated units would win an important military honor. I reminded him of his typing problem, but he introduced me to his new clerk typist, PFC Meyers.

An Improbable Series of Risky Events

The day after I temporarily rejoined Charlie Company, I was polishing my boots in the barracks when two MPs—military police—entered and shouted, "Private Lindberg!"

Startled at hearing my name in the mouths of MPs, I instantly stood up and raised my hand. The MPS approached and with no further explanation said, "Come with us, please." At least they were courteous. The fifty or so other soldiers in the building and one drill sergeant, Fernstrom, watched the MPs escort me into a jeep.

"I don't know what you've done, but you're in real trouble now," Sergeant Fernstrom yelled at me.

We drove for a few minutes to a low-lying administrative building, and I was ushered into an empty room with a half-dozen tables and many unused chairs. A nod indicated that I should take a seat. After waiting for a few minutes, a first lieutenant entered and took a chair opposite me.

"Do you know why you're here?" he asked.

"Not a clue."

"Well, turns out you're suspected of cheating on your GT test. Probably trying to qualify for a better army job, they think. Anyway, you're here to retake the test all by your lonesome. The MPs here will watch you carefully to make sure you don't cheat again."

I had no idea why the military would think I had cheated on its version of an IQ test. In fact, I had no idea how well I had done. Obviously, quite well.

"Why do they think I cheated?" I asked plainly.

"Well, for one thing, you got a perfect score of 144. No one except General Westmoreland has ever done that." Westmoreland was the commander of United States forces in Vietnam. "Think you can do it again? We'll soon find out."

I wondered what would happen to me if I did poorly, or even less well. A dishonorable discharge? A stint in the brig? The Army would likely use this test as proof of dishonesty instead of evidence of a fluke or a scoring error.

Nervously, I took the test. After a return trip to my barracks, Sergeant Fernstrom got in my face and asked, "What'd you do, son?"

"Apparently, I passed a written exam and they wanted to congratulate me," I answered.

Fernstrom marched off shaking his head and muttering something like, "Damn college kids."

I didn't have time to conjecture what this misadventure was all about because in a couple of days I was going to be recycled back to zero week. But I had an idea that would keep me out of stupid duties like KP and night watch. I did some research in the company day room and discovered a photo of a particularly dramatic mural in the Presidio. That afternoon, I showed it to the company commander, suggesting that I could reproduce that painting on a long and barren wall in the company mess hall if he could supply the paints and brushes. This could be his ticket to winning the upcoming competition.

The captain agreed to cancel his recycling decision so I could start painting immediately. He also exempted me from all forced marches, bivouacs and night watches so our important artistic pursuits would not be hindered. On the day of the big competition, the post commander awarded the captain of Charlie Company its top honor. I felt like a character in Joseph Heller's famous satirical war novel, *Catch-22*.

Reproducing an army mural in the mess hall of my boot camp company was better duty than forced marches and bivouacs.

An Improbable Series of Risky Events

On graduation day from basic training, we were all lined up in ranks awaiting written orders that would dictate our fates. Everyone was hoping for two weeks leave to see loved ones before moving on to advanced infantry training (AIT) or being shipped directly to Vietnam. The Army was so anxious for fresh troops on the battlefield that all but a handful of soldiers in our company were sent immediately to AIT, guaranteeing they would soon have the chance to put their new fighting skills to work.

I received two weeks leave and a new military occupational specialty (MOS)—TV production specialist. After leave, I would be heading to Fort Benning to make movies for the US Army—or so I thought. In 2023, Fort Benning was renamed Fort Moore to remove ties to a Civil War white supremacist general after whom it had been named. I will continue to call it Fort Benning, not to honor a dishonorable general, but because it was the name in use while I was there.

After graduation, Charlie Company's commander sought me out to explain my unusual orders. "You're a lucky man," he told me. That test they made you retake? Well, you did great. Scored 143, practically a perfect score. They must've thought it would be a waste to get you blown up by mortar as you stepped off the plane in the Nam. Good luck to you. Turns out I'm going back there for another tour."

"Good luck to you too, sir."

My proficiency at taking tests had probably saved my life. I would never set foot in Vietnam, but my Army career was about to veer off course in a most unexpected way.

* * *

I flew back to Minneapolis immediately for a two week leave. Karen and I rented a private cabin on Christmas Lake in Excelsior, Minnesota, to have some privacy. Our relatives celebrated my good luck with us, and Karen at last could make some plans for the next couple of years. We decided that after I got settled into my new military job, I would rent an apartment or small house off-post in Columbus, Georgia, and then she would move down to be with me. Since my employer was the US Army, however, nothing went as planned.

I arrived at Fort Benning and temporarily moved into a barracks for draftees who were getting settled on post. On the second day, I went to the television production facility to report for duty, but they had no record of me or my assigned position. In fact, the staff told me they had no job openings at all. What had happened? No one knew. But the major in charge said he would notify the Pentagon, which would figure out what to do with me. In the meantime, I could stay in the "holding company" where I had placed my belongings.

"What's a holding company?" I asked.

"It's where you sleep until new orders come through," I was told. "Most troops get reassigned to Vietnam."

My stomach churned with this depressing turn of events, so I wandered around the post trying to reorient my brain to the rejiggered reality. Finally, I drummed up the courage to call Karen with the bad news.

"You'll figure something out," she told me. "You always do. The Army doesn't want to waste you."

My opinion of the Army's ability to make good decisions, however, had plummeted. If I waited for the Army to decide where to put me I would be condemned to an ambush patrol in Vietnam. By the second day, fearing that new orders would be arriving at any moment, I set out to find a better job job at Fort Benning. I figured the Army was just a big company, and in my short career at Somerset Limited, I had effectively called on many big shots at big companies.

In the Army, the big shots were officers—majors, colonels and generals—and largely inaccessible to lowly enlisted men like me. But there was one place on post where these big shots often congregated, the Fort Benning Officer's Club. Open only to officers, this watering hole for military big shots was seldom frequented by generals, but I didn't need these highest-ranking officers to help me out. The problem was gaining entry as an enlisted man.

The Officer's Club at Fort Benning, Georgia.

I decided to try anyway. One evening, dressed in civilian clothes, I entered the club pretending I was with a family group. Presumably, one of them was an officer. No one was checking military IDs at the door, so apparently civilian friends and relatives were welcome. After entering, I peeled away from the group and approached the bar where I noticed a single man seated in khakis. The oak leaf cluster on his uniform indicated he was a lieutenant colonel, a rank right below colonel, often called "full bird" colonel for the eagle on his uniform. The graying officer was nursing a scotch on the rocks.

I took a seat next to him and said in my most confident voice, "Busy night, huh?"

The officer turned to me, and I was sure he detected that I was an enlisted man. "It'll be busier later," he said. "I'll be gone by then."

I held out my hand. "Sorry for interrupting your thoughts, but I'm Gary Lindberg." *Was I sounding too desperate, too pushy?* I wondered.

He shook my hand, saying, "Lt. Col. Hanks. Nice to meet you, Captain…"

He was fishing for my name and rank. I was too young to be a major, so he assumed I must be a captain. It seemed pointless to concoct a charade with someone I hoped would help me, so I modified the lie I had prepared. "Not an officer, actually," I confessed. "Just a private. Entered with another party…" I gestured toward a table now occupied by the family I had accompanied through the door. "…but the conversation got a little boring."

Hanks nodded. "Well, you can't buy a drink here on your enlisted man's ID, so what will you have? My treat."

It turned out that Hanks had been an officer in the army all his adult life but had hit his ceiling for advancement. He was divorced—army life was hard on marriages, he told me—and his children were all adults scattered around the country. Now awaiting retirement, he had accepted a cushy job running a secret school housed on the officer's golf course.

After three drinks, the lonely lieutenant colonel confessed that his school was part of a military experimental program called Project 100,000, which Defense Secretary Robert McNamara had initiated the previous year. Today, the program is often referred to as McNamara's Folly. The program was secret because it was so controversial. To meet the army's escalating battlefield requirements, 100,000 young men, previously unqualified for the draft because they fell below mental or literacy standards, were recruited or drafted each year. These unfortunate new soldiers were then provided with six weeks of literacy education in which clandestine schools, like the one Hanks supervised, taught reading, writing and basic arithmetic skills.

The mostly Black men of this so-called "Moron Corps" helped provide the necessary cannon fodder that deflected the political horror that would result if the government eliminated student deferments or called up the reserves, which were then sanctuaries for mostly White males. Instead of a certificate, graduates of this program, dubbed "New Standards Men," usually received a one-way ticket to Vietnam. In 1989, the consequences of Project 100,000 were summarized in a study sponsored by the Department of Defense, which stated:

> Comparisons between Project 100,000 participants and their non-veteran peers showed that, in terms of employment status, educational achievement, and

> income, non-veterans appeared better off. Veterans were more likely to be unemployed and to have a significantly lower level of education. Income differences ranged from $5,000 [to] $7,000 in favor of non-veterans. Veterans were more likely to have been divorced.

In the Officer's Club that evening, however, I knew none of this, except for what Hanks described in general terms as the mission to educate illiterate draftees. One comment he made caught my attention, though.

"My problem right now is that I am supposed to have more military instructors than I can find. Most of my teachers are officers' wives with teaching certificates. Only one is military."

"Maybe I can help," I said hopefully. I described my predicament with the television production group.

"Do you have a teaching certificate?" he asked.

"Well, no, not actually. But I have a BA degree in journalism and went to graduate school in market research."

"Hmmm, that might work. Journalism is related to literacy."

I bolstered my case by telling him my GT score, which he could confirm if necessary. He promised to "fly it up the flagpole at the Pentagon" and let me know. In the meantime, he could put a hold on other orders until he had an answer.

A week later, Hanks left a message for me at the holding company office. I met him at the Officer's Club, and he gave me the good news that I had been approved to teach at the Project 100,000 school. Immediately, I called Karen and told her she was going to become a southern belle. Then I started looking for a place to live. There were few off-post choices, and most were small, depressing assemblages of gray cinder blocks. I chose the best of the lot at 2934 Dalton Street, and my parents sent me money for the deposit.

* * *

While I thought things were looking up, Karen had just been contacted by the IRS in Minnesota with alarming news. We owed the government back taxes on the stock I had taken when starting Somerset Limited. The sum was staggering. Always the good wife, she decided not to share this with me. Instead, she reached an agreement with the IRS in which we would meet with its office in Columbus, Georgia, after we got settled there. After all, the IRS agents and we all worked for the same employer now—the US government.

I flew home to get Karen, and we packed our Fiat to the brim with clothes and household items we thought we'd need. The one necessity was my old, window air conditioner.

When we arrived in Columbus, Georgia, I took her to our new home. Unfortunately, she hated it. I hadn't seen the bungalow for several weeks, and my mind clearly had shined it up to a much more pleasant place than the reality of it. Chipped tile floors throughout. Uninsulated exterior walls. The pungent smell of mold and mildew. Doors that wouldn't open all the way. Cupboard shelves containing the carcasses of dead roaches. Broken locks. Windows stuck shut with paint. My noisy air conditioner only cooled the bedroom. In other words, standard army housing.

After her tour of the premises, Karen turned to me and kindly said, "Well, better than a tent." I knew this was debatable.

We had some work to do, and Karen was determined to find a job in Columbus so we could pay our bills and possibly upgrade our life. I was earning just over a hundred dollars per month from the Army plus a fifteen-dollar uniform allowance. Yes, we needed some additional revenue.

Fortunately, Karen was charismatic, skilled and employable. Within a couple of weeks, she had landed a job as secretary to Bobby Waugh, the marketing director of Columbus Mills, a major carpeting manufacturer. Her every waking moment at home was spent making our hovel livable, but the task proved impossible.

Since we had only one car, which I needed for transportation to my Fort Benning office and occasional meetings, Karen figured out how to take the local bus to her job, a twenty-minute ride. In

Minnesota, she had often traveled by bus, so this seemed like no big deal. But she noticed that almost all the passengers on her route to Columbus Mills were Black. She didn't mind, but noted how the distribution of Blacks to Whites in Columbus was quite different than in Minneapolis.

When she mentioned to her co-workers that she was riding the bus to work and back home every day, they were astonished that a White female would have the guts or stupidity to ride a public bus anywhere. Buses were for Blacks, they pointed out. One of Karen's co-workers said that if she had to take the bus to work, she wouldn't work. Karen's bus route ran through a ramshackle section of Columbus with narrow, tiny houses, many with refrigerators on their collapsing front porches. She was stunned by a kind of poverty she had never witnessed before. Prejudice was rampant, and one colleague, commenting on that section of town, told Karen, "Can't you see they just live differently than we do?"

I think Karen started to feel like a Freedom Rider in reverse.

* * *

The day after reporting for duty at the secret school, I entered a classroom for the first time. Facing me were about twenty raging and belligerent students. All of them knew they had been drafted semi-illegally and had already been publicly demeaned by their drill sergeants as the "village idiots." They also knew that this program added six weeks to their basic training, which meant it would be fifteen weeks before they could see their loved ones.

Most of these students were larger than me and none were physically restrained. I felt like a lone Christian thrown into an arena filled with lions. But there was something even more fear-provoking than my students.

I had received no training in the project's curriculum or the teaching techniques to be used. All the school's teachers were left to fend for themselves. I had not even seen the reading materials provided until a box of books showed up on my desk that first day of my first six-week cycle of instruction.

I tore open the carton, hopeful that the army would have provided specially developed reading materials aimed at young adult readers. My heart fell as I pulled out copies of elementary reading primers with titles like *Pete on the Farm* and *See Spot Run*. How would my adolescent and adult students react to being handed such profoundly insulting books written for eight-year-olds? These materials would certainly provoke antagonism, perhaps even violent protest by my students, who had already been humiliated by disparaging name-calling. These materials could never produce a conducive environment for adult learning.

It occurred to me that my students probably viewed me as a symbol of scornful military authority. I was at the front of the class in a military uniform even though I was anti-war, anti-draft and generally anti-authoritarian. I needed to transform my students' view of me and somehow erase their embarrassment at being given children's books to read.

On this first day of my first class, I walked to the center of the group and took a chair. I apologized for how they were being treated as inferior. I explained my background and how I also had been "kidnapped" by the draft just as they had been. I invited them to laugh at the silly books the army had provided us, explaining that I had been previously unaware of which books would show up. I invited them to share their personal stories about how the draft had disrupted their lives and relationships, their fears and anger. Most importantly, I told them that I was committed to using their time wisely during our classes by teaching them skills they could use for the rest of their lives.

I sincerely hoped that the military was not recording my not-so-military speech.

This impromptu dialogue was not exactly a kumbaya moment, but most of the students seemed willing to give me a chance. I promised that I would come up with something more enjoyable for their lessons than *See Spot Run*.

But what would that be?

After class, I had a brainstorm, which I shared with the other five teachers. I explained a little experiment I wanted to try and asked if they would each be willing to donate five dollars to seed the pilot phase. Everyone opted in.

Late that night, when I was sure no one would see me, I drove down a stretch of 13th Street adorned with small specialty shops selling everything from jewelry to porn. At random, I chose an adult bookstore and spent our love offering on dirty books. I chose only novels since long text was required for reading instruction. My theory was simple. If I could provide my students with material that was more relevant and more interesting, their eagerness to gain literacy might improve.

An adult novel with one of the tamer covers.

It worked! The next morning, student faces lit up when seeing the salacious covers and titles of these novels. This was the next best thing to a packet of condoms and a pass into Columbus, the town next door to Fort Benning. As grade level reading scores improved starting in the third week, the other teachers—even the officers' wives—joined in the experiment. It felt good to be accomplishing something positive for these young men. Soon, the faster learners became tutors for the slower ones. While some of the students were clearly mentally disabled, most were simply unschooled by choice or an unjust society.

* * *

In early July, a very hot and humid month in Georgia, a plastic glass melted on our stovetop, which was not turned on. Karen decided that we had to find another place to live. I learned that another house had just become available just down the street—a much nicer place, except the bathtub had been plunked into an ill-fitting hole in the bathroom floor through which our cat could escape. With Karen's income, we could afford it, so we applied and got approved.

But then Karen told me about our tax problem.

At our first meeting with the IRS agent in Columbus, we learned the extent of our problem, which was my fault as usual. When founding and financing Somerset Limited, I had chosen to take additional shares of stock for my role as founder and in exchange for a lower salary. Because I was an insider, my shares were "lettered," meaning that I could not sell them for several years. This restriction was to prevent the founder from raising a pile of money, quickly selling the shares to gain cash and then absconding with the proceeds. Unfortunately, to the IRS, my shares had taxable value even though I couldn't sell them to obtain cash to pay the taxes.

We owed the IRS a great deal of money and had no available assets to offset our tax debt. In the end, we were asked to give the IRS a budget listing all our monthly expenses and income. Each month, after food and shelter, we had about thirty dollars left over—"fun money," we called it. Truly, it was more like suicide prevention.

Every month, the IRS took most of our fun money. Fortunately, we could see movies in the post theater for a quarter per ticket.

* * *

Things were coasting along at the school. One student in my third cycle, Tyrone, was reading at a high school level by the end of his six-week cycle and was actively assisting me in class. His story was one of heartbreak, however, and haunts me to this day. He had been a third-grade student in Prince Edward County, Virginia, when the state chose to shut down public education after the supreme court in Brown v. Board of Education declared segregated education unconstitutional. For six years, Black students in the county received no formal education. This was the longest that any school district had ever closed its schools to avoid integration.

In 1964, when the county schools were forcibly reopened, Tyrone was placed into the ninth grade because of his age, never having been taught how to read. Discouraged, he dropped out and in 1967 was drafted as one of McNamara's Misfits. Though society had failed him, he was now a member of the Moron Corps.

Years later, while researching a historical novel at the Library of Congress in Washington DC, I visited the Vietnam Veterans Memorial for a very personal reason—to see if Tyrone's name was engraved on the wall, which would reveal whether he had survived Vietnam. As instructors, we were never informed about the fate of our students.

I found Tyrone's name on the wall and couldn't stop crying.

My Lai

I still had fourteen months to serve when Lt. Col. Hanks informed the school's staff that the army was closing the school. With that much time left, I could be levied to Vietnam for a standard thirteen-month tour. Suddenly, Karen and I were again thrown into turmoil.

Hanks contacted the television production unit, but they still had no job openings. I begged my resourceful officer friend to find something for me, and three days later, Hanks came up with a possibility.

Fort Benning was the home of the 4th Infantry Division, the Airborne School with its drop towers for training paratroopers, the Army Infantry and Armor schools, the Scout Dog school for training combat canines, the 75th Ranger Regiment, Infantry Officer's Candidate School (OCS), 17th Special Tactics Squadron of the Air Force, and much more. Almost all returning Vietnam vets came to Fort Benning before discharge. Most soldiers were assigned to The School Brigade (TSB), one of the largest in the world.

The legal affairs of the entire School Brigade were handled by a legal unit comprised of a commander (a captain), defense and prosecuting attorneys (usually lieutenants minted from the civilian lawyer marketplace) and a chief legal clerk. Through a stroke of good luck, the chief legal clerk had just re-upped and had been assigned to a position in Vietnam, so a new legal clerk was needed.

During the previous six months, I had taught at the secret school and Hanks had gotten me promoted three pay grades—from Private

(E1) to Specialist (E4) during that short period. If I accepted this new position, I would become the chief legal clerk in about six weeks and receive another pay grade increase to Specialist (E5), which would be necessary to serve in that MOS. This would be a spectacular army career rise for a draftee during the Vietnam era.

The catch was that I had only two weeks to gain a passable knowledge of the entire Uniform Code of Military Justice (UCMJ), the foundation of the system of military justice for the US armed forces.

That seemed doable—I'd just have to read the UCMJ and comprehend it—so I said yes.

* * *

It's not so much that I can still remember my first day in my new job, but that it is impossible to forget it. The legal unit was in a small building at the base of the three jump towers used for dropping paratroopers in simulated jumps. When I entered the building for the first time, Captain Frenzel was seated at his desk flanked by judge advocate (JAG) Gonzalez, who I would learn served mostly as a defense counselor, JAG Martin, who was a prosecutor, and Specialist E5 Brooking, the outgoing chief legal clerk.

"Lindberg, I take it? Welcome aboard," Frenzel said, gesturing toward an open chair. "We're informal here, so no saluting higher-ups we work with. We're in the middle of something important right now, so if you don't mind, we're going to finish up."

I silently took a seat and watched as Frenzel flipped a coin. Gonzalez called heads, which was correct. Apparently because he had lost, Frenzel then flipped the coin again. This time, Martin called *heads*, but it came up tails.

"Shit," Martin said quietly. "Guess I'm the loser. We'll see what happens."

I must have looked confused. This was not the kind of behavior I expected from military attorneys.

Frenzel attempted to relieve my perplexity. "A very complex and important case just dropped in our laps," he explained. "It's so important that the Pentagon asked us not to file charges until they decide if we should, which means they're contemplating dropping the thing altogether. We've looked over the case, and we understand the political ramifications, but we've decided to file charges no matter what the Pentagon says. We have jurisdiction, but defying the Pentagon could have other consequences, as you can imagine."

I looked over at Martin and said, "So you earned the right to sign the papers if the Pentagon says don't?"

Martin nodded.

This is going to be a very interesting assignment, I thought. Soon, I would learn that this monumental incident would become known as the My Lai Massacre. Years later, the movie *Platoon* would be inspired by it, according to the producers, though the storyline departed significantly.

* * *

Inside every filmmaker is someone who wants to make a "real" movie, so out of frustration and boredom, I wrote a screenplay for a feature film. This was fun the IRS couldn't take away. Our legal unit had a new Xerox copier, so I hijacked it for making photocopies of my script to send to Hollywood producers. One of the recipients on my list was Academy Award-winning cinematographer/director Haskell Wexler. I didn't expect any results from my efforts—I was mainly killing time—but a month later I got a phone call from Wexler who told me he loved my screenplay and wanted to buy an eighteen-month option—a contract that would give him exclusive ownership of my work for a year-and-a-half during which he would try to get studio backing to make the movie. He was soon going to be flying through Atlanta. Could I meet him at the Hyatt Regency there?

I pulled some strings to clear my schedule and drove the hundred miles to Atlanta. Wexler was a friendly, non-intimidating, gray-haired man armored head-to-toe in denim and carrying an aluminum camera case instead of a satchel. We talked in the hotel lobby for two hours, he gave me a copy of an option agreement for my science fiction/thriller, and I signed. The agreement gave me back all rights if the movie didn't get funded before the option period ran out, and I could keep the option payment. A week later, we got a check in the mail from Wexler's production company for $2,000.

* * *

With autumn came deer hunting season. I was still a bowhunter, and since I could hunt anywhere in the country free on my military ID, I decided to drive across the river to Alabama where an army buddy had bragged about the fun he had hunting swamp deer. That sounded great, so I packed up my gear, put on my civvies—paisley pants, sandals and a puffy shirt to look as unmilitary as possible—and headed for the swamps. By nightfall, I was hungry, so I stopped at a roadhouse with multiple RC Cola trucks parked outside.

The busy interior was roaring with chatter, and my lungs instantly rebelled against the stink of cigarette smoke, but my stomach was growling. All the tables were taken, so I headed for an open seat at the bar. Suddenly, the room seemed to shift into another dimension. The patrons all stopped talking. As I slowly turned my head, I noticed that every set of eyes in the bar was staring at me. Glaring, actually. My hippie look had apparently inflamed the locals who had not yet settled on a lynching. I knew better than to wait for the vote.

A hulking bartender approached with squinting eyes that seemed to ask, "What the hell are you doing in here?" On the wall behind him was a poster—not a jokey one.

DON'T BE HALF A MAN
JOIN THE KU KLUX KLAN

My appetite disappeared. Thinking quickly, I asked the bartender if I was on the correct route to my destination, and he nodded. Then I swiveled on my stool and walked casually out the door and to my car, glancing behind to see if anyone was following me. My rear tires scattered gravel as I pulled onto the main road.

I have never since stopped for a burger in Alabama no matter how I was dressed. And no, I don't remember anything about my hunt.

* * *

By early 1970, as I was settling into my new job as chief legal clerk of The School Brigade, Karen was bragging to her boss about my creative marketing skills. Suddenly, I was working as a part-time marketing consultant for Columbus Mills. I started out inventing new names for carpet colors—much harder than it sounds—then graduated to writing and designing printed marketing materials.

At my military job, as I learned more about the UCMJ, I became more useful for the brigade's numerous company commanders, who had endless consulting and paperwork needs for courts martial and Article 15s (non-judicial disciplinary procedures). By doing favors for these captains, including the commander of Headquarters and Headquarters Company, to which I was attached, I earned return favors including mid-week passes for personal travel. This allowed me to design and supervise displays for carpet showrooms in Chicago and San Francisco and to coordinate marketing activities with my client's Atlanta-based ad agency. By the end of my stint in the Army, Karen and I were making more money than when we were at Somerset Limited.

* * *

All this frantic, free-lance activity kept me busy, but my Army job was heating up as well. Second Lieutenant William Laws Calley, Jr. was confined to post and charged with the 1968 murders of 109 unarmed South Vietnamese civilians in the village of My Lai. The murders took place during a massacre purportedly led by Calley and Capt. Medina in which up to 500 elderly men, women, children and infants, all from allied South Vietnam, were systematically slaughtered. Oddly, the Fourth Geneva Convention excluded allied civilians from being classified as protected persons in an international armed conflict. This meant that Calley and the soldiers under his command could not be legally tried as war criminals.

An Improbable Series of Risky Events

Photo taken by United States Army photographer Ronald L. Haeberle on March 16, 1968 in the aftermath of the My Lai massacre showing mostly women and children dead on a road. Public domain: (https://commons.wikimedia.org/wiki/File:My_Lai_massacre.jpg.)

My job as chief legal clerk in the jurisdiction of this court-martial required me to take sworn statements from Calley and members of Charlie Company, the unit under Calley's and Captain Medina's command. I also catalogued most of the evidentiary photographs, which were brutally graphic. I gathered and organized other evidence, compiled research on supporting and hostile witnesses and served as liaison between Calley and his civilian attorneys. I attended many days of testimony at the first court martial. Upon first meeting Calley, I was reminded of another murderer I had known—Ronald Steeves, who had brutally slain the sister of his girlfriend. Both showed a remarkable lack of remorse and unusual candor about their actions.

In Calley's first Fort Benning interview for the record, he told us that he had worked at a variety of common jobs before enlistment, including as a bellhop, dishwasher, insurance appraiser and railroad conductor. His military test scores were high enough to qualify him for acceptance into Officer Candidate School (OCS) at Fort Benning, so he had been at Fort Benning before. His military records described him as an average officer, but interviews with other members of Charlie Company complained that he lacked common sense and could not read a map or use a compass correctly.

Lieutenant William Laws Calley, Jr.

In my private conversations with Calley, he revealed an impulsive side that seemed triggered by a desire for recognition. He told me about an incident that occurred in June 1969, about a year after the My Lai massacre. It was an incident he was intensely proud of and believed was deserving of respect. The incident began innocently with Calley and two other officers in a jeep near Chu Lai Basse Camp. They passed another jeep containing five unkempt marines and pulled it over.

Calley told me he shouted, "You soldiers better square away!" I can still see him acting this out for me.

One of the marines, probably drunk, yelled back, "We ain't soldiers, motherfucker, we're marines!"

The ensuing fight ended when one of the officers pulled out a pistol and fired a shot into the air, but some physical damage had already been inflicted. The two officers were briefly hospitalized, and Calley was badly pummeled. At their courts-martial, the marines pled guilty with a stipulation that they had not known Calley and his cohorts were officers. In describing this event, which also appeared in his record, Calley told me he still resented the lack of respect shown by the marines.

Because I often accompanied Calley to meetings and arranged for various comforts and courtesies during his post confinement— even under the UCMJ he was considered innocent until proven guilty—he sometimes opened up to me when he remained closeted to other officials. This caused me to wonder about another charge the army had made against him that we had been ordered to shelve, one that was never revealed to the public until years later.

Before the March 1968 massacre in My Lai, a platoon led by Calley had entered another village and seized a Vietnamese male who Calley believed was a spy. Lacking evidence, Calley decided to frighten the man into a confession.

Calley told me he ordered the American troops to encircle a well in the center of the village. He dragged the supposed spy to the well and repeatedly beat the man with the stock of his M-16 as the suspect continued to insist he was not a spy. Calley admitted that he had finally lost patience and ordered one of his privates to toss the limp and battered man into the well before firing several rounds into him.

The army had taken many sworn statements from soldiers who had witnessed the event. Calley explicitly told me the charges against him in this case were true but showed no remorse. Yet, the Pentagon decided to drop all charges in this murder case to avoid the appearance that the military was piling on.

Since the massacre, Calley had become a kind of public folk hero sparking a national "Free Calley" movement that claimed the lieutenant had shown courageous allegiance to his country and was being persecuted as a scapegoat for the government's failed policies in Vietnam. Several weeks after I was discharged, when Calley was finally convicted of the premeditated murder of 22 Vietnamese civilians and sentenced to life in prison, nationwide protests over his conviction erupted. A song, "The Battle Hymn of Lt. Calley," sold over 200,000 copies. More than 5,000 angry telegrams were sent to the White House. Flags in Florida were lowered to half-mast in protest. Numerous army veterans turned in their medals in disgust.

A month after Calley was sentenced, President Nixon bowed to public pressure and ordered him released from the stockade and placed under house arrest. Four months later, the lieutenant's sentence was reduced, and two years after that was reduced again after he was returned to the stockade. On November 9, 1974, he was released on parole. He had served four months in a stockade despite being found guilty for killing twenty-two Vietnamese civilians.

Captain Medina, Calley's direct superior and the commander of Charlie Company, was treated even more gently. The Criminal Investigation Department (CID) determined that more than 300 Vietnamese civilians were killed under his leadership. Some soldiers testified that Medina had directly killed civilians on three separate occasions and had frequently abused noncombatants. Nevertheless, he was only charged with assault with a deadly weapon and premeditated murder.

Following his court-martial, Medina was acquitted of all charges due to an emphatically sympathetic court and the unexplained withdrawal of a key witness, Michael Bernhardt. Despite the acquittal, Medina was denied a long-promised promotion to major. After his trial, Medina acknowledged that he "had not been completely candid to avoid disgracing the military [and] the United States."

As in many legal cases both civilian and military, the full, true story of what happened in My Lai never came out. From my unique position at the center of the investigation and court-martial, I learned in confidence many of the hidden pieces, but certainly not all of them.

Burning Vietnamese bodies at My Lai can be seen at the lower right corner. Public domain: https://commons.wikimedia.org/wiki/File:My-Lai_Haeberle_P33_BodiesNearBurningHouse.jpg.

After gaining this knowledge, I had lost confidence in the truthfulness of most, if not all, of what we know about political decisions and organizations, historical events and people. Later experiences have caused me to be skeptical of celebrity escapades and lives, job applicant resumés, even family anecdotes, many of which are just legends or false beliefs. In the absence of critical thinking, I've come to believe that most of what we are told is a combination of misinformation, disinformation, public relations, omissions of critical facts, superstitions and bias. But the truth is out there, as the *X-Files* TV series promised, if we look hard enough.

I did not arrive at this cynical point-of-view lightly. The My Lai massacre case was one of my first confrontations with the reality that truth is hard to find because it is often at the bottom of a cave-in. Like the Watergate tragedy, the massacre was bad enough, but it was almost immediately followed by a cover-up that attempted to bury the horrible truth so deeply that no amount of excavation could find it.

On March 16, 1968, Task Force Barker, led by Lieutenant Colonel Frank Barker, launched an assault on the village of My Lai, a village that inaccurate intelligence tragically claimed was the headquarters of the ferocious North Vietnamese 48th Vietcong Battalion guarded by a highly trained enemy unit of up to 280 soldiers. Against this superior force, which proved to be fictitious, Barker sent his weakest unit, Charlie Company, which was led by two sparring officers, Captain Medina and Lieutenant Calley.

A previous unit led by Medina had suffered 25 percent casualties in ninety days and had never been in a real firefight. Calley's inexperienced platoon had lost eighteen soldiers without having a straight-up firefight. All these losses had come from snipers, mines and booby traps.

If he believed the intelligence about My Lai, Barker was either one of the most incompetent commanders or one of the dumbest in Vietnam. That he was both is confirmed by the fact that he misplaced other tactical units at such distances from each other that they were of no support to Charlie Company during the My Lai incident.

Two days earlier, Charlie Company had lost its beloved Sergeant George Cox, the motivational backbone of Calley's platoon. Before Charlie Company's assault on the village, Captain Medina stirred up the emotions of his men by saying they were going to get "those bastards" who had killed Sergeant Cox. He urged the war-torn soldiers to be unusually aggressive and merciless. Based on the false intelligence, Medina promised that there would be few if any noncombatants in My Lai because civilians would have left for the local market before the assault was set to begin at 0730.

Disturbingly, some intelligence officers at 23rd ("Americal") Infantry Division headquarters knew that the 48th Vietcong Battalion was not in My Lai. Classifications on the use of radio intercepts, however, would prevent them from divulging the Divison's location to Task Force Barker. The 48th was in fact some distance away, licking its wounds in the mountains west of Quang Ngai following punishing battles in the Tet Offensive.

Today, it's fair to compare this Vietnam-era intelligence breakdown to the CIA's bogus report of weapons of mass destruction in Iraq, which led to the disastrous US invasion and to the Israeli failure to foresee the kibbutz massacres and kidnappings by Hamas on October 7, 2023, which resulted in hundreds of Israeli deaths and the devastation of the Gaza Strip.

* * *

We would have never heard of My Lai except for several courageous individuals, including Warrant Officer Hugh Thompson who was flying one of several observational helicopters above My Lai during the massacre. As the ground operation commenced and Charlie Company opened fire on the villagers, Thompson dropped smoke cannisters to mark the positions of wounded Vietnamese civilians needing medical assistance.

Warrant Officer Hugh Thompson.

After returning to the village from a refueling stop, Thompson and his crew noted that the wounded civilians they marked had all been shot dead. As he hovered over a wounded Vietnamese woman, he watched in horror as a soldier approached the woman, prodded her with his boot, then shot her in the head.

Several minutes later, Thompson saw a group of children hiding behind a woodpile from an approaching American soldier. In a totally unauthorized move, he landed the chopper, jumped out and appealed to the soldier, later identified as Lt. Calley, to help the civilians. Calley simply replied that he was "putting them out of their misery." Shortly after Thompson lifted off, Calley gunned down the children.

Furious, Thompson landed again, telling his two door gunners to train their guns on Charlie Company troops who were in pursuit of a dozen Vietnamese women, children and elderly men. After calling in assistance from other choppers, Thompson successfully organized an impromptu rescue mission that dropped off the group about four miles away. These victims were among the few survivors of the massacre. Around noon, Hugh Thompson fiercely confronted his section leader about the atrocities and filed an action report with company commander Fred Watke.

The army retaliated against Thompson. Beginning immediately, Thompson's assigned missions were increasingly dangerous. Over the next eleven days, his various helicopters were shot down four times. On a fifth shoot-down, during a mission from Da Nang to Chu Lai, the helicopter's fall from air space broke his back, and Thompson narrowly escaped an attack from local Vietcong. In April, however, he was incongruently awarded the Distinguished Flying Cross for his actions at My Lai. He promptly threw away the award. Eventually, he would provide critical testimony to help expose an attempted cover-up of the My Lai atrocities.

During the ensuing months and years of investigation and testimony, Thompson was celebrated as a hero by some but demonized and berated by many others for committing "unpatriotic acts" and "undermining authority." In 1998, his heroism was documented for posterity when he was awarded the Soldier's Medal for courage and valor, which he kept.

* * *

One of the first enlisted men from Charlie Company to candidly talk about the massacre was PFC Paul Meadlo from Indiana. Two days after the My Lai incident, after being ordered by Calley to move swiftly through an area known to be heavily mined, Meadlo stepped on a landmine and lost a foot. He was sent back to the US, treated and discharged. I took his sworn statement in preparation for Calley's court-martial, and he tearfully told me that he considered his dismemberment to be God's punishment for the horrible injustices he had committed at My Lai.

Later, in an interview with Mike Wallace, Meadlo described how he and some other soldiers had moved about forty-five noncombatants to the center of the village under orders from Calley. "Men, women, children, babies," he said. "We made them squat down, and Lieutenant Calley came over and said, 'You know what to do with them, don't you?' ... I took it for granted that he just wanted us to watch them. And he left and came back about ten or fifteen minutes later and said, 'How come you ain't killed them yet?' And I told him, 'I didn't think you wanted us to kill them, that you just wanted us to guard them.' He said, 'No, I want them dead.'"

Meadlo choked up, then continued. "[Calley] stepped back... and he started shooting them. And he told me to start shooting. So, I started shooting. I poured about four clips into the group... I fired them on automatic, so you can't... you just spray the area, so you can't know how many you killed, cuz they were going fast. So, I might have killed ten or fifteen of them."

Meadlo described how the soldiers led another group of eighty villagers to a ditch "and Lieutenant Calley told me, 'Meadlo, we got another job to do.' And so he walked over to the people, and he started pushing them off and started shooting them... Men, women and babies." Meadlo estimated that about 370 civilians had been killed.

So defenseless were the victims that only one American soldier was injured. Private Herbert Carter shot himself in the foot so he would be medevaced out of the killing grounds and avoid participation in the massacre. He may have also been feeling some guilt since he was the soldier who had tossed the falsely accused Vietnamese "spy" into a well and watched as Calley shot him.

* * *

Sergeant Ron Haeberle, an army photographer assigned to follow Charlie Company on this fateful day, was on the ground during the massacre. Haeberle was armed with just two cameras—one for official army use and his own camera for personal use. The official black-and-whites primarily showed routine stuff—soldiers interrogating villagers and burning huts. The personal color photographs, however, revealed piles of bodies, including many children, that had been shot to death. In perhaps his most famous color photo, a group of My Lai women and children defensively huddle together, fear in their eyes. Seconds after that photo was taken, according to Haeberle's later testimony, everyone in the photograph was ruthlessly killed by Charlie Company soldiers. Haeberle claimed to have witnessed at least 100 similar murders, and he documented many of them.

Haeberle submitted the official black-and-white images to the army but retained the incriminating personal photos fearing they would be destroyed if turned in. After he was discharged, he decided to share some of his war photos with various clubs, associations, even a high school. In November 1969, the *Cleveland Plain Dealer* published a small selection of his photos showing dozens of Vietnamese women, children and elders lying dead or awaiting their imminent execution. Haeberle had destroyed the images of soldiers in the act of killing civilians to protect their identities. Nevertheless, his images provided invaluable visual evidence of illegal and unforgiveable acts.

Seldom mentioned by the press or at court-martial was the fact that Lieutenant Colonel Frank Barker was observing the slaughter of civilians from a scout helicopter above the gunships flown by Thompson and others. His reports, which I had read, were distinctly at odds with the facts that emerged later.

During the morning massacre, Barker reported that he had no cause for alarm because a call from Captain Medina at eight o'clock had told him that fifteen Vietcong had been killed. At eight-thirty, Barker updated that statistic to eighty-four Vietcong killed. In fact, no Vietcong were ever found dead or alive in the vicinity of My Lai, only native civilians.

Two days after the massacre, the cover-up began due to increasing reports of atrocities. Lieutenant Colonel Barker joined Brigadier General Young, Major Watke and Colonel Henderson in a crisis meeting that resulted in Henderson receiving orders to thoroughly investigate the My Lai incident.

Henderson's investigation included a second interview with Hugh Thompson and two other aviators, a conversation with Captain Medina and another fly-over of the My Lai battlefield. Two days later, Henderson reported to General Young that the investigation had yielded nothing suspicious or out of the ordinary. The formal written report stated that twenty civilians had been killed and Thompson's allegations of mass exterminations were false. Nevertheless, Henderson instructed Barker to conduct a formal inquiry, a most unorthodox order, since Barker would be investigating a task force that he personally commanded. Predictably, Barker's report concurred with Henderson's.

Twelve days after the massacre, Barker filed an official report declaring the My Lai operation successful. "This operation was well planned, well executed," he wrote. "Friendly casualties were light, and the enemy suffered heavily. The infantry unit on the ground and helicopters were able to assist civilians in leaving the area and caring for and/or evacuating the wounded."

Less than two weeks after I was discharged from active duty and just before Calley was finally convicted, Colonel Henderson, the highest-ranking officer in this debacle, was court-martialed for his role in the cover-up. The trial lasted sixty-two days with testimony from a hundred witnesses. On December 18, 1971, he was acquitted of all charges. Later, he publicly admitted that he had not conducted the investigation he was ordered to lead but instead had handed it off to Lieutenant Colonel Barker.

In my informed opinion, Barker, who had a birds-eye view of the massacre from a helicopter, would have been court-martialed and convicted if he had not died in a suspicious helicopter accident. During the Vietnam War, there were few head-on collisions between American helicopters. Three months after the massacre, however, a chopper carrying Barker "collided" with another one carrying Captain Michles of Bravo Company, a second unit in Task Force Barker that on the day of the massacre destroyed a smaller nearby village before joining up with Charlie Company at My Lai. I could find no evidence that the army ever formally investigated this head-on collision.

It is perhaps noteworthy that photographs of all the officers charged in the My Lai incident, including those both convicted and acquitted, are available on the Internet, except for Lieutenant Colonel Frank Barker. His picture is conspicuously absent.

* * *

I spent many sleepless nights trying to expunge the grotesque images and horror stories from my mind. Sometimes, I struggled to switch my attention from the brutality of war to the relative insignificance of carpet marketing. Fortunately, Karen and I developed friendships in Columbus that provided support and often comic relief. Karen's boss and his wonderful wife, Dottie, offered assistance and moral support when needed. Lt. Gonzalez, a JAG officer specializing in defense counseling, invited me to his apartment to lie on the floor and listen to the Moody Blues while smoking pot.

Besides the My Lai massacre case, we also had a lot of other routine legal work. Most surviving Vietnam vets with time left to serve returned to Fort Benning. Almost all of them were psychologically or physically wounded, but few were diagnosed and offered medical help. It's hard to remember any who did not have a drug or alcohol problem. Because discipline in Vietnam was lax or nonexistent, many vets returning to the US didn't or couldn't understand that they would be held accountable for their actions on post. But they were required to conform to military standards for the duration of their service, even if it were just a month or two.

Our legal unit had a continuous stream of Article 15s and courts-martial for relatively minor offenses such as lighting up a joint in the post library, failing to salute officers, violating uniform standards and disorderly conduct after a round of drinking. Some of these could result in a dishonorable discharge, which meant the soldier would lose all military benefits and have an indelible stain on his record that would be visible to every potential employer.

To me, this seemed terribly unfair for the masses of walking wounded on the post. I believed that if the army refused to simply discharge these Vietnam vets upon return, at least it should cut them some slack. So, I lobbied the JAG officers in our unit to help some of these guys out with a stronger legal defense, and they agreed, finding some unusual loopholes and language inconsistencies in the UCMJ. Since I had developed a close relationship with many of the company commanders by doing them favors, I found many of them agreed to reduce or drop charges for some of their soldiers as payback for their service. During my year in the legal section, I think we probably preserved an honorable discharge for about fifty soldiers, and I feel good about that.

* * *

After a year of antiquing in Georgia and neighboring Alabama, financed by our enhanced earnings the previous year, Karen and I had accumulated some beautiful furniture. Fortunately, the army was required to hire movers to transport all our possessions back to Minnesota at no cost to us. On the evening before my discharge, Karen and I packed up what the moving van was not transporting and tried to get some sleep. We were so excited to go home!

The next morning, we drove with a car full of personal items, including our cat, to the Infantry Center headquarters. Karen waited in the car while I sat through a half-hour of arm-twisting to convince me to re-up for another year or two. At last, the discharging officer surrendered, reminding me that I was still in the reserves for six years and giving me an envelope with a bunch of official papers. My active military career was over, and we headed off for a two-day winter drive to Minneapolis.

Reentry to Civilian Life

When a returning spacecraft reenters Earth's atmosphere, it risks destruction unless its heat shield provides sufficient protection and there is a soft landing. Our heat shield was a dream of life away from military domination and our soft landing would be at my parents' home, where Karen and I would stay until we had recalibrated our lives. Honestly, it was a bit weird living in the same basement apartment that Georgia and I had shared and from which I had been exiled. At times, I felt caught in a loop. Was my life progressing or just endlessly repeating itself?

Fortunately, we weren't with my parents long before finding an upper duplex unit at 4136 Aldrich Avenue in south Minneapolis. Coincidentally, Barbara Long, one of Karen's old friends from high school and church, lived on the first floor with her two-year-old son, Adam. This softened our splash-down considerably.

Restless to reenter the film business, I sought out my old company, Somerset Limited. Because I had been drafted, law dictated that I was entitled to get back the job from which I had been so abruptly removed. Shortly after my departure, it had become more difficult to take a company public in Minnesota, so Somerset had become an attractive commodity for individuals looking for an existing, publicly held corporate shell.

Ted, the man I had installed as a caretaker president during my absence, had betrayed all the co-founders by engineering a hostile takeover that replaced our board of directors and caused all my co-founders to leave. After the takeover, the company's business of film production had morphed into real estate development. Somerset was now building condominiums near Duluth, Minnesota. I was aware of this from annual reports and financial statements sent to me as a shareholder. What no one at the altered company seemed to know was that their previous president had just been released from active military service and wanted his old job back.

I went to the company's new offices and approached the receptionist with an expectant smile. I knew Somerset would never bring me back as president, but it would be fun to push their buttons.

"Hi," I said, "I'm Gary Lindberg, your new president. I'm here to see my office."

I wish I'd had a camera. The receptionist stared at me dumbly, as if I had spoken in a foreign language, then said, "Excuse me. What was that again?"

"Maybe I should speak with your current president. I'm his replacement," I explained.

The receptionist fidgeted for a moment, then said, "Ummm, follow me please." She left her desk and escorted me into an adjoining conference room. "I'll be right back. Coffee?"

I shook my head. Barely a minute later, a rotund, gray-haired man walked in and sat down across a table from me. He introduced himself as the president of Somerset and said, "So what's this about replacing me?"

My time as chief legal clerk of The School Brigade had taught me the value of preparation for conversations about legal matters. I briefly explained the history of Somerset Limited and my role in founding it. I showed him my stock certificates. I gave him a copy of the pertinent statute guaranteeing me a return to my old job if it still existed, which it did, the proof of which was the gentleman sitting across from me.

Clearly, the current president was shaken. I suspect he knew little or nothing about me or my rights. "I recognize your name now," he said. "I thought you were just one of the stockholders. What is it you want?"

"Well, an office for starters. And an explanation of what you've done with my company. We can discuss the rest after that."

We agreed to meet later that afternoon after he'd consulted with the company attorney, who joined us at our three o'clock consultation. The meeting was quite brief. Somerset did not want me as president, and I did not want to run a real estate development business. By mutual consent, we agreed that Somerset would buy back my shares. This did not make Karen and me rich, but the settlement allowed us to have some capital to further ease our reentry.

* * *

I was burning with desire to revive the "glory days" of Somerset, though in truth there had not been very many of them. In my mind, we were just getting started at the company when I had been drafted.

My main colleague had been Greg, who had been with me on the Gopher Yearbook. Greg was truly a master cinematographer and editor. I believed the two of us could co-found another successful production company.

Greg was hard to find, but through conversations with mutual friends, I learned that he had become despondent after the Somerset debacle and had withdrawn to a simpler life away from the pressures of business. I found him living in a tent on the bank of Apple River in Somerset, Wisconsin, with his wife and children. He was working as a plasterer.

Reluctant to go back to his previous life in filmmaking, my entreaties finally succeeded. We decided to keep this version of a company simple—just the two of us. No investors. In searching for a company name, we finally settled on using our middle names—mine was Russell, after my father, and Greg's was Manning. Thus, Russell-Manning Productions was born, and I designed a logo for it.

Always supportive, Karen joined us as a salesperson, and she was good at it. In viewing several office locations, I met Jim Michael, the owner of the Oak Grove Hotel near Loring Park in Minneapolis. Jim owned other downtown real estate as well as Lynnville, an alcoholism treatment facility in Jordan, a southwest suburb. I learned later that Jim's wife was a recovering alcoholic. Jim officed in the basement of the hotel, which also housed the social club for actors and associates at the nearby Guthrie Theater, one of the nation's preeminent regional theaters.

Jim and I struck up a friendship. Because he was also intrigued by media production, Jim gave us serviceable space next to his office at a nominal price. Before long, I persuaded Jim to invest in the production of a series of successful dramatic films about alcoholism. As research for the first one, which I wrote and directed, I lived as a patient for a weekend at Lynnville and experienced firsthand the physical and emotional trauma of substance abuse on families.

During my weekend at Lynnville, three near-death cases of individuals who had detoxified in the Minneapolis drunk tank were delivered to Lynnville. They were mostly still incoherent, slick with vomit and retching from withdrawal—truly humanity at its lowest point. My heart went out to them all and their loved ones.

During the production of a film about female dual addiction to pills and alcohol, we learned that Karen was pregnant. Our son, Brendan, was born January 22, 1972, after his mother suffered thirty-six hours of painful back labor.

Combining business with personal joy. Karen holds our son, two-day-old Brendan, next to a prototype of a greeting card innovation we called a card-vase.

Karen was such a good sport. I had just collaborated on a greeting card innovation with Bolger Printing. To promote it, Karen agreed to let us shoot a photograph of her with two-day-old Brendan and the card, which surprisingly was also a vase. It contained a plastic sleeve that could be filled with water and a bouquet of flowers. The prototype message I wrote was, "LOVE | GOOD THINGS GROW OUT OF IT."

The day that Karen and Brendan came home from Northwestern Hospital, instead of celebrating one of the happiest days in a parent's life, I invited business associates to my home for a business meeting. Afterward, at my mother's request, we drove Brendan to the nursing home where my ailing Grandma Averill was living. We wanted her and grandpa to meet Brendan before her condition deteriorated. Like I said, Karen was a good sport.

Brendan was a colicky baby. He fussed often and cried loudly for long stretches. Our pediatrician suggested phenobarbital in a baby bottle, and it worked. At last, the entire family could get some sleep.

During the summer of 1972, we bought a two-story house at 4808 Lyndale Avenue in south Minneapolis. Russell-Manning was building a reputation, but Greg and I were not yet making much money. "I made more as a plasterer," Greg complained one day. A few weeks later, another filmmaker offered Greg a full-time position at a decent wage to join him, and my partner left. Suddenly alone in the business, I decided to shelve the company and find a job with an existing company.

Fortunately, in early 1973, my reputation quickly earned me a job as creative director for a large production company called Creative Center. This company did some film production, but its main business was producing multi-image shows for business meetings. Creative Center had great clients like Pillsbury (now absorbed into General Mills), 3M, Burger King and many others, which all spent huge sums to entertain and inspire their sales forces at elaborate meetings in fun places.

I quickly learned the ropes of multi-media production and was soon writing all the shows and executive speeches for these extravaganzas. My boss, Bob, had invented technology for synchronizing and controlling scores of slide projectors and film sequences into sophisticated presentations with a high WOW! factor. Bob had also invented a unique inflatable theater system that allowed us to set up exotic multi-screen environments inside hotel ballrooms. For a creative person like me, Creative Center offered a gigantic playground.

Unfortunately, Bob was not a good businessman. After close to two years with him, he came to me one day and said he had decided to let most of the staff go, including his two sons. When asked, he showed me his books. Creative Center was essentially bankrupt, and I resigned so he would not have to fire me.

I had made one particularly close friend at Creative Center. Bruce, the production manager, was an experienced producer with great client relationship skills. I suggested to Bruce that we start our own production company, and he agreed. Not able to come up with a better name, we called it Russell-Manning Productions. After all, I already had a logo for that name. We asked Bob if we could approach his former clientele, and he gave us permission. So, we were able to start business with First Bank System (later called US Bancorp) as our first customer in March 1975. This was so much better than starting from scratch.

In the meantime, my second son, Scott, was born at Southdale-Fairview Hospital in Edina on July 13. Brendan greeted his new brother more enthusiastically than I had greeted my infant sister years earlier. In the following years, I could have eliminated some of my adventurousness and elevated my threshold for boredom to make room for the enjoyment of family. I could have spent more time with my boys, showing them that a Lindberg man didn't have to be emotionally distant like their grandpa or his father. But to my everlasting loss and theirs, my focus remained on the pursuit of adventure and success. How I wish I could go back.

* * *

The explosive success of Russell-Manning went to my head. Increasing business pressures caused me to spend more time traveling, producing films and growing my "empire" than I did with my family. The company moved into more elaborate offices in Butler Square downtown, where my glass-enclosed office overlooked an atrium carved out of the timbers of a historic warehouse.

During this period, I met two individuals who would be influential in my life. The first was Pablo, a handsome and charismatic Bolivian architect who had a small office on our floor. We would become close friends and would share some extraordinary adventures together in future years, one of which would threaten my life.

The other person was a performer who went by one name—YANNI. I watched him perform one day surrounded by synthesizers in the fireplace pit of a ground floor bistro called Joe's Saloon. The young, slender Greek with flowing black hair mesmerized me with his astonishing music, all originals. He was literally a one-man band, and the band was a powerhouse of sound moving from hard-driving tunes to sweeping, romantic melodies.

During a break, I chatted with "Yanni the Synthesizer Wizard," as the hand-lettered sign called him, and we became good friends. Yanni Chrissomallis, born in Kalamata, Greece, to a wealthy banker, had followed his brother to the Twin Cities and attended the University of Minnesota earning a BA degree in psychology. His love of music, though, sidetracked him into a popular local rock band called Chameleon, but he quickly grew tired of the rock music he was playing. A fresh, new kind of music was swirling in his head, and he was intent on getting it out. A few FM stations had started playing tapes of his songs on late night shows, and the music was attracting a small but dedicated fan base.

After our first meeting, Yanni and I spent a lot of time together. Often, I would go to the small house he shared with his brother in a northern Minneapolis suburb. He had a parrot named Caesar who greeted me by name when I came to visit and would often fly over and land on my head. His talons sometimes unintentionally hurt my scalp, but I never said anything to Yanni or Caesar.

When Yanni learned I had a film company, he was excited, because one of his dreams was to score movies. He didn't know at the time that his bright future would be in recordings and extravagant concerts. In the meantime, I persuaded him to teach my son, Brendan, how to play keyboards. The rest would unfold over time.

* * *

As Russell-Manning continued to grow, we bought our own building on Park Avenue near downtown Minneapolis and improved a sound stage already present in the back of it. Our increasing national reputation earned us steady business from major accounts such as Coca-Cola and John Deere, where I had assisted on my first motion picture production.

Feeling financially secure and anxious to exhibit my self-made success to the world, I was ready for a new home. By this time, Karen and I owned a two-story house in south Minneapolis, but Karen had seen a remarkable house for sale near Minnehaha Creek. It was a replica of a Moorish castle with tall, stained-glass windows capped by a copper dome and columned second-floor balconies.

Inside, a spiral staircase led upward to a prayer balcony that overlooked the entrance guarded by a massive front door. The sunken living room was two stories high. The second-floor bedroom, with its fireplace, opened onto a terrace that overlooked the living room. The house was a movie set situated on Aldrich Avenue in Minneapolis, and we couldn't resist buying it.

For the first time, I became involved in domestic activities—repairing cracked walls, buying furniture to match the home's Moorish theme, laying new ceramic pavers in the front room. My father, an expert at redecorating, helped with plastering and painting. To my dismay, I now realize that my renewed interest in family affairs had more to do with my need to publicly proclaim my success than to appreciate my loved ones.

My beautiful wife, Karen, seated in the living room of our castle.

We certainly enjoyed this special home, though. Our sons loved all the hidden spaces and the balconies outside their bedrooms. And we all made peace with a ghost that resided within. Karen and I threw wonderful social events in the castle, and every year the house was opened to the public for neighborhood tours. It took over a year for us to learn that the house was thought by many to be cursed. Some referred to it as the "Divorce Castle," because every couple that had owned it had suffered a divorce. Eventually, Karen and I would sadly succumb to that curse.

Rocket Man

Gary Hudson, a good friend since the 1970s, was a brilliant young man with a dream. He believed it was possible to design and build low-cost rockets to deliver payloads and eventually humans into low earth orbit. This could be done by private industry, he thought, at a cost far below the wasteful investments NASA was making.

Gary had found college so boring that he'd dropped out after three years. He already knew most of what they were teaching. Like me, who had started a film production business having never made a movie, he was dedicated to changing the aerospace industry having never so much as lit a Roman candle. But he was wickedly smart, so I teamed up confidently with Gary, the rocket man.

A very young Gary Hudson holds my sister's dog.

In my limited free time, I started helping Gary publish a quarterly magazine called *Foundation*, named after Isaac Asimov's science fiction series. Gary's brainstorm was a counterculture publication inspired by the periodic *Whole Earth Catalog* and featured eclectic essays, articles, occasional fiction, some product reviews and an idealistic emphasis on individuality, creativity and norm-busting. It was very much a quarterly journal of ideas.

I was introduced to Gary by a mutual friend, John Bolger, owner of Bolger Printing, a company in Minneapolis that printed *Foundation*. I had met Bolger through my sister, Bonnie, who then worked for an ad agency that frequently used Bolger's services. Bonnie hadn't known Gary Hudson until they both attended a party at my castle along with a dozen other select friends and associates.

This was a typical 1970s party with wine, cheese fondue, pizza slices and free-for-all conversation ranging from UFOs and interstellar travel to the latest project adventures of my company, Russell-Manning Productions. Eventually, as the wine bottles emptied, we sat around in my castle's sunken living room and played a parlor game someone suggested but no one else had heard of called "light as a feather, stiff as a board."

I'm not sure which guest volunteered, but that brave soul was instructed to sit in a straight chair while four others—Bonnie and I were two of them—stood around her in a circle, stacking our hands above her head for about twenty seconds until all eight hands were warm. Then we recited the phrase "light as a feather, stiff as a board." Immediately, we lowered our hands, palms down, with the two pointer fingers of each hand extended. In perfect synchronization, we placed our fingers either beneath the volunteer's shoulders or beneath her knees and then began to lift. Effortlessly, we levitated the woman off the chair—light as a feather—before setting her back down.

Astonished, everyone now had to try this, and everyone had success. Because our group was comprised mainly of overachievers, someone suggested we try lifting a car. We toasted that idea and poured out of the house, finding a Volkswagen bug parked on the street. I hoped no neighbors were watching as four bold guests went through the "light as a feather" ritual, placed their fingers at the corners of the front and rear bumpers, and tried to lift the car.

The car didn't rise, but eight fingers showed bumper creases.

Someone suggested that perhaps the trick didn't work on German automobiles, so another parked car was chosen, but it didn't rise either.

Disappointed but still merry, our little band reentered the castle for more wine and a short lecture by Gary Hudson with no spoiler alert. Our fingers were stronger than we thought, he told us, and the weight of the volunteer distributed over eight sets of fingers would feel lighter than expected for each person doing the lifting. It was pure physics, he told us. Later, I think that no one but me would remember his explanation, just the magic of levitating a person in my front room.

Despite his intellectual buzzkill, Gary and I became close and deeply respectful friends. Over time, while Gary was perfecting designs for a reusable rocket that could be built without government support or interference, he and I were also finding cooperative projects that perhaps were not practical but at least could satisfy our creative urges.

The first of these involved the popular science fiction novel *Dune*. Gary and I were both fans of the book, which had defied attempts to adapt it for the big screen. Director David Lynch had tried in 1984, but the scope of the novel made his movie version more of a highlights reel than a coherent story. And since CGI was not available then, many of the effects were laughable.

In 2000, the Syfy channel had attempted a mini-series version of *Dune*. Despite threadbare production values due to the low TV-budget of the series, this version told more of the story, and international sales earned the producers a sequel in 2004, *Children of Dune*.

Alejandro Jodorowsky's LSD-like vision of the novel was never made but had a script the size of a phone book written by *Dune* author Frank Herbert himself. Orson Welles was under contract to play the Baron, and H.R. Giger (of *Alien* fame) was signed for production design, but alas, it was never made.

The Denis Villeneuve 2021 version of *Dune* recognized that it would take at least two long films to tell the original story. Fortunate to be produced after CGI effects had matured, the film is a marvel of beauty and inspired storytelling.

Imagine, then, that in the mid-1970s, two unknown script-writers with no funding obtained an option to the movie rights for *Dune*. Gary and I were given an option like the one I had assigned to Haskell Wexler for my screenplay while serving in the US Army. During the option period we hoped to find financing based on our brilliant screenplay and produce the movie ourselves. Apparently, the Herbert estate considered the book unfilmable, so they asked for no option fee. The challenges of writing the script, of course, were daunting—only primitive effects were available at the time. The number of characters was massive and the story was voluminous.

Gary and I co-wrote a screenplay, and it was pretty good, certainly faithful to the book. But predictably, we came up short on financing. Occasionally, in my old age, I pull out the script and read a few pages to bring back wonderful memories of working with my good friend.

Another Gary Hudson project, this one even more ambitious, literally made it to the launch pad. Long before Elon Musk's SpaceX or Jeff Bezos's Blue Planet, we decided it was time to build a working version of a Gary Hudson-designed low orbit rocket to prove that a private company could change the space business with a reusable craft. Our vision was two-fold. First, we intended to replace the space shuttle with a more practical vehicle. It would have a short turnaround time between flights and would be capable of placing payloads like satellites into orbit at a lower but still profitable cost. Second, we wanted to inaugurate space tourism.

In our opinion, when first launched, the space shuttle already had been obsolete, heinously expensive, wrapped in nested economic lies to appease taxpayers and congress, and hopelessly compromised on its first fire. Our rocket, we hoped, would be the antidote.

Achieving the dream proved, as always, to be more difficult than expected. After stealing away my assistant, Anne Roebke, and then marrying her, Gary and Anne ultimately moved to Sunnyvale, California, a more fertile area for the kind of engineering talent that would be needed. To support his family, Gary packaged himself as a futurist and persuaded some large companies like IBM and 3M to pay him for lectures. This helped him gain a reputation and keep the dream alive.

His talks to the scientists and engineers of these companies were intended to be provocative, to stimulate imaginative thinking in the corporate ranks. In the 1970s, he often lectured about the future of tele-tourism, in which earthbound individuals would don a special helmet with a video screen at the front. Their head movements would synchronize with cameras placed, say, on the moon or a lunar rover, so the tele-tourist could drive remotely while sitting in his armchair. This, of course, anticipated the current reality of motion sensor technology gaming.

Gary would also speak about asteroid retrieval for mining—sending rockets to capture passing asteroids. The only uncertainties, he would explain to his captivated listeners, related to questions about where the asteroids should be positioned. "An asteroid 100 meters in diameter contains, among other things, a billion dollars' worth of nickel and three years' supply of cobalt," he would explain. "If you put the asteroid in orbit while you mine the elements instead of bringing them to the surface, you don't have to deal with the problem of gravity."

Gary's lectures and published papers caught the attention of an investor. David Hannah, a Houston-based real estate investor, had coincidentally acquired an interest in the commercial potential of space. "Until Gary came along," Hannah later told the press, "I was convinced that the only one who could launch rockets was the government."

Hannah persuaded a few friends to join him in putting up $1.2 million to build and send a rocket into space. The first $400,000 would fund the rocket design phase, and the rest would pay for building and launching the vehicle. A successful, privately built rocket that was launched into low earth orbit, they all agreed, would certainly attract another larger round of investment.

As self-appointed CEO—Chief Encouragement Officer—of Gary's company, I knew that the biggest challenge for my friend would be not technical in nature but economic. Technically, it was easier to build a rocket engine than a jet engine. Gary named the project and the rocket Percheron because, like that breed of workhorse, the rocket had to be big and dumb. It had to be cheap enough to justify the cost of launching small payloads and just reliable enough to not lose too many of them.

Gary attracted two talented, adventurous engineers to Project Percheron—David Ross and Clif Horne. Then Jim Fruchterman, who was working on a PhD in electrical engineering at Stanford, came aboard. "Hudson was talking as a matter of course that he was actually going to build rockets outside of NASA," Fruchterman later explained. He needed to give that a shot.

Over a few months, numerous designs were discussed and rejected. Near Christmas of 1980, the design finally coalesced about the same time that investors were pushing the team to get a working prototype on the launch pad as soon as possible. The pressure increased on everyone.

The body of a rocket, compared to its engine and nose cone electronics, is mostly just a hollow tube filled with fuel. In Percheron, the upper portion held liquid oxygen. A welded plate separated the liquid oxygen from kerosene stored in the lower half. Both sources of fuel would have to be pressurized to 150 pounds per square inch (about the pressure of 10 atmospheres) to burn properly, so the welds securing the shell and the plate separating the two tanks would need to be entirely leakproof. One way to test those welds was to fill the rocket with water under pressure.

In early February, Ross arrived for this pressure test in a swimsuit, goggles and fins. As it turned out, he was dressed appropriately. Water poured from all parts of the rocket. The welds had to be redone by a different contractor, but the schedule and budget unfortunately did not permit a second test, which built more suspense around the venture.

Mounting pressures also limited testing of Percheron's engine. "I regard it as unimaginable that you would set off a rocket with tons of propellants in it without any prior experience, but that's pretty close to what we did," Fruchterman admitted later. There simply was no other option given the low budget of the operation.

A scale model of the engine was built and fastened to a test stand at Fremont Airport south of Oakland. Performance of the first test firing failed to record the necessary data, so the team tried again. An excess of liquid oxygen prevented the second firing of the two-foot model from reaching maximum power. "Not an engineering success," Fruchterman explained, "but given the money, it had to do."

In May of 1981, Gary dispatched a team to Matagorda Peninsula south of Houston, a narrow strip of land running parallel to the Gulf Coast. They brought in generators, compressors, a four-wheel-drive vehicle, a small mobile home, and a van full of electronics. Federal officials, curious about the unusual activity on the normally uninhabited land strip, suspected the team of being drug runners but soon learned the truth was even more exotic. Later, when word leaked out about the extraordinary nature of the undertaking, press helicopters invaded the strip.

Unfortunately, some members of the family that owned the peninsula did not want a rocket launched from their land. On June 24, a deputy sheriff served Fruchterman with legal papers, forcing the team to abandon its endeavor. Besides losing four weeks of preparation, the relocation required barging all the equipment further south to Matagorda Island, which was owned by Percheron investor and American Liberty Oil Company Chairman Toddie Lee Wynne, Sr.

This island was essentially a cattle ranch pocked by ponds containing alligators, the largest of which was named Ralph. A nineteen-foot-high test frame was soon erected and anchored to concrete pilings extending three feet into the island soil. Ralph had to be baited to another location with chicken carcasses so suction pipes could be installed in his pond. These pipes would flow cooling water through the stand's metal structure to prevent heat damage from the test firing.

On Tuesday, July 7, the finished Percheron prototype was placed on a special trailer and trucked from Sunnyvale to the New Mexico state line where it collided head-on with red tape. Unfortunately, no one had obtained a special permit to truck an over-length rocket through the state. The driver, Don Ambrose, was told to book a motel room for a couple days while the paperwork was processed.

The Percheron rocket took up a few spaces in a parking lot.

Impatient, Ambrose hijacked the parked truck after dark and headed toward Matagorda, sticking to back roads so he would be less likely spotted by law enforcement. When he arrived, the press was waiting. The privately funded Percheron Project had become the biggest thing to hit Texas since Hurricane Jeanne.

On July 31, 1981, the rocket was bolted to the test stand and at a quarter past two, 3,700 pounds of liquid oxygen were pumped from storage tanks into the upper portion of the rocket. Sixteen hundred pounds of kerosene were sent into the lower tank. At twenty past four, engineers began pressurizing the tanks, and by a quarter to five, the pressure in both had reached 137.5 pounds per square inch without a leak. The welds had held.

The team had planned to conduct two test firings of the engine. The first firing, a "burp" test, would last about five seconds. If this static test went well, the rocket would be launched over the Gulf.

After a five-minute countdown, at 5:50 the igniter button was pressed.

Nothing happened.

A minute later, the team tried again, but still nothing happened. The burp test had fizzled. After relieving the tank pressure, the team checked the rocket and discovered that kerosene had leaked into the engine, wetting the igniter and causing the failure.

The next test firing was scheduled for Wednesday, August 5, 1981. This time, the igniter was wrapped in a plastic trash bag to keep it dry. An ABC News helicopter hovered nearby to record the event.

After a short countdown, the igniter button worked, and smoke erupted from the rocket's base. Then the button was pushed to open the liquid oxygen valve, and a split second later another button opened the kerosene valve. The first two stages shot into the sky, but the third stage exploded into a magnificent yet apocalyptic explosion.

Failure to launch.

Long after all the grass fires were put out, NASA asked for permission to gather and analyze the debris for any meaningful data that could be gained. Its conclusion, many months later, was that the rocket would have successfully launched but for one failed part, the three-dollar valve controlling the flow of kerosene. Most likely, it had simply frozen up in Matagorda's high humidity.

A three-dollar, off-the-shelf part had prevented us from becoming the first private commercial space company in the world. It's always the little things, isn't it?

After the crash, Gary went on to have successful careers in space technology and his second passion, gerontology research. He co-founded and served as chief architect of Gravitics, a space station manufacturing company; was founding partner of Oisin Biotechnologies, which is developing a liposomally-delivered gene to remove senescent cells from the body and possibly reduce or eliminate aging; and served as president/truste of the Space Studies Institute.

The Glensheen Murders

My mother, who had drawn me into so many unique experiences during my youth, was still at it. Unwittingly, she maneuvered me into a fascinating Minnesota murder mystery.

The infamous Glensheen murders had occurred in a large mansion in Duluth, Minnesota. The 39-room, 22,000-square-foot mansion had been built by Chester Adgate Congdon on twelve acres of Lake Superior waterfront property. Congdon, a lawyer who had made his fortune in the Minnesota taconite mining industry, named the estate Glensheen.

At seven o'clock on the morning of June 27, 1977, two people were found murdered at Glensheen. The first was Congdon's oldest surviving daughter, Elisabeth, who had inherited the estate. Due to Elisabeth's health condition—she was paralyzed on one side following a stroke—her fortune had been placed in a trust. The second victim was Velma Pietila, a nurse filling in for another caregiver who had been providing full-time care for Elisabeth. At the time, Elisabeth was the wealthiest woman in the state.

Elisabeth had been suffocated by a satin pillow and Velma beaten with a candlestick. Originally, the deaths were thought to be the result of a robbery because Elisabeth's bedroom had been ransacked, a jewelry box had been stolen and Velma's missing car was found the next day at the airport.

When I first read about the murders, they seemed like a real-life version of *Clue*, the board game—"Colonel Mustard killed in the drawing room with a candlestick." The opulence of Chester Congdon and his Glensheen Estate coupled with a double homicide won headlines across the nation, but I never expected the story to personally reach me.

The roots of this murder began in 1932 when Elisabeth, who could not bear children, adopted the daughter of an unwed mother in Tarboro, North Carolina. Elisabeth changed the girl's birth name, Jacqueline, to Marjorie. Though Elisabeth raised her daughter in the elegant Glensheen mansion, and the girl attended expensive Dana Hall Prep School in Massachusetts, it was clear from the beginning that Marjorie was a troubled child.

At sixteen, Marjorie was sent for a stay at the famous Menninger Clinic in Topeka, Kansas, a prominent center for treating serious mental illness. The clinic diagnosed her as a sociopath, meaning she exhibited little empathy, struggled to tell right from wrong, and often felt justified in performing actions she recognized as wrong. Today, this is called antisocial personality disorder (ASPD).

Two years later, Marjorie found herself estranged from her family and married to Richard "Dick" LeRoy in St. Louis, Missouri. When LeRoy was transferred to Minneapolis, the couple moved to my suburb, St. Louis Park, where Mom would soon open an art gallery.

In 1960, Dick LeRoy was still working from a small office above a strip mall called Miracle Mile, which I frequently visited, but despite having seven children with Marjorie, the marriage was now failing fast. Marjorie was an inveterate liar. A neighbor once said that she could "make up fibs faster that anyone could keep track of." Marjorie was also a compulsive spender. Even more dangerous, she was a firebug. When her home in Marine on St. Croix, Minnesota, burned down, she was suspected of arson, but the matter was mysteriously dropped.

By 1976, Marjorie had married again. Her new husband, Roger Caldwell, was of no financial consequence, their home had been foreclosed on, and Marjorie's trust fund had been exhausted by her indulgent spending. They were desperate for money. But Marjorie knew that upon her mother's death, she would receive eight million dollars from the estate.

Three days before the murders, Marjorie signed papers authorizing her husband, Roger, to receive $2.5 million of her share. After the murders were discovered, evidence found on the scene and later in the possession of Marjorie and her husband led to Roger's arrest. He was charged with first degree murder of both women, and the next day Marjorie was charged with conspiring to murder her mother. Roger was convicted on both counts and given two life sentences.

Two new developments, however, were introduced at Marjorie's trial. An expert witness disputed a fingerprint on an envelope that linked Roger to the murders. (Years later, DNA on the envelope was found to match Roger's.) Additionally, a witness from Roger's trial came forward and changed her story. She had seen Roger elsewhere on the day of the murder, she said, casting doubt on his availability at Glensheen to commit the crime.

Marjorie's grandmotherly performance during her trial also had an impact. She sat calmly knitting at the defense table during testimonies and brought a birthday cake to court for one of the lawyers. It must have been difficult for the jury to see this kindly woman as someone who would kill her own mother.

Marjorie was acquitted, but then another twist occurred. In 1982, the Minnesota Supreme Court overturned Roger Caldwell's conviction based on the new evidence introduced at Marjorie's trial. Instead of retrying Roger, the prosecutor offered him a plea deal. If he confessed to second-degree murder, his sentence would be converted to time served, which was only five years. On July 5, 1983, Roger was released from prison. Five years later—twelve years after the murders—he committed suicide.

Marjorie's children filed a civil suit for their right to their mother's inheritance, arguing they could prove she had been involved in the murders. Marjorie settled with her children out of court for a stipend of just $40,000 per year from the trust. Moving to Mound, Minesota, she became linked to another mysterious death. While Roger was in prison, Marjorie befriended a married couple, Wally Hagen, and his ailing wife, Helen. Marjorie was the last person to feed Helen before she died, and Helen's children claimed Marjorie had poisoned her. The case never went to trial, but Wally inexplicably became Marjorie's third husband. Later, Marjorie was charged with bigamy because she had failed to divorce Roger before marrying Wally.

In the following years, Marjorie served two prison terms for arson. After spending fifteen years in prison, she was then arrested for computer fraud and forging an $11,000 check on the account of a man who had died while under her care. She was later accused of murdering her third husband, Wally, who had died the day after Marjorie was convicted of setting an RV on fire in Ajo, Arizona, but those charges were eventually dropped.

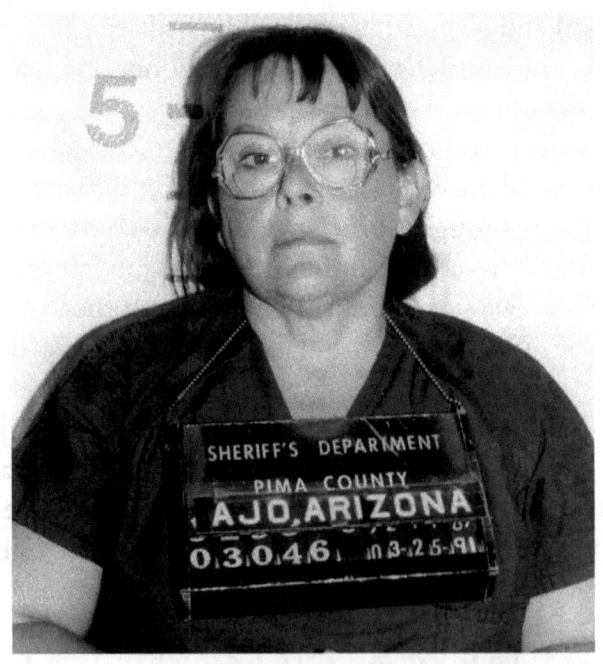

Marjorie after her arrest for burning down an RV in Arizona. Charges were later dropped.

This is where my mother entered the story and brought me into it. When visiting Minnesota, Marjorie sometimes went to

Elayne Galleries in St. Louis Park to buy art. My mother owned the gallery with my father and sister. Before long, Mom developed a relationship with Marjorie because, well… Mom liked everyone. During one conversation, my mother mentioned she had a son who was a writer. "Maybe you should talk to him about writing a book from your point of view," she suggested. "You could explain the truth behind everything that happened."

Marjorie liked the idea, and soon she and I were having discussions, some of them lengthy. She seemed candid and unremorseful, as you would expect from a sociopath. I was drawn to the story because Marjorie had been at the center of one of the most famous murder mysteries in Minnesota history and there were still numerous unanswered questions. Did Roger act alone? Was someone with him at Glensheen? How involved was Marjorie? Why was nurse Velma killed? How did Marjorie's third husband really die? Why did she give up the wealthy and comfortable life that had been given to her?

I don't like walking away from unsolved mysteries, but I'm sure I made the right decision in declining this opportunity. Marjorie was a very unreliable source of information, so any book based on her recollections would lack credibility. I was interested in getting to the truth of this mystery but had no interest in repairing Marjorie's reputation with shaky evidence and deceit. I also worried that if she didn't like what I wrote, my house might burn down.

In the summer of 2017, the History Theater in St. Paul, Minnesota, staged a musical about the murders called *Glensheen*. Its performances were sold out, but Marjorie was never in the audience. I did see the show, and it was entertaining, but like many stories "inspired by true events," it had little to do with the true story, which had already become mostly legend. The music and lyrics were written by Chan Poling, who was a previous colleague of mine and the widower of Eleanor Mondale, daughter of former vice president Walter Mondale.

The History Theater billed the show as "A Crackling Musical with a Wicked Edge." Its website featured this promotional blurb:

1977. An heiress, kind and generous, is found dead in her bed. Her night nurse, lying lifeless on the staircase. A robbery? A clumsy break-in? A conspiracy? A scandal! The Congdon family tragedy splashed across the headlines of every newspaper in Minnesota. But what really happened on that fateful night at the Glensheen Mansion? Whodunit? Witness this dark musical that tackles the tale with wicked dialogue and evocative music.

Eventually, the Glensheen property and mansion were given to the University of Minnesota Duluth to own and operate. While the mansion is open to the public for tours, docents have been instructed not to mention the murders to avoid disturbing the guests with the grisly tale.

The Great Rockwell Heist

So many things in my life were now happening at once—one mystery after another, adventures overlapping each other, all while figuring out how to manage a growing company. Then, tragedy struck the family art gallery.

On the evening of February 16, 1978, eight months after the Glensheen murders, over five hundred patrons gathered at Elayne Galleries for the largest show of original Norman Rockwell paintings ever held in a private gallery. Rockwell would have been there himself but had fallen ill. He would pass away nine months later. The exhibit featured eight original Rockwell paintings as well as numerous signed limited editions. A small dock scene attributed to French impressionist Pierre-Auguste Renoir was co-featured at the insistence of its owner, Buddy Verson.

Elayne Galleries had earned a nationwide reputation for handling Rockwells. Six of the original works were on loan for the show, but my family owned the other two. In the '70s, art had become a popular investment opportunity, and the exhibition was expected to attract the kinds of collectors who would be interested in buying the gallery's Rockwells.

My family had taken extraordinary measures to guard against theft. A contractor had installed a special sonic alarm system and "theft-proof" locks. The Pinkertons were hired to guard the building for the duration of the show. Mom's and Bonnie's knacks for turning a show into an extravaganza guaranteed a large turnout, but this time a publicity blitz reached deeper into the collector community.

The day prior to the show, however, the entire family became unnerved when three men who looked nothing like art lovers entered the gallery amidst the hubbub of preparations and began looking around. One of them left his sunglasses on while inspecting various artworks, a suspicious act. They split up, also viewing the various windows and doors in the gallery, then converged around the Renoir. Dad overheard them discussing the kinds of security that would be required to protect such a painting. Mom called them "cocky." After about half-an-hour, the men left. Dad followed them to the parking lot and made sure they saw him writing down the license plate number for their 1976 Chevrolet Impala. Dad was certain they were casing the gallery.

After the show, the gallery was locked up, the alarm was switched on and the Pinkertons came on duty. Nevertheless, thieves punched out the "theft-proof" lock, cut electricity to the alarm system and stole all but one Rockwell and took the Renoir, all within several minutes. The 1978 value of the paintings was about a half-million dollars, much more today. The ease and speed with which the theft took place suggested familiarity with the security system components, exceptional skill or insider complicity. It was and still is the largest art heist in Minnesota history and is well-documented in a book, *The Great Rockwell Heist,* by Bruce Rubenstein.

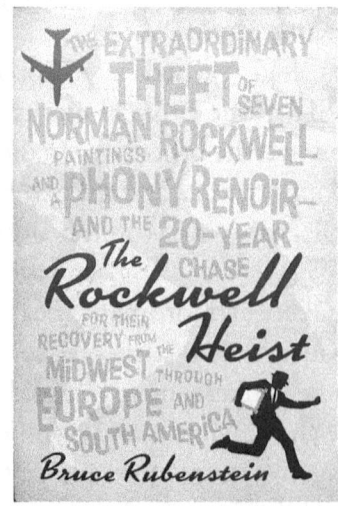

Likely, a hitch in the plan or an unexpected interruption had occurred preventing the eighth Rockwell from being stolen. But where were the Pinkertons during the time of the theft?

The St. Louis Park police figured the robbery had taken just fifteen minutes or less to accomplish. After tracing the license plate number Dad had documented, the police learned the Impala had been bought and sold three times during the previous month. The only previous owner who could be found was cleared of involvement.

The FBI's art theft unit took a keen interest in the burglary and developed a theory that it had been spearheaded by someone with inside knowledge of the gallery and the show who then had hired professionals for the theft. They also thought there was a tie to an organized crime ring operating out of Miami that was known to sell stolen art.

News of the heist spread quickly, and tips from all parts of the country started coming in. Most came from cranks, but a few were plausible. Psychics regularly came by the gallery offering their services for a fee.

On the first anniversary of the unsolved theft, a local newspaper article and a couple commemorative TV news features prompted an unusual tip. It was deemed credible because it correlated with the inside job theory even though the female tipster had just been released from a mental institution. The paintings, she said, had never left the gallery. They were still hidden between the hung ceiling and the roof beams.

My sister called me after FBI agents explored that tip. "A couple FBI agents just tore into our ceiling looking for the Rockwells," she told me. "At least they were apologetic when they didn't find anything, but they left a mess."

There were three "insiders" the FBI considered for the crime. The first was Robert Horvath, who had owned one of the Rockwells and was a frequent customer of Elayne Galleries. Unknown to my family, Robert and his brother, Paul, were in the business of money laundering and distributing marijuana from 1975 to 1979 and were also accused of tax evasion. The FBI believed that Robert may have been buying and selling art to launder money and could have organized the theft of his own painting to deflect suspicion of his involvement.

Even though the gallery had urged Robert to insure his painting for the show, he had declined. After the theft, however, he threatened to sue the gallery for his loss, but he never did.

The second suspect was Mom, the ultimate insider. To the FBI, Elaine Lindberg was in a better position than anyone to stage the burglary. She could collect insurance on some of the paintings and keep them all for later sale on the black market. The FBI noted that Mom had a relationship with Robert Horvath and other unscrupulous people in the art world, though Mom did not know the backgrounds of these individuals.

The FBI was especially interested in Mom when they learned about her relationship with Buddy Verson, who owned the stolen Renoir. They had met in 1976 at a gallery exhibit of the works of artist Charles Bragg. Soon after that meeting, Verson bought a Bragg and two Rockwell lithographs from the gallery. Two weeks before the big Rockwell show, he had approached Mom with a proposition.

A Spanish- and English-speaking cabin attendant for Northwest Airlines named Sonia had tipped off Buddy that a valuable painting—which turned out to be the Renoir dock painting—was available at the bargain price of $15,000. He proposed that Mom meet Sonia in Miami where she would be taken to the painting to authenticate it. If the artwork was genuine, Mom would be authorized to negotiate a price and close the deal.

My mother had been the authenticator and/or intermediary for many such transactions, so this was not that unusual. She agreed and flew to Miami with cash and a blank check signed by Verson. Sonia picked up Mom at the airport. On the way to Withers Warehouse in Coral Gables where the painting was located, they picked up a Spanish-speaking man, Rolando, who claimed to own the painting. With Sonia translating, he explained that he had been an art collector in Cuba but had fled after the Castro revolution, taking only the Renoir with him. He needed cash, so he was willing to sell the Renoir cheap.

At the warehouse, a third man named Caesario Concannon appeared and showed a different painting to Mom, asking her to identify the artist.

"Picasso," Mom said, assuming this was a crude test.

Caesario nodded, then removed the Renoir from a small vault. Mom spent a half-hour with the painting, investigating everything from the brush strokes to the canvas to the stretcher bars and frame. She did a "blue light test" and a "varnish test," which were both positive for the types and dates of materials used in the painting, and then declared it authentic. Mom started her bid at $8,000 but finally agreed to $10,000, considerably below the asking price. A check would not do, however. The owner insisted on full payment in cash. Also, a second signature from the seller would be needed to release the painting, and that signer was flying in the next day from Santo Domingo.

Mom called Buddy, who agreed to fly to Miami the next day with cash. Mom flew back to Minneapolis the next morning before Buddy arrived at the airport. She didn't see the painting again until Buddy brought it to the gallery on February 13 so it could be displayed. Immediately, Mom noticed a scratch in the upper right corner that had not been there when she had examined it in Miami. Buddy said he had been showing the painting to friends and suggested it must have been scratched when passing it around.

Buddy insisted that the painting be exhibited during the upcoming Rockwell show. Mom disagreed because it was inconsistent with the Rockwell theme, but finally agreed to exhibit the work in a separate room. After all, she told me, having an original Renoir would add some luster to the exhibition.

Over time, the FBI removed Mom from the suspect list.

The third person on the FBI insider list was Buddy Verson himself. The FBI had found too many "coincidental" links between Buddy, the two men at the Withers Warehouse and Sonia, the flight attendant. In different combinations, these individuals had been involved in art transactions of forged works.

Clearly, a scratched, fake Renoir had been swapped for the original painting Mom had authenticated. Sonia was transporting stolen art and forged art on the planes she flew, and the others were con men who capitalized on the works. It was important for the Renoir to be stolen with the Rockwells because it was a fake, otherwise it would eventually be identified as such.

At this point, my mother, an expert in written and painted forgeries and a policewoman in a previous life, agreed to assist the FBI in a sting operation. The fascinating details are in the book, *The Rockwell Heist*, but the conclusion to this adventure remains unsatisfying. The big fish managed to get away, including Sonia. As author Rubenstein put it:

> Dark-eyed Sonia, with her cocaine, her gangster friends, and her mysterious aura, is the most intriguing person among those whose identity is known, but at this point in the story she floats off like a bubble and pops. It turns out that even the name by which she's remembered might be wrong.

Buddy Verson's story, however, ended abruptly. On March 29, 1978, he had a heart attack and died while jogging at his athletic club. He was just forty years old. We thought his death was highly suspicious.

The Rockwell saga continued to unfold for twenty-one years, disappearing for a while and then reappearing with some strange tale or tip, an offer from a con artist to return one of the paintings for a fee—always a forgery—or an FBI break in the case that turned out to be a dead end.

Bonnie never lost focus on the paintings, though. It wasn't the monetary value of the works that drove her interest, but her need, like mine, to solve the mystery by finding the paintings. Eventually, the FBI figuratively washed its hands of the case, and an agent returned many of its case-related files to Bonnie.

"So, you're saying, you're done and now it's completely up to me?" Bonnie asked the agent.

"Pretty much," the agent responded.

"Maybe I should take this case to *Unsolved Mysteries*. They love poking into cold cases."

"That's a good idea," the agent said dismissively before leaving.

During this long stretch of frustration and red herrings, other dramas would also occupy my attention.

Sea Serpents and POWs

During the late '70s, I was feeling the crushing pressure of supporting a staff that would grow to fifty talented people. We either had too few production contracts or more than we could satisfy, yet every two months pay checks had to go out. I was spending much less time doing creative things like writing and directing and too much time with administrative tasks. I was burned out, and opportunities for side hustles like the Glensheen story, which did not fit into the business of Russell-Manning, made me think about what I really wanted to be doing. During my years at Russell-Manning, I had won over a hundred national and international awards, including two Grand Awards from the New York International TV and Film Awards competition, but winning more honors had become an unsatisfying goal that merely sustained the status quo.

At home, I was ignoring my wife and failing to be an attentive father. Karen, I'm sure, was increasingly distraught by my long hours, my anxiety over finances and my distractions, which she knew could separate me even further from my family. At times, she teasingly referred to me as "Uncle Gary" in front of the kids. Frankly, I was feeling trapped on all sides. And yet, instead of simplifying my life, I pushed forward in the opposite direction, deciding to steer the business into entertainment projects—a high-risk proposition. Today, as my own elder, I am dismayed at my own shortsightedness.

I had two business partners—Bruce, my original partner, and Bill, a minority partner who had married my sister in 1978. I suggested my new vision of entertainment films to them with mixed responses. Bruce felt we should maintain the successful model of corporate communications that we had worked hard to establish. Bill, a photographer and cinematographer, was attracted to the idea of branching out. For the time being, we agreed to maintain the status quo, but I continued to focus on a way to escape the tyranny of contract production work.

* * *

My yearning to make a "real" movie had finally overwhelmed me, but I knew that it would have to be a low-budget affair, one for which I could realistically find funding. Echoes of the Loch Ness Monster documentary we had produced back in the Somerset Limited days still haunted me. The problem with all documentaries, in my opinion, was that they were generally passive viewing experiences. Some used dramatic reenactments to boost entertainment value and tension, but these fake interludes contrasted with the real-life nature of true documentary footage, producing a dissonance I found irritating and disingenuous.

A second problem was that in documentaries about expeditions in search of something new or unexplained, the "something new" was seldom found. After a big build-up, the audience would be left with a tangle of circumstantial evidence and no payoff. Older readers may remember April 21, 1986, when Geraldo Rivera hosted a live, two-hour CBS broadcast special during which gangster Al Capone's walled-off underground room in Chicago's Lexington Hotel was finally blasted open to reveal the much-anticipated startling contents. Thirty million viewers tuned in to find the room empty except for some debris.

What if someone produced a wholly fake documentary? I wondered, recalling the famous Orson Welles radio show dramatizing the famous H.G. Wells novel *The War of the Worlds* as if it were a live news event. If a film could be shot to look like "found footage," and audio recordings could be produced with realistic sound effects mimicking documentary audio, a producer could at last be free of the constraints of truth telling and use the documentary form to tell a narrative story. You could shoot handheld, jerky, out-of-focus footage cheaply and it would actually have a desirable, realistic effect. Such a film would be cheap to produce but would require great care in the construction of the storytelling and creation of credible "real life" pictures and sound.

I crafted a story about a National Geographic photographer, Paul Martin, who had become hooked on tales of a contemporary, sea serpent-like creature off the shore of Baffin Island—the fifth largest island on earth—in the Canadian territory of Nunavut. He traveled there to capture evidence, conducting interviews with local Inuit peoples and discovering collected objects that resembled large dinosaur eggs and soapstone Inuit carvings of a long-necked animal rising from the sea.

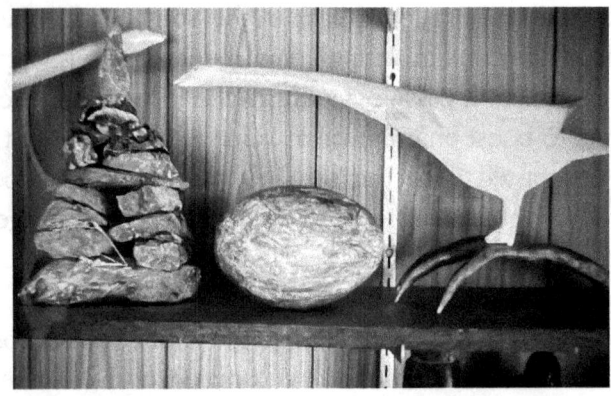

In my story, while interviewing an Inuit woman in Pangnirtung, photographer Paul Martin spots this "dinosaur" egg (top image) on the woman's shelf, being used as a decoration. He also finds this Inuit soapstone sculpture (bottom image) depicting an encounter with a "sea serpent."

We hear his audio-recorded notes and his final words as he pursues a strange creature in a small fishing boat, a journey from which he never returned, though we can hear the destruction of the boat by a large creature and the screams of Paul and his companions on tape. I hired props people to produce the eggs and carvings and asked my good friend, Warren Frost, to play the role of Paul Martin in some pre-production photos to be shot on Baffin Island for pitches to potential investors. In 1972, Warren had played the key role of Dr. Hayward on the David Lynch TV series *Twin Peaks*, which was co-created by Warren's son, Mark Frost.

Actor Warren Frost, portraying photographer Paul Martin, pretends to be recording notes while scanning the horizon of Baffin Island.

Warren and I spent over a week on Baffin Island, flying into Frobisher Bay in early September and then hiring a bush pilot to take us to the Inuit village of Pangnirtung on the shore of a magnificent fjord that cut into the arctic circle. We accomplished a lot of necessary pre-production work and took important photos, but the big drama occurred on our last day when we were notified that dense fog, a precursor to winter, was rapidly approaching. We were told that a plane was coming to get us and a small group of Japanese cliff climbers. If we did not leave on this plane, we might be stuck in Pangnirtung for weeks.

The aircraft, an old DC3 cargo plane with folding chairs strapped to the floor, landed on the rock-strewn strip of land alongside the fjord at low tide. We had twenty minutes to load up and take off before the tide flooded this makeshift airstrip. By the time all ten of us were boarded, the fog had filled the narrow fjord, which was surrounded by 5,000-foot cliffs. The pilot taxied to the farthest accessible inland point on the beach, then turned around to make his seaward run for a take-off.

As fog entered the fjord, Paul Martin, played by actor Warren Frost, boarded the rescue DC3 with a group of Japanese cliff climbers for an escape from Pangnirtung. This event was not scripted, but a genuine rescue. Photo: Gary Lindberg.

Bouncing over the rocks, the DC3 built up speed and finally lifted off. Looking out the window, I suddenly saw the rocky face of a cliff appear just off the wingtip. Fearing we would fly into the cliff or scrape off a wing, I screamed—at least I tried to—but then watched in amazement as the pilot steered the craft close enough to the cliff to keep it within eyesight but not so close as to remove a wing. He used the cliff as a guide until we were out of the fjord and over the Cumberland Sound. Thank God for experienced bush pilots.

For all the effort and adventure, I was never able to raise enough money to produce this "found footage" pseudo-documentary, which would have been the first of its kind. Eighteen years later, a movie with the same found footage concept, *The Blair Witch Project*, was released, and its worldwide gross box office receipts were $248.6 million.

* * *

Since Russell-Manning was still purring along, I decided to add two employees to the payroll. Marc Kramer had been a principal at Creative Casting for a few years. This was an agency we often used for auditioning and hiring on- and off-camera talent. Annemarie Osborne, the founder of Creative Casting, had decided to close her business to pursue other interests, and Marc had become available as a sales rep and production coordinator. Marc and I became best friends and stayed close until he died in 2023. Annemarie and I continued to have many adventures together, as you will see later in this book.

I also hired Chuck Whitney, a man with no production experience, chiefly because he had such an interesting life story and seemed very trainable. Chuck had served three years as a marine during the last period of the Vietnam War and then had worked as a hospital administrator with the American Refugee Committee (ARC), which was headquartered in Minneapolis. ARC had sent him to the Ban Vinai Holding Center in Thailand to supervise the delivery of healthcare to Hmong refugees who were fleeing persecution in Laos, their homeland, because they had assisted the United States during the Vietnam War conflict. When the US vacated Vietnam and Cambodia, the Hmong were left unprotected militarily and diplomatically. Many had crossed the Mekong River into Thailand for their safety.

During his two years providing care for Hmong refugees, Chuck had become close friends with many Hmong resistance fighters.

These were experienced Hmong fighters who would travel into Laos and escort women, children and elderly Hmong to the safety of Ban Vinai. Chuck's remarkable discoveries of war crimes and attempted genocide would present to me a new adventure of epic proportions.

I acquired the rights to Chuck Whitney's life story even though I wasn't sure what to do with the agreement after signing it. It was certainly the stuff of a riveting book, I thought, or possibly a movie. While I was still responsible for keeping Russell-Manning intact, my heart was now in the inspiring and important story I had just acquired. Torn in multiple directions, I let Karen carry the burden of raising our sons practically alone—one of the most unfair decisions I had ever made.

As I continued to obsess over Chuck's story, which I believed was a door into the entertainment industry, my marriage was slowly coming apart. In the fall of 1981, Karen told me she thought it best if we separated. I was so excited by the possibilities facing me and stressed over business pressures that my first thought was, *Well, that would relieve me of the guilt of failing to meet family expectations.* Karen had unwittingly offered me a way to simplify my life. But it meant admitting my failure as a husband and father.

Looking back on this pivotal moment from the perspective of an eighty-year-old man, I can now see the selfishness and cowardice in my response. I was so anxious to relieve my stress without losing my opportunities that I agreed to sacrifice my family. That night, I cried myself to sleep. I had failed a second time to have a successful marriage. But I did not reverse course. Karen and I remained friends with some hurt feelings, and many years later, when discussing why we had divorced, neither of us could explain. I think both of us were just burned out. Ironically, the divorce was final on Valentine's Day, 1983. We agreed on joint custody of our sons, though they would live primarily with her. She got the castle, and I got the company. Both of us, however, lost a piece of ourselves.

My tunnel vision had prevented me from seeing, or admitting, the toll my addiction to drama would have on Brendan and Scott.

* * *

Russell-Manning continued to roll, but increasingly I was obsessed with Chuck Whitney's story and the possibility of developing entertainment projects. But first things first. Chuck's story had led to some startling revelations that tugged at my heart as a Vietnam-era veteran.

During his prolonged service at Ban Vinai, a tent city with over 50,000 refugees, he had gained unprecedented acceptance by the Hmong community because he, alone among other American aid workers, chose to live in the camp and learn to speak Hmong. "I spoke it rather lamely," he told me. In his continual treatment of diverse illnesses, he had noticed a trend. Many of the ailing refugees had symptoms consistent with tuberculosis, a potentially fatal bacterial infection.

Chuck began to administer hard-to-swallow pills containing rifampin, pyrazinamide and ethambutol, a standard regimen for treating TB. But over many weeks, he saw in most of these patients a steady deterioration of their health and too often a fatal outcome. If the TB pills were not helping, he thought, then perhaps these sick people were suffering from some other undiagnosed ailment. But what?

In trusted conversations with Hmong resistance fighters he had befriended in the camp, he heard first-hand stories of Russian helicopters spraying out a sticky, yellow substance over the mountainous Hmong villages and fields. Shortly after a dump, the villagers would begin to get sick—vomiting and diarrhea, sudden weight loss, intense fatigue, loss of appetite. These were symptoms of tuberculosis, but they also coincided with the dropping of some kind of chemical on the Hmong people and their food sources. Many of the villagers died of dehydration because of the loss of fluids. And survivors who ended up at Ban Vinai, perhaps, were being incorrectly treated for TB.

Chuck sent this information up his chain of command to no effect, so he decided to solve the mystery himself by obtaining a sample of the malevolent "yellow rain" that was reportedly falling on the Hmong. If it was poisonous, there would be a remedy, and the samples could also be evidence of attempted genocide.

Several resistance fighters volunteered to reenter Laos and get a sample for Chuck, but he needed first-hand observation of the intentional distribution of the substance and careful collection of uncontaminated material for later analysis. He decided to accompany the resistance fighters into Laos, knowing that the US had no diplomatic relations with the country at that time. Laos was a black hole, and if an American went in and disappeared, that was usually the end of the story.

With a small resistance team, Chuck surreptitiously entered no-man's-land in early May, 1981, and after several hours reached a small Hmong village. He was prepared to stay for a few days, as there was no way of knowing if or when the Russians would spray the village or nearby rice fields. The plan was to avoid staying in the village and away from the fields in case helicopters attacked with their toxic cargo.

Late in the afternoon, the team heard a chopper on the horizon, then saw its distinctive shape moving toward another village several miles away. Hurriedly, Chuck and the team made their way toward the neighboring village and caught a glimpse of the helicopter releasing a gentle spray over the buildings. Chuck took photos, then handed a surgical mask and a pair of rubber gloves to each team member as they approached the village, cautioning them not to touch any contaminated surfaces with their skin.

The foliage around the village was lightly coated with a moist, yellow substance that Chuck carefully scraped into a series of vials and put into his backpack. He had what he had come for. The team reached the Mekong after dark and found their concealed boat. Eluding the Thai border patrol, they crossed the river and entered Ban Vinai. Chuck remembered sleeping well that night.

Chuck only had three months of duty left in Ban Vinai before returning to Minneapolis. His military experience caused him to be wary of officially turning in all the samples, so he divided the collection vials into two small groups. The first group he sent in a diplomatic pouch to the state department with a detailed letter explaining the suspected nature of the biological samples. Because it was illegal for Americans to enter Laos, he claimed that he had been given the samples by incoming Hmong refugees. He kept the second group for himself in case the first samples disappeared.

He never heard from the state department, and when he sent a request for confirmation of receipt and an analysis of test results, he was told no such package had ever arrived. It was simply missing. *Incompetence or suppression of evidence*, Chuck thought.

When at last it was time for him to leave Ban Vinai, he taped the remaining small vials to his leg. Wearing long pants, he smuggled them into the US. In Minneapolis, he rented a small house with worn furniture and started thinking about finding a job. He knew that a chemical analysis of the samples would cost more money than he had, but he was uncomfortable keeping the samples in his house. After the first set of samples had vanished, he was fearful that the government might be onto him. His name had been on the vials in the diplomatic pouch.

Feeling rather paranoid, he buried the remaining samples in his backyard and concluded that the vials would only prove Russian complicity in the expected poisoning if the chain of custody for the samples was protected. He needed an important, big-name partner to help him credibly bring this evidence forward.

After returning one evening from a day of job hunting, he found his house broken into, his drawers and cupboards emptied onto the floor and multiple holes dug in the yard. Someone had been searching for the samples. Fortunately, the buried samples had not been found.

Feeling greater urgency, Chuck contacted the head of ABC News and gave them his story. They agreed to pay for a chemical analysis and credit Chuck for his role in the affair if the analysis proved to be yellow rain.

A news team flew to Minneapolis and filmed Chuck digging up the buried samples, then followed the samples as Chuck flew them to a laboratory for analysis. The network TV giant produced a television documentary called "Rain of Terror" that aired December 21, 1981. It featured Chuck and blew the lid off the excuses that yellow rain was simply a substance found in the natural world as had been conjectured. Rather, it was a chemical weapon made of fungus toxins and created by the Soviet Union. The US secretary of state at the time, Alexander Haig Jr., admitted that the Soviet Union had given the weapon to the Viet Cong and Pathet Lao (officially the Lao People's Liberation Army) to exterminate the Hmong.

The *New York Times* ran a lengthy story on December 18 making this statement:

> Yellow rain is a term coined to refer to chemical warfare agents dropped from the air. A derivative of polyethylene glycol, the man-made chemical was identified by Dr. Joseph Rosen, a Rutgers University chemist who analyzed the sample for ABC News. Dr. Rosen said he was "100 percent certain" that the substance was not found in nature. The discovery appears to buttress assertions that chemical warfare agents have been dropped in Southeast Asia and to undercut suggestions that the toxins found in previous samples of yellow rain resulted from normal biological processes.

Chuck received no compensation for his efforts, but as promised, ABC paid his travel expenses and the costs of chemical testing. He still had no job, however. This was when he approached Russell-Manning Productions, and I offered him a paid internship. Our company now owned his life story, but we had no idea of the strange places this story was going to take us.

* * *

Chuck was a fast learner and hard worker, a genuine asset to the company. Within several months, we hired him as a full-time employee. I continued to personally meet with him about his remarkable story, taking careful notes of details that might be useful in developing a book or a movie. As we gained trust and rapport, I slowly evolved into a kind of Father Confessor. His many years in battle and refugee support had taken a toll on him emotionally.

An Improbable Series of Risky Events

While in the marines, he had seen bloody battle as a medic, of course, but his last year was the most emotionally taxing. He had been reassigned to Graves Registration, a safer position but extraordinarily depressing. Graves Registration was the military's bowdlerized term for processing corpses. Every day he had to handle mutilated bodies and body parts, try to identify which marine they belonged to, then tag and package the remains for storage or shipment. Physical risks were minimal, but the psychic damage, he feared, was indelible. He suffered more depression during that time than when he was in the field caring for the wounded. Death was all around him.

He had signed up with ARC because it was a way to use his combat medic knowledge to help the living, and also because a counselor had told him that serving others could help him focus less on his own problems. He had not expected to connect so strongly with the Hmong, and his mission-oriented training had allowed him to find a purpose—to stop the genocide.

Unfortunately, his military and healthcare experience were not immediately transferable to civilian employment, which explained his eagerness to start at Russell-Manning as a low-paid intern. He knew he would work his way up the ladder.

I vividly remember the afternoon Chuck first talked about American POWs and MIAs. His reference to prisoners of war and soldiers missing in action startled me. My army instincts, dormant for over a decade, were suddenly revived. I had army friends who were taken prisoner in Vietnam or had gone missing, but the prospect that some unreturned marines were still alive had never crossed my mind during interviews with Chuck because I was obsessed with the yellow rain storyline.

According to the US government, all POWs had been released or had died, and all MIAs had either been accounted for or had long been presumed dead. But Chuck told me this was not true—some MIAs still existed as POWs in Laotian jungle compounds. They had been captive for over a decade, he said, but the US government didn't want to address the thorny issue so it either covered up the facts or simply could not accept the truth.

"How could you be sure there were still Americans held captive in Laos?" I asked him.

"Some of the new refugees entering Ban Vinai had been held in remote jails in the jungle alongside American soldiers and got to know them," Chuck told me. "Some were captive for months because they were Hmong and the Pathet Lao hated them."

The Pathet Lao was a communist organization in Laos closely tied to the Vietnamese communists of northern Vietnam. The Hmong, as allies of the hated US, were considered enemies by the Pathet Lao. Stories of POWs and MIAs alive in Laos seemed farfetched to me at the time, so I pushed Chuck for more information.

"Obviously, you believed these stories," I said. "Are you sure they weren't just trying to gain favor with you?"

Chuck opened a folder. Obviously, he was prepared for this line of inquiry. He showed me a list of about thirty American names with a number next to each one.

"Many Hmong prisoners escaped. The Americans with them were usually too weak to accompany them. When I met these incoming Hmong escapees to screen them for health issues, they told me about the Americans left behind. Some Americans gave their names and army serial numbers so if the Hmong person made it to freedom they could get word to family members that they were still alive."

Chuck showed me a list he had transcribed, along with some scraps of paper on which names and numbers were scrawled to remember them.

"Check out these names for yourself," Chuck said. "They're all POWs and MIAs still alive in Laos, unless they recently died."

Over the next week, I checked the names against public records. All of them were listed as MIA and most of the serial numbers were accurate, though a few were slightly off, perhaps due to misremembering. My skepticism diminished.

In my next interview session with Chuck, he showed me a tattered, hand-drawn map. "This is the most recent one I was given by a resistance fighter. It shows where one of the Laotian jungle jails is located," he explained. "I believe there are Americans being held there, but the compounds move every six months or so. This circle here, near the jail, is a village with a name that translates into 'Silver City.' This compound should be easy to find and check out."

"What are you suggesting?" I asked.

"Nothing. Just putting the info out there. But I should also tell you that I had a talk with a guy named Barnes, a former army special forces agent, who said he had gone into Laos on a mission to discredit stories about remaining POWs and instead discovered an armed camp with about forty men who looked like Americans."

Information released later by the US government showed that the validity of these Hmong accounts was entirely possible. When the Paris Peace Accords were signed in January 1973, all US prisoners were supposed to be released under "Operation Homecoming." The United States Department of Defense (DOD) listed 311 Americans as missing in Laos. One month later, however, the North Vietnamese gave US officials a list of prisoners of war in Laos that revealed only nine Americans—seven servicemen and two civilians. While tamping down discussions about Americans still in captivity, US agencies believed that as many as forty-one Americans may have been held prisoner by the Pathet Lao. As late as July 2019, the DOD's Defense POW/MIA Accounting Agency listed 286 Americans missing in Laos, of which 263 were classified as requiring further pursuit, twelve were deferred for unspecified reasons and eleven were labeled as non-recoverable.

In my research for this book, I found a declassified/sanitized UPI story about Barnes, who had testified before congress about the mission mentioned by Chuck. The article, quoted verbatim below, revealed details of the mission.

> A former Army special forces agent told Congress he saw possibly 45 American prisoners of war in Laos on a 1981 mission intended to disprove reports of U.S. servicemen held captive in Southeast Asia… Barnes testified that he and three other Delta Force members were recruited for a secret mission arranged by Army Col. James "Bo"

Gritz... aimed at discrediting accounts of remaining POWs reported by Robert Garwood, a marine private accused of collaborating with the Vietnamese during his own captivity.

Barnes further testified that photographs and some audio was captured of these servicemen but "the information was seized by the Defense Intelligence Agency and US embassy personnel and has been suppressed by the CIA."

My years in the army had softened my heart to the plight of our soldiers, most of them young. I could not bear to hear such persuasive talk about the possibility that some of these soldiers were still captive in Laos after more than a decade. Now that I had this information, I would have to make a decision. Should I ignore it and go about my life, or do something to aid those MIA/POWs?

I chose the second option. But the next question was—do what?

"You know it's illegal for unassigned Americans to even enter a Hmong refugee camp, let alone sneak into Laos," I told Chuck.

"And don't forget dangerous," Chuck added.

"Russell-Manning isn't a mercenary force, so we're not going into Laos on a rescue mission. We aren't even 100 percent sure there are Americans there."

"Agreed."

"Anyway, who would take our word for it? The government says these American captives don't exist."

"On paper, they don't—unless we had hard evidence, like I did. Remember those samples of yellow rain?"

I could see where this was headed. Russell-Manning didn't have a spare armed special forces unit to lend, but we were experts at producing visual media. If we could train a Hmong resistance team in photographic techniques, then equip them and send them into Laos, maybe they could get pictorial evidence of surviving MIAs held captive by the Pathet Lao. Certainly, that would have to be taken seriously by the government. Or the mainstream news media.

At this same time, I was coincidentally in the process of starting a new division of the company to specialize in producing entertainment. I had already recruited the executive director of the Minnesota State Arts Board, John Ondov, to join the effort, which we planned to split off as a separate entity in the future. I proposed my Laotian mission to John and my other partners, Bruce and Bill, and all but Bruce were enthusiastic about it. Bruce volunteered to keep the commercial side of the business running.

To carry out our Ban Vinai mission, we would need financing, lots of specialized photographic equipment, assurance from a major news outlet to publish our evidence if we were successful, and cooperation from the Hmong resistance in Thailand. John was a great help in finding and reaching out to the families of MIAs who lived in the Midwest. We invited them to a presentation about our audacious plan, and their response was enthusiastically supported by donations for expenses.

I contacted Les Crystal, the head of ABC News, who had previously greenlighted Chuck's exposé about yellow rain. After hearing me out, he agreed to fulfill a request for photographic equipment and materials if we would give ABC News an exclusive to any genuine evidence we obtained. Our "ask" included still cameras and film, Super 8mm cartridge-load movie cameras and cartridges, infra-red cameras for night shooting, and other miscellaneous equipment for field film processing and other tasks. Within a couple weeks, cartons of photographic supplies started showing up at Russell-Manning headquarters.

Chuck's job was to make a list of pharmaceuticals and other medical supplies that were chronically in short supply at Ban Vinai. Chuck planned to obtain Hmong cooperation by bartering a truckload of healthcare supplies.

* * *

At the same time, we were planning our mission to obtain photographic evidence of living American MIAs in Laos, another group was planning a private mission that we worried would interfere with ours. The Green Beret lieutenant colonel named James "Bo" Gritz, who had led the Barnes mission to discredit POW reports, had become a celebrity based on his inspirational story of heroism during a Vietnam mission he often boasted about.

In a speech Gritz made in 1981 to Vietnam veterans in Buffalo, New York, he told the dramatic story of a soldier named Sgt. Hoaglund who took his own life in a 1965 battle. He said the following exact words transcribed for posterity and published later by the *Washington Times*.

> As happened all too often, we landed right in the middle of the lion's den. While fleeing from the pickup zone, SFC Hoagland was hit by one of many machinegun bursts that cracked by our ears. It was as if we were all hit when Hoagland went down, his legs shattered. There wasn't a moment's hesitation. We all crashed back through the heavy jungle to encircle our comrade. Hoagland was frantic, not from pain or fear, but because he knew, as we all did, that to stay meant certain death or capture.
>
> Even as we stacked magazines and straightened pins on our grenades, bullets began cutting bark and vines all around us. Still, we could all hear Hoagland screaming, "Get out of here, now!" But the men couldn't bear to leave Hoagland there alone. Hoagland's unspoken devotion and love for his buddies was stronger than life itself. With a whispered goodbye and a last look at his friends, Hoagland put his AR-15 to his head and, before any of us could react, pulled the trigger, eliminating in a twitch of a finger any need for all of us. He had not died alone and yet we had a chance at life.

Even worse, on March 29, 1983, the *Washington Times* exposed the Hoagland story as a fraud when reporter Whitt Flora wrote:

> The trouble with Gritz's story, according to Army records and eyewitnesses, is that the soldier mentioned did not commit suicide, the battle did not take place where and when he claimed and, finally, Gritz wasn't even there.

This was certainly not the first use of fake news to accomplish a goal, but it proved that even a lie, if told often enough, can influence countless people to believe it is true. While we were secretly planning our covert operation, Bo was making a splash in the media with this falsified story to raise money for a bold rescue of American POWs. One of his stated plans was to invade Laos on the backs of elephants to surprise the Pathet Lao and save the American soldiers. He raised money from some right-leaning celebrities. William Shatner bought his life story for $10,000. Tough-guy movie star Clint Eastwood contributed $50,000 and lobbied his actor pal, President Reagan—who had used mercenaries such as Oliver North to do what the US government could not legally do—for government help.

On November 27, 1982, Gritz, who must have had a change of heart since finding that POW camp a year earlier, attempted a scaled-back and failed extraction mission, sans elephants, code-named Operation Lazarus. On the third day in Laos, the team was ambushed. Radio man Dominic Zappone was captured and later ransomed. Two hired Laotian guerillas were killed and three wounded. The team lost all its equipment to the enemy including two high-speed code transmission devices.

In early February, Gritz made another attempt to enter Laos. A few days later, two team members were arrested by Thai police for possessing an illegal radio, the latest in US-made spy gear, with a powerful transmitter that could be used to send messages from Laos directly to Washington, suggesting possible government support for the mission. Two weeks later, Bo Gritz turned himself in, taking sole responsibility for obtaining the radio equipment. In Thailand, the spy-equipment charge carried a possible five-year sentence, but all the defendants were given suspended one-year sentences, fined, and deported from Thailand.

On November 15, 1986, Gritz was refused entry into Thailand upon his arrival at the Bangkok airport, but a week later he sneaked in through the southern border with a false passport. He was arrested and deported for the second time in a month. Back in the US, Bo faced an FBI investigation for possible violations of the Neutrality Act and regulations on the export of high-technology equipment.

Bo Gritz later in life.

Bo's reckless and unsupported claims of surviving POWs threatened our mission's credibility and also embarrassed the Reagan administration, which was attempting to improve ties with the Thai and Laotian governments. Bo's rash plans made everyone involved in more serious efforts look foolish by association. Fortunately, we already had all the money, equipment and support we needed to launch. Within several weeks, Chuck Whitney and my partner Bill caught a flight to Bangkok with a lot of excess baggage—the photo supplies.

The duo rented a truck and stowed the cartons of equipment in the back. Stopping at several large pharmacies, they used funds provided by MIA families to purchase a quantity of drugs and medical supplies. Fortunately, in Bangkok at that time, you could buy any kind of drug over the counter without a prescription.

They stayed in a hotel that evening and left the next morning for the eight-hour trek to Ban Vinai. They did not have official passes to enter the camp or deliver their cargo, but in Thailand, cash was the only pass you really needed. Chuck's contacts were waiting for them inside the camp and helped to unload the goods.

Bill Carlson (left) and Chuck Whitney in the Ban Vinai camp.

Bill had prepared a demanding curriculum for the team. Using still cameras, they learned to load and unload rolls of film in the dark, control exposures and focus on fast-moving targets like disks thrown into the air. With the super-8mm cameras supplied by ABC News, they practiced quickly switching out film cartridges, steadying their shots to eliminate jitters, and controlling the zoom function of the lenses smoothly to ensure that more frames contained useful content, not blurry imagery. They learned how to charge batteries in the field, clean their cameras and lenses and provide basic maintenance.

At the outset, our greatest fear was that, even if we were successful in locating a Laotian POW camp, the photos obtained would be of insufficient quality to prove anything. Actually, that was the greatest fear only until the team started cleaning their weapons on the last day. Seeing the variety of lethal firearms each member would carry reminded Chuck and Bill that this was going to be a dangerous mission and some team members might not return. For the Hmong resistance, however, this was just another walk through no-man's land. It was heartening to know that each of the team members had survived countless firefights with the Pathet Lao, but also frightening to know they had been in countless firefights.

The plan called for Chuck and Bill to return home after completing the photo training. But Chuck decided he couldn't let his Hmong friends undertake the risks of a mission that he would not be taking. He decided to stay in country and accompany the team into Laos.

When I learned of his decision, I was enraged. This was an unnecessary risk. He was breaking our agreed-upon rules of engagement. I had been willing to set everything up, get the players in place, and then watch from the sidelines knowing my American team was safe at home. But now my key player was going to march into harm's way, changing the extent of my responsibility. What if Chuck was captured or killed? What if he just disappeared?

It occurred to me how easily I had accepted the high risks for the Hmong team members as if their lives were less important than that of my friend. These people also had friends and family in the camp who worried about them and would severely mourn their loss if tragedy struck. I started to understand why Chuck could not abandon the team and flee to the safety of his home in Minneapolis while they were risking their lives in the jungle for our mission.

Bill returned to home base. Chuck stayed in touch with me as events unfolded in Thailand. During phone calls, he told me that after Bill had left the CIA had begun a "massive buildup" of personnel in Bangkok and Ban Vinai as if expecting some kind of incident. The Thai Border Patrol, which guarded the Mekong River, was on high alert. For several weeks, his news was a torrent of frustration about all the activity, which made a stealthy crossing of the Mekong by a team of eleven people impossible. I often wondered if the Bo Gritz dustups had caused all the fuss.

One night, Chuck called at midnight Minneapolis time. "Gary," he said, "things are still pretty hairy over here, but I've been in contact with the Border Patrol and they're now willing to let us cross into

Laos if we can barter some radio equipment. Most of their walkie-talkies are on the blink."

"You sure they'll honor their word?" I asked.

"No—it's Thailand, after all. But it's our best chance to get this thing underway. I'm pretty tired of just sitting around the camp."

"Send me the specs of what you need. I can probably raise some money to buy stuff if I can find it available somewhere. Call me in two days and I'll let you know."

"Okay. If you get the equipment, ship it to me ASAP at the Trocadero Hotel in Bangkok. They know me here."

I contacted our donor list of MIA families, and they came up with the money. I found usable radio equipment at an army surplus store, paid cash, and express shipped it to Bangkok.

Two nights later, Chuck called. I told him to watch for his shipment.

"Great," he said. But he sounded down.

"What's the matter? Something happen?"

"An old friend of mine, Kit Green, was staying in the room next to mine. Worked for the CIA. They found him dead in his room this morning. Likely an assassination."

Our mission seemed to be going off the rails, and I felt helpless. If Chuck hadn't stayed in Thailand, the mission would have come to a screeching halt with all the obstacles.

Chuck called again, but I wasn't available, so he left a voice message. He had received the equipment and expected to cross the Mekong soon. Two days later, he left one last message. "I'll make it short. Crossing tonight. Wish us luck."

* * *

All communication then stopped.

Remorse plagued me. What had I done? I'd gotten my friend killed, that's what.

I talked to the MIA families and told them that Chuck had not made it back from Laos, and I'd heard nothing from the other team members. I notified ABC that we had come up with no evidence of surviving POWs. I tried to get on with business as usual, but I struggled. Then, about two months after my last call from Chuck, a woman came to the front door of Russell-Manning and dropped off a package. She had just returned to ARC headquarters after a stint working as a nurse in Ban Vinai. She had been asked to deliver the package to Russell-Manning Productions when she got back to Minneapolis.

Bill and I were frantic to see what was inside. Maybe it was photographic evidence of American POWs in Laos. Could it be that Chuck's sacrifice had not been in vain?

The package contained one of the super-8mm movie cameras with a partially shot film cartridge still inside. Our hearts were racing as Bill extracted the cartridge. Soon we were able to view it.

The projected image began with all ten members of the Hmong resistance team posing for the camera, which meant Chuck had probably been the cameraman. They had their arms around each other and were smiling and laughing, then the camera zoomed in on close-ups of each of the men. Suddenly, though, there were no more images. Apparently, the cartridge had jammed in the camera. At some point, someone must have decided it should be returned to Russell-Manning for repair, so the nurse obligingly delivered it to our door. The few images we saw were a bittersweet reminder of our well-intentioned but unsuccessful mission.

Another four months drifted by as I spent my time setting up our new entertainment company, Media Ventures. The plan was to raise capital to finance and produce entertainment film projects beginning with shorter films for educational and cable-TV distribution, then venturing into feature films for movie theaters—the dream of all filmmakers.

It was fall and a little brisk outdoors as I was walking through downtown Minneapolis to a business meeting. As I glanced across the street to my left, I saw what at first seemed to be Chuck Whitney's doppelganger. As I studied the man, who was walking parallel to me, I became certain it was not a lookalike but Chuck himself. But how could this be? Surely, if Chuck had returned safely from Thailand to Minneapolis, he would have reached out to me!

I raced across the street and grabbed Chuck by the arm. Surprised, he stopped and looked at me, clearly unprepared for this confrontation.

"Chuck!" I said. "We all thought you were dead. Where have you been? Why didn't you call?" I wanted answers right now.

"I'm sorry. I should've called you," Chuck said, glancing around for an escape route. "It'll all make sense when you hear the whole story. But I can't talk right now—I'm late for a thing. But I'll stop by your office tomorrow morning, and we can debrief. Still in the same place?"

"On Park Avenue, yes," I said.

And then he was off. I didn't move—just stood there wondering what had happened.

Chuck didn't come to the office the next day, or the day after that… or ever. But now I knew that he was alive and in Minneapolis. I tried to find him but came up empty—until three weeks later.

My wife and I were watching the evening news on KSTP-TV when we saw news footage of Chuck Whitney in handcuffs being walked out of a small house by police. We both leaned forward. Yes, that man was definitely Chuck. The newscaster was saying, "… Chuck Whitney, arrested for the murder of his roommate, whose body was found in a rolled-up carpet in their home's garage."

This adventure could not have taken a more bizarre turn. Within a minute, however, I knew that Bill and I would be facing a serious threat. Our mission had been mostly illegal. American citizens were not allowed into a Thai refugee camp without authorization. We had smuggled boxes of drugs into Ban Vinai. We had recruited an illegal Hmong resistance team to assist us. We were attempting to expose state department lies about American POWs and MIAs. We could be facing serious charges.

Within weeks, we were contacted by the police department, the sheriff's department and the FBI. We gave verbal statements that were true though redacted. Fortunately, law enforcement seemed more focused on the exotic murder than the specifics of our mission.

A few months later, charges against Chuck were dropped because of insufficient evidence against him. He disappeared and I never saw him again, so he never explained what had happened in Thailand. From conversations with others involved in the chain of events, however, I pieced together my theory of what had gone wrong. I suspect Chuck had somehow been recruited into the drug trade in Thailand, which some CIA agents had supported for a cut of the proceeds. I don't think it was a coincidence that Chuck's "old friend," CIA agent Kit Green, had been staying in the room next to Chuck when he was murdered, probably over a drug deal. Chuck, who struggled with PTSD, was certainly capable of making misguided decisions, and in the drug trade, these decisions can follow you home—in Chuck's case, all the way to Minneapolis. Was Chuck's roommate a participant in drug dealing? I don't know, but he and Chuck Whitney, previously a national hero, certainly suffered the consequences of some remarkably bad decisions.

Chuck's acquaintance and rival, Bo Gritz, also burrowed down the rabbit hole when his deepening anti-government rage propelled him into extremism. As an early leader of the "Patriot" movement, he gave paramilitary SPIKE training to thousands of zealots, ostensibly preparing them for a coming Armageddon. As a propagandist, his bigotry whipped many impressionable fanatics into frenzied rage fueled by misdirected fears of a nonexistent Jewish-controlled "New World Order" and the displacement of Whites by minorities.

In September of 1998, after his wife had abandoned him, Gritz attempted suicide. Paramedics found him in a military uniform adorned with medals on a gravel driveway next to his GMC pickup. He had shot himself in the chest with a .45-caliber, semi-automatic pistol at a survivalist compound he had established in Idaho near countless militia groups. He referred to the compound as a "constitutional covenant community." The man who was the model for Sylvester Stallone's *Rambo* movie, who had run for president in 1992 under the slogan "God, Guns and Gritz," who had trained thousands how to kill their enemies, had somehow failed to kill himself, but again he had attracted an abundance of publicity, his Holy Grail.

Wife 3: Gloria

After I split up with Karen, I moved into a small house my parents owned across from the gallery. Everyone there loved to see my sons when they came to stay with me, which was often. Pete, my sales manager at Russell-Manning, assumed the responsibility for finding me a girlfriend. As a single and inveterate skirt chaser, I think he wanted a male companion for his amorous escapades. Because of my despair at failing at marriage a second time, however, I was reluctant to meet someone new.

As a persuasive salesperson, though, Pete talked me into a blind date "just to see what it's like." He would meet me at the bar in the Sofitel Hotel in Bloomington, Minnesota, and his current woman friend, Diane, would join us there with her friend, Gloria. The friend was a retired nurse who now sold medical devices to doctors. "It will be fun," Pete promised.

I showed up, promptly as always, but Pete had already called Diane to say that he couldn't make it. He described me—blonde, close to forty, carrying a black male handbag—and told Diane to watch for me. She and Gloria looked around the bar, and Gloria nodded at me, looking a bit lost and depressed, telling Diane, "If that's him, I'm leaving."

Of course, that's precisely when I spotted two women at a table and approached, asking if one of them was Diane. I remember Gloria's expression of disappointment. Obviously, she was not interested in me, but I took a seat anyway just to be polite.

And that's how I met my third wife, though getting to the wedding was not easy. Gloria and I hit it off immediately once we started talking. She was witty, I was funny, and we both enjoyed wordplay. She seemed confident and sassy, worldly in a non-threatening way and told interesting stories. Pete had been right. It was fun to meet someone new.

After about an hour, everyone had to leave, and I walked Gloria to her car in the parking lot, hoping she wouldn't think I was a stalker. I was too timid to suggest another meeting, so she simply drove off. A week later, I mustered up the courage to call and ask her out. She picked up the phone at work and politely declined. Later, she would tell me that her boss, whom she was hoping to marry, could hear the conversation and started pointing to his ring finger, indicating he was ready to ask the big question. He never came through, though.

After six months, summer had arrived, and Pete told me that he and Diane were taking his boat out on Lake Minnetonka. Diane thought Gloria would like a boat ride, and he suggested I might want to enjoy the lake too.

Well, Gloria had already brushed me off, so I declined but was persuaded to change my mind. Again, Gloria and I had a wonderful time together, and as the sun was setting and I was standing behind her on the stairs to the galley below deck, I put my arms around her. That's when I fell in love with Gloria, the start of another tale with a surprise ending.

Gloria and I started doing everything together, and unwittingly I hijacked her life into a series of bizarre adventures. I soon met Jennifer, her live-in teenage daughter from a divorced husband. The divorce had given custody of Gloria's younger son, Brant, to her ex. I thought about marrying Gloria, and she urged me to, but I was already a two-time loser, so I stubbornly held out while wondering if I could ever sustain a meaningful relationship.

Then, suddenly, Brant was given up by Gloria's ex and his second wife. They now had children of their own. Brant, a child wounded by his parents' divorce, suffered another disturbing change of venue after being sent back to live with Gloria.

Two months later, after a brief holiday in Mazatlán, I fell ill. Thinking it was just a case of Montezuma's Revenge, I grit my teeth, expecting it to go away, but the stomach cramps became almost unbearable. Gloria urged me to rush to the ER. I stubbornly refused because I had important business guests coming to Minneapolis the next day. The illness escalated, and within a few hours I went into shock. Gloria slipped back into nurse mode and somehow drove me to the ER where I arrived unconscious.

Gloria and my ex-wife had become friends (I know that sounds implausible, but then, my whole life is), so she called Karen—technically still my wife—and then rushed to the hospital. The attending physician diagnosed me with acute diverticulitis and ordered emergency bowel surgery.

After a time in the recovery room, I was taken to a private room where I could have visitors, but only immediate family. Gloria and Karen approached a nurse, who asked how they were related to me. Both of them said, "His wife." Confused, I am told the nurse gave them both a strange look and allowed them in. I'm sure the nurse didn't want to get drawn into *that* drama.

During the colon resection, twenty-one inches of my lower intestine had been removed. It took weeks to recover. Without Gloria's intervention, I'm sure I would have died.

Four months after that, a more serious tragedy struck. As Gloria was making french fries from scratch, the kettle of oil caught fire, and she instinctively pulled it into the sink, turning on the faucet to quench the flames. The explosion rattled the house, shook the cabinets, blew a hole in the ceiling and knocked me over a railing into the living room. Gloria suffered severe steam burns on her face and arms. When I reached her on the oil-slick kitchen floor, I could see her skin blistering.

The kids and I got her to my car and packed ice cream containers and ice around her to mitigate the burns. I tried to pick up a police escort by speeding, but the police are never around when you need them. I stopped only once—at a busy intersection. Trying to lighten the moment, I turned to Gloria and said, "You certainly are a hot date."

Despite her misery, she gave me a generous smile—one of the many reasons I loved her. She endured many weeks of painful recovery. But as always, she maintained a positive attitude, even during the excruciating daily debridements. Shortly after the incident, I moved in to help care for her, but in truth I was little help.

Even so, I never left.

All this was occurring while I was starting a major entertainment company, Media Ventures, which I hoped would produce a series of significant films. As usual, I was in way over my head, and the stress was killing me. Besides business pressures, Brant was struggling with me as a surrogate father. I think both of us had territorial issues and each felt Gloria was favoring one over the other.

One afternoon, Brant and I had an argument over some trivial thing neither of us can remember. Brant packed his little suitcase and a few other favorite things, then stacked them by the front door, begging his mom to drive him back to his "real Dad's" place. Looking at that little guy begging to get away snapped me out of my momentary adolescence, and I started behaving like an adult again.

Brant and I worked it out, even ended up hugging—just like Mom and I had done when I was a kid. I recognized that this was my acquired way of seeking intimacy with my wonderful soon-to-be stepson. Would I ever be able to have a close relationship without the warm-up act?

Now that I was living with Gloria and helping raise her children, guilt surfaced about how I'd been neglecting my own sons. I was spending less time with Brendan and Scott than the stepchildren I was living with. The imbalance was due to my overstuffed business schedule and my proximity to Brant and Jennifer, but to my sons I knew that it must seem like purposeful negligence.

Shortly after the dust-up with Brant, eleven-year-old Brendan called sounding very depressed. The conversation ended with an ultimatum. If I married "that woman"—meaning Gloria—Brendan said he would never see me again. This was a frightening proposition, since I felt myself sliding headfirst into a collision with a third wedding.

I had made a total mess out of my life. How could my partners and employees and investors ever expect that I could run a complicated media company and produce multi-million-dollar feature films if I couldn't manage my own life? How could a third wife avoid burnout from all the drama I was certain to bring her into? How could I maintain my own physical and mental health?

I was in too deep, of course. Many people were trusting me to sort everything out and ultimately succeed brilliantly because "that's what Gary does." Regrettably, there was no easy escape from all my entanglements. And things were soon going to get much more complicated.

* * *

In the midst of all my entrepreneurial yearning, it was easy to forget the legendary Rockwell art heist that had shocked us more than twenty years earlier. While the FBI had lost interest and Bonnie occasionally had to beat back con artists and forgers who offered to sell back fake "stolen" paintings, an intriguing new lead came in. Suddenly, my despair was relieved for a spell as the conclusion to an unfinished mystery tantalizingly awaited.

Five years previously, three faxes originating in Lisbon had been received at Elayne Galleries on the letterhead of Galerie Schreiner, Inc., which purportedly had art galleries in Lisbon, New York and Basel, Switzerland. At the time, our operating theory based on numerous sources was that after the theft the stolen artworks had likely made their way to Lisbon. After failing to unload them, we believed the thieves concluded that to realize a profit, the paintings had to reenter the new world with a stopover in Brazil. This is why the faxes piqued our interest. The sender wanted the paintings returned to Lisbon so a sting operation could recover them. The first fax dated April 28, 1993, contained this ominous message:

> Dear Mrs. Elayne. The case is too complicated to deal with alone. We'll have to join forces. I fear we have to deal with a gang.

The next day, Mom received a phone call from the gallery owner in Lisbon, who said he wanted assurance that Elayne Galleries represented the owners of the paintings, which she gave him. Then, the Lisbon caller said, "I believe your paintings are being held by the federal police in Brazil."

The previous day, this man had claimed the paintings were being held by a gang. A day later, they were in the custody of the Brazilian police. Of course, in Brazil there was almost no distinction. The immediate contradiction, however, diminished the credibility of the gallery owner.

Strangely, the day of the Lisbon call, Bonnie had taken a call from a man named Fulvio Minetti who claimed to be a State Farm Insurance agent but also owned a travel agency and money exchange in Rio de Janeiro. He confirmed the gallery owner's story about the federal police and said he had some shady Brazilian contacts that could get their hands on the paintings for a price.

Bonnie contacted the FBI with this information, but they dismissed the calls as hoaxes. She called Minetti and told him that the FBI was skeptical about his story. He became angry that the FBI had been contacted, worrying that his "contacts" would back out if they knew that the FBI had been alerted, but agreed to fulfill Bonnie's request for photographic proof that the paintings were in Brazil. She suggested they include a dated local newspaper in the photos as in hostage pictures.

Astonishingly, the photos arrived in the mail with a current Brazilian newspaper clearly in the shots. Various visual indicators convinced Bonnie and Mom that the paintings were genuine and in good condition. Unfortunately, Brazil had not signed a UNESCO agreement that required its citizens who were recipients of stolen art to surrender the works even if purchased in good faith. In other words, the person in Brazil who possessed the Rockwells had no legal risk or requirement to return them.

Finally, Minetti proposed that Bonnie travel to Rio with a half-million dollars in cash from which he would get a 10 percent commission. After some haggling, the price came down to a quarter-million dollars if the transaction took place by July 5, 1993, the date that a loan secured by one of the paintings came due.

By this time, our family was worn out from the Rockwell drama, particularly Bonnie. The gallery was not going to pay that much to retrieve paintings that were stolen from it, especially since most were owned by other parties, some of which had already received an insurance settlement. It looked like our search had finally come to an end, though we still wanted the paintings returned.

That Was Then, This Is Now

Despite the general dysfunction in the Lindberg family, Media Ventures, my new entertainment business, finally launched, and we raised money to produce our first three non-sponsored titles. I was eager to leave the business communications business behind, so I offered to sell my share of Russell-Manning to my partner, Bruce, and let him make monthly payments for it. After all, *that was then, this is now*.

The first film produced by Media Ventures was an hour-long children's special for cable-TV called *Sometimes I Wonder*. It was a short drama about two little kids who run away from home because of their parents' preoccupation with a new baby. They show up at their grandma's ranch and learn some valuable lessons. When they watch a new foal being born, they realize how much attention a new life demands and choose to return home. The story resonated with me because of my harsh feelings about having a new sister arrive in my household many years earlier

I directed the show and brought my sons to the horse ranch in Thousand Oaks, California, to see how a movie was made. Brendan was nine and Scott about six. In the movie, grandma was played by famous Broadway actress Colleen Dewhurst, who had twice married actor George C. Scott and lived to talk about it. Before casting her, I sent Colleen the script and then traveled to New York to watch her opposite Jason Robards, Jr., in the comedy *You Can't Take It with You* at the Plymouth Theatre. I loved her performance as Olga, a Grand

Duchess of Russia who had fled to America before the Revolution and was now working as a waitress. I met Colleen backstage after the show, and she agreed to be in our little film, which she found "sweet."

The second film was an adaptation of a highly successful play developed and performed by the Illusion Theater in Minneapolis. Called simply *Touch*, it was aimed at elementary school children and boldly addressed the issue of sexual abuse, teaching children how to distinguish "good touch" from "bad touch" and giving them permission to say "no." An innovative approach used adult performers to play both adults and children, which audiences found highly entertaining. I directed the film version and cast TV actress Lindsay Wagner (*The Bionic Woman*) as an on-screen narrator and performer. For several months, the VHS version of the film was the highest-selling educational title at Target, its principal retail outlet, and was widely distributed to schools.

We didn't know at the time, but the world-famous Children's Theatre in Minneapolis, generally recognized then as the premier such theatre in the world, had become a den of pedophilia under its founder and former director John Clark Donahue. The same year we released *Touch*, Donahue was convicted on three counts of criminal sexual conduct. I was proud to have been associated with a much-needed antidote to the problem.

During my years at Russell-Manning, I had developed a relationship with Donahue and many members of his administrative and artistic staff and often cast adult and child actors from the Children's Theatre. Until the disturbing charges were filed, I'd had no knowledge of the atrocities being committed at this jewel in the crown of Twin Cities artistic endeavors. But later in my life, I would learn much more about the terrible toll of these atrocities on the children and how so many of my friends were responsible directly or indirectly.

The third film in our financing package was *The Power of Purpose* produced by David McNally, an Australian motivational speaker who had joined Media Ventures as a fundraiser. A passion project for David, the inspirational documentary was about Terry Fox, a young man who had suffered the amputation of a leg because of cancer. Not one to give up, Terry then attempted to run the equivalent of a marathon every day across Canada on a prosthetic leg to raise money for cancer research.

We acquired rights to thousands of feet of footage shot by Canadian news channels and obtained many family photos and home movies from Terry's family. We did most of the editing in Toronto, though I directed Christopher Plummer's narration in New York, which was nearer his Connecticut farm. Terry had died of cancer after reaching the two-thirds point of his journey. He exceeded his goal of a million dollars. To date, over $850 million has been raised for cancer research in Terry's name through the annual Tery Fox Run held across Canada and around the world. When we showed the finished film to investors, I saw many moist eyes as the lights came up.

* * *

During this stretch, so much was going on that my mind fogs over when trying to remember it all. What stands out the most, though, was the death of my mother—the queen of the Lindberg clan and a force of nature. Or, as I have sometimes said, just "The Force." She had become ill quickly with a serious cardiac event, and I got word of it during a Vikings game in Minneapolis.

Her death was eerie because she had an implanted pacemaker, and although she was pronounced dead, her heart kept beating, and I kept hoping that life somehow would be magically restored. I wished she and I could have had one more argument so we could hug and kiss and make up as in earlier days. I worried about how Dad would get along without her.

At the funeral, Scott played a haunting guitar solo that left everyone in tears. His brother, Brendan, had grown very close to his grandma by working at the gallery, and he was devastated by losing the woman who was like a second mom to him.

During this time, Brant remained educationally feral. He was exceptionally bright but also extremely unmotivated; alert to his surroundings and creative in solving difficult problems but lacking self-confidence; friendly but highly independent, even obstinate. One day, when about twelve, having been warned not to be late for school, he overslept and simply drove his mother's car to school, arriving on time—an odd way of showing seldom expressed responsibility. Though he had the makings of a genius, he was flunking out of school.

Jennifer, on the other hand, was a social butterfly. In high school, she started wearing business suits and carrying a briefcase, mimicking her mother's business attire. I loved having a stepdaughter, but I feared the temptations and abuses that young women were subject to in society. She proved to be up to the task.

It was just after my birthday in 1983, while thinking about Gloria and our growing family, that I realized how our lives had become inextricably linked. I casually said to Gloria, "I think we should get married. What do you think?"

She looked surprised, then said, "How soon?"

"Well, it's almost the end of the year. Maybe before New Year?"

"Let's talk to our accountants and see which year would be better for taxes," she said, always practical.

The accountants agreed that 1984 would save us money compared to a 1983 wedding. "I suggest New Year's Day," Gloria said. "Why wait? My church will still be decorated, so no worries coordinating that. And you'll always remember our anniversary date."

So, it was settled. We had a small wedding of less than a hundred friends and family, including all four of our children. Gloria wanted the reception before the wedding, so everyone brought food and we ate in the church basement, then the women helped with the dishes while the men cleaned up. When everything was tidy, we all moved to the sanctuary, which was still adorned with beautiful angels and lights. On January 1, 1984, I again became a married man—hopefully until death parted Gloria and me. This being my life, however, I should have expected that even marriage to a woman I dearly loved would become very complicated.

* * *

My business pressures continued, as I was quickly consumed with finding money for an even more ambitious Media Ventures project—a full-length feature film for movie theaters, cable-TV and foreign markets. Our trial run with three successful shorter films had been successful. Now it was time for the big screen. We had promised this milestone to investors. Now we had to deliver.

I judged the teenage market to be the easiest to reach with a movie. Teenagers bought more movie tickets per person than any other age group. But teen movies were typically horror flicks or raunchy sex comedies like the emerging *Porky's* franchise. I desperately wanted to produce a more mature movie for teens, one about relationships, perhaps a meaningful coming of age story—something I would be proud to show my family. The current model for this was a successful film titled *The Outsiders*, based on a young adult novel by S.E. Hinton. A casting model had also emerged in the form of a group of young actors known as the Brat Pack, which included Emilio Estevez, Anthony Michael Hall, Rob Lowe, Andrew McCarthy, Demi Moore, Judd Nelson, Molly Ringwald and Ally Sheedy.

I looked up Hinton's YA novels and discovered she had written four. Besides *The Outsiders*, Francis Ford Coppola had directed *Rumble Fish* and Buena Vista, a Disney company, had released *Tex*. The fourth Hinton book was *That Was Then... This Is Now*, a beloved novel often assigned as reading in high school English classes. The rights to this book appeared to be available, and its notoriety among teens meant it had a pre-sold audience. I knew I could pitch this to investors.

Alas, we learned that the book had been optioned about a year earlier. Emilio Estevez, one of the stars of *The Outsiders*, had fallen in love with Susie Hinton's books. His father, actor Martin Sheen, had purchased an option on *TWTTIN* (as we started to call *That Was Then... This Is Now*) and gave it to his son as a birthday present. Emilio and his best friend, Tom Cruise, wanted to play the two leading roles—boys who grew up as brothers but weren't. They had co-written several drafts of an adapted screenplay, but no studio had offered financing.

I found out that a man named Brandon "Randy" Phillips of the Arnold Stiefel Group in Beverly was Emilio's manager, so I called him. At the time, Randy was also managing Prince, rock stars Rod Stewart and Billy Squire, actress Maria Conchita Alonso (*Moscow on the Hudson*), two-time Academy Award-winning screenplay writer Bo Goldman (*One Flew Over the Cuckoo's Nest* and *Melvin and Howard*) and others. Randy's partner, Arnold, was a powerhouse in the industry and a friend of most studio heads.

I had noticed Randy had no film production credits and guessed he might be looking for one to round out his credentials, so I told Randy I was prepared to raise the financing for *TWTTIN* and give him an executive producer credit if Emilio would agree. He suggested a face-to-face meeting with Emilio in Los Angeles.

I took the meeting accompanied by my co-founder John Ondov. Emilio's option on the property was going to run out in a few months, so he seemed eager to do a deal. By the end of our meeting, he agreed to star in the film for a fraction of his usual fee. He also agreed to co-write the adaptation with me, but he wanted full screenwriting credit. At the time, he knew that his best buddy, Tom Cruise, was heading toward leading man status while he clearly was not, so a production credit—particularly a creative one like screenwriter—would help him keep pace and be a steppingstone to a future behind the camera.

Randy urged me to also find another executive producer with a successful track record to help bridge the credibility gap with investors. I found such a person in Alan Belkin, the man who had discovered karate star Chuck Norris and produced Norris's first highly successful films. Each of Alan's movies had made money, a great story for investors. After a couple highly detailed phone conversations, we struck a deal with Alan and began to put together our deal and presentation materials for investors.

Finding money in Minnesota for a feature film was tough. Most wealthy people in the state had never considered making such an investment. The economics of the movie business was a foreign world to them, and investors don't like investing in deals they don't understand. There was no Minnesota tradition of locally produced movies making money. The Coen Brothers had financed and made their first movie, *Blood Simple*, in Minnesota (I had made a small investment to encourage them), but it had returned none of the investment capital.

Curiosity in our offering delivered wealthy prospects to our presentations, but too few investments. This being Minnesota, though, everyone wished us well. Unfortunately, Emilio's schedule of film commitments had left a narrow production window for *TWTTIN* during the late summer of 1984. Despite the slow growth of investments and with the groundless belief that we would get financed, I started the scripting process to stay on schedule.

Emilio and I set aside six weeks to write the screenplay. This would require a dedicated, nonstop effort. I traveled to Santa Monica, where Emilio was living in a small apartment to stay out of the public eye. The place was like an old folks' home. None of the seniors who lived there had ever heard of Emilio Estevez, so no one pestered us. I brought a computer and printer with me. Emilio had never used a computer, so I did the keyboarding. He was astonished at how easily we could modify text and still have a clean document.

Every morning, he and I would meet at his apartment, drink juice and slam down a vitamin pack, eat a pastry and go for a vigorous walk to the beach and back. Then we would work until midday and go to a local restaurant, usually Zucky's, for lunch. After that, we would work diligently until dinner time. That's when some of Emilio's movie star buddies, the ones not currently shooting a film, would stop by and read the dialogue we had written that day. Hearing these words come out of actors' mouths helped us craft more realistic dialogue. At times, since I was fifteen or more years older than these youngsters, I felt more like the adult chaperone—not that they were up to any mischief. Surprisingly, except for an occasional beer, none of them were using addictive substances.

We finished the script, but Media Ventures had not made much progress on fundraising. I didn't want to go back to Randy and Emilio with a failed effort to finance the project, so I decided to go after some of my old Russell-Manning clients. Some were CEOs of huge companies and had the resources. At least this group of prospects knew my capabilities and might have enough confidence in me to chip in some money. And one of them did.

Myron was CEO and majority shareholder of the nation's largest chain of hair salons, putting his net worth at several hundred million dollars. Through some error of insight, he believed I was a genius. I didn't tell him right off that I had only raised a third of the necessary funds and time was running out. But over several long conversations, he decided to invest a significant sum. It was not all we needed, but I hoped that his participation would encourage other wealthy investors to follow.

Even though we weren't fully financed—actually, we couldn't use any of the funds until we crossed the finish line—it was time to hire a director and audition actors for the other parts. We settled on Christopher Cain as director because he had rapport with many of the Brat Pack boys—he had been their softball coach as well as a film director (*The Stone Boy* starring Robert Duval). Chris's son, Dean Cain, played Superman on the 1993 TV series *Lois & Clark: The New Adventures of Superman*.

Emilio was lobbying for his brother, Charlie Sheen, to play the best friend part, so I flew out to join Chris for the audition. Charlie was a fine actor, but not right for the part. We did hire Emilio's youngest brother, Ramón Estevez, for a small part.

For the female lead, we auditioned Cyndi Lauper, a singer known for *Girls Just Want to Have Fun*, who wanted to branch into acting. We deemed her too eccentric for the role and kept looking. Eventually, we cast an obscure New York soap actor from *One Life to Live*, Craig Sheffer, as the best friend; Kim Delaney, a Daytime Emmy-winning actress from *All My Children* as the female lead; and Morgan Freeman in his first significant role in a feature film.

From the left, Emilio Estevez, Craig Sheffer and Morgan Freeman.

Emilio had to fit the production of *TWTTIN* into a narrow slot between *The Breakfast Club* and rehearsals for *St. Elmo's Fire*. If we were not ready to start production on schedule, the entire project would run off the rails. Still without full financing, I was being pressed by all my trusted advisors to cancel the project. The odds were high that we would come up short and have a lot of expenses to pay.

The anxiety was crushing, but I saw this as my one big chance to make a real movie, so I told the staff to instruct all crew members, who were from all over the country, to arrange their flights into the Twin Cities. We booked the entire three-story St. Paul Holiday Inn to house the 150 crew members and actors. The green light was flashing—and we were still $850,000 short of releasing the funds.

With just three days to go before production would begin, I decided to call my friend Myron and beg him to put up the remainder of the budget. His receptionist told me he and his wife were on vacation at a resort in the Poconos.

Desperate, I called the resort, but he wasn't in his room, so I left a message. Several hours later, he hadn't called me back, so I placed another call—and he answered! But I can't say he was very happy about having his holiday interrupted.

I had nothing to lose, so I candidly told him my dilemma and asked him to put up the rest of the money. He thought for a minute, then said, "OK, I'll do it, but I want better terms for this money. I want to get it back before any other investor starts being repaid. Also, I don't have a blank check here, so have someone get that to me along with an agreement I can sign."

I had no idea how to accomplish this, but agreed anyway. The clock was ticking. I immediately called the attorney who had worked up the investor agreements for the project, and together we concocted a legal way for Myron to invest this last tranche and be first in line for reimbursement.

My best friend, Marc Kramer, was working as production accountant on the film, so I asked him to coordinate getting the new Myron agreement from the attorney, fax it to Myron, then get a blank check from Myron's assistant and jump on a plane to the Poconos.

We had two days to get everything done, but we did it. Marc picked up a signed check for $850,000 and we deposited it six hours before the deadline for releasing funds.

Unfortunately, we had just completed the easy part.

From the left, my stepson Brant, Emilio Estevez, and Gloria's daughter, Jennifer. Before and during the shoot, Jennifer had a wonderful time escorting Emilio and other cast members around the Twin Cities.

The Blizzard

I was told by seasoned crew members that despite the numerous shooting delays, crew and actor meltdowns, city permitting mix-ups, weather issues, accidents and health problems, technical difficulties, script changes and financial overruns, our shoot went better than most. Such is the nature of making a movie. It is an exercise in problem-solving. A few times I came close to firing the director for a host of reasons, wishing I had opted to direct the movie myself. But I knew I had been too burned out by all the financial and pre-production issues to take on such a responsibility. Producing alone had almost killed me.

A blurry photo of me (left,) director Chris Cain, and Spanish cinematographer Juan Ruiz Anchia on a frigid morning before sunrise.

In the end, we finished the shoot with a joyful wrap party, and everyone went their separate ways. All that was left was, well… everything else. Editing, sound effects and mixing, screening and testing, and then the most important part—finding a distributor to market our movie to the public.

* * *

Shortly after we finished shooting, my ex-wife Karen called and asked if Brendan could live with Gloria and me for a while. She had gone back to college to earn an advanced degree, and she believed her pressures and parental absences were having a negative effect on our son, who was "acting out" in undesirable ways. I was eager to have my son living with me despite my busy life, so I consulted with Gloria, who readily agreed.

Almost immediately, Brendan moved into our little house with Brant, Jennifer, Gloria and me. What a wonderful early birthday present he was! We were packed in tight, though, especially since Brendan had brought with him his German Shepherd, Bruno. Brendan told me that school kids had been picking on him, and the big dog made him feel more secure outside of class. Bruno was sweet but not the brightest dog. He stood tall enough to knock things off the coffee table when he wagged his tail, which he did constantly. We were going to need a bigger house, so we started looking.

A couple weeks later, Gloria and I both announced on the same day that we had found our "dream home." We first drove to Gloria's find, and I realized it was the same house I had fallen in love with. The five-bedroom Tudor sat on an acre of land in Plymouth, Minnesota, with deeded access to a small lake behind it. Each of the kids could have a separate bedroom with one for guests. After a quick tour, we bought the house, and shortly after Christmas, the five of us moved in.

We quickly discovered that blending a family was hard work. Jealousies and tensions abounded as our three children tried to sort out new family relationships, territorial boundaries, hurt feelings and hormonal changes—all with a father who was gone much of the time pretending to be a big-time movie producer. Gloria was left to manage the motley bunch as best she could. She must have wondered how she had been swept into such an erratic and unmanageable life.

After a few months in the big house, Gloria confronted me with an unexpected dilemma. As the manager of our household finances, she had paid all our bills from the previous month on time by check, but suddenly those checks started bouncing for insufficient funds. When she checked our the bank balance, all our money was gone.

I called the bank and was told that American Express had legally seized all our cash assets to cover the unpaid balances on all the Russell-Manning company credit cards. Further investigation showed that my former partner, to whom I had given my business equity in exchange for monthly payments, had not only made no payments but had managed the company into a declared bankruptcy. Bruce had also filed for personal bankruptcy, so he would not be liable for any company debts, including Russell-Manning's mortgage payments. Since I had failed to remove my name as a guarantor of the American Express accounts, I was personally responsible for all that debt plus everything else the company owed to creditors. With the remaining balance on the mortgage, the total debt was close to three-quarters of a million dollars.

Gloria was furious with Bruce and even angrier at me for failing to pay attention to the details. Personally, I felt crushed, but I did what I always did in crises, I went to work negotiating with creditors to reduce debt and arrange payment schedules. Our real estate mortgage was for a specialized building with a studio in the back end and no viable tenant with Russell-Manning gone. It was not likely to sell quickly.

It took many months, but eventually I worked out payments that would take us about seven years to pay off. The only alternative, filing for personal bankruptcy, didn't seem fair to the creditors since I was in fact legally responsible. Gloria and I decided to just do the right thing. She certainly had a right to be unhappy about our circumstances, and over time I found ways to accelerate the paybacks.

* * *

In the meantime, Chris Cain was supervising the edit of *TWTTIN* in Los Angeles and at last presented the "director's cut" to our team for review. Randy Phillips brought in Keith Olson, a well-known record producer, to score the show. Keith's work would eventually earn him more than 39 gold, 24 platinum, and 14 multi-platinum album certifications. He worked with Fleetwood Mac, Ozzy Osbourne, Santana, Pat Benatar, Grateful Dead, Foreigner and many other artists.

We booked Saul Zaentz Studios in Berkley, California, to prepare and synchronize sound effects, lay in music tracks, record dialogue replacement loops and do the final sound mix, which is the blending of all these audio elements together at proper levels. Our sound mixer was Mark Berger, who had just won the Academy Award for best sound for *Amadeus* and had previously worked on *The English Patient* and *Apocalypse Now*. We were honoring our pledge to investors to bring in top artisans to make the best possible film.

By now, John and I were hanging out a lot in LA, making noise about our Minnesota company and trying to stir things up for another film deal after *TWTTIN* was completed. Nothing causes more excitement in Hollywood than a new source of money, and we were starting to be seen as that source. This meant that people who had no time for us earlier were now eager to talk.

* * *

A columnist for the *Hollywood Reporter* I will call Joan, though that is not her real name, decided our midwestern roots were a breath of fresh air and took us under her wing, making some introductions and posting an occasional reference to Media Ventures in her trade publication. Most likely she had some designs on becoming a producer herself and thought we might fund her films or possibly hire her in some producing capacity on our next project. Nevertheless, she invited us to some interesting parties.

One gathering I will never forget was at Joan's house on the outskirts of Beverly Hills. John Ondov and I had just reviewed the director's cut of our film when she called and said she had some interesting guests coming to her house for a small dinner party. Would we like to join them? They would be good contacts for the future.

We showed up at eight and met the other guests—a man I could not place named Marjoe Gortner and the actor David Carradine and his wife. Marjoe had gained public attention in the late 1940s when he was just four years old and his parents had arranged for him to be ordained as a minister. His parents claimed he had received a vision from God during a bath and immediately started preaching. Those who heard him claimed he had an extraordinary combination of oratory skill and showmanship learned, apparently, on his evangelist father's lap at Pentecostal tent meetings. He had an astonishing memory, able to recall lengthy passages of scripture on demand, and was unintimidated by large crowds of strangers. It was said that he had led thousands of doomed souls to salvation in Jesus Christ. On the revival circuit, he brought celebrity status and large audiences with cash for offerings to the events. He continued to preach until he was about sixteen.

Later, resentful of his lost childhood, Marjoe denounced his spiritual gifts, claiming that his father had invented the vision story and taught him how to mimic his fellow evangelists' speech styles and dramatic gestures. He told reporters that his parents used mock drownings to compel him to perform as taught, choosing not to beat him as bruises could be noticed during public appearances. By the time he reached sixteen, he had amassed a fortune of approximately three million dollars through various cons, including the sale of so-called "holy" articles, but his father had suddenly absconded with the money.

In 1972, he participated in an Academy Award-winning documentary called *Marjoe* that exposed the duplicity, deceit and trickery he and other evangelists used to extract money from the pockets of the people they were supposed to be saving. Eventually, he started a career in acting, making use of his performing talents. He landed some roles in TV shows and low-budget features.

After dinner, Marjoe pitched John and me on a personal film project called *The Revivalist* based on incidents from his life. As we soon learned, project pitches occur whenever film people meet.

Marjoe demonstrated a vocal technique used by evangelists that combined rhythmic and hoarse breathing, rising and falling volume, and eventually a peculiar quavering of the voice that literally sent chills through me. He delivered a one-minute sermon as a revivalist, and by the time he was done, I was ready to march forward if he'd made an altar call.

The other guest, David Carradine, was a casual, long-haired dude who had become famous for his role as a karate master in the TV series *Kung Fu*, one of the first in a long line of martial arts shows. He came from a prodigious acting family that notably included his father, John Carradine, considered one of the greatest character actors in cinema history, and Keith Carradine, a singer and actor appearing frequently on stage, TV and in movies. In recent years, David is perhaps better known for his appearance as Bill in Quentin Tarantino's *Kill Bill Volume I* and *Volume II*.

David was musically gifted, and after dinner at Joan's, he and his beautiful wife sat at a piano and we all sang show tunes together. Some wine may have been involved. He was less direct than Marjoe about his goal for the evening but indicated that he would enjoy a private conversation at the right time, which never occurred. Sadly, in 2009, David was found dead in a Bangkok hotel room closet. He was naked and hanging with a curtain cord round his neck. Thai police suggested the lack of a suicide note indicated he may have died from accidental suffocation due to auto-erotic asphyxiation.

* * *

At about this time, I approached Karen about having Scott move to Plymouth to live with his brother. We discussed many pros and cons, and Karen was torn by the thought of sending her second son to be with his father. After great deliberation, we decided it was the right decision, and if things didn't work out, we could always reverse course. Karen and I loaded up two cars—hers and mine—with Scott's belongings and drove him to his new home.

At only nine years old, Scott arrived at the big house with a forlorn expression that was temporarily erased by warm embraces by his brother, father, and new family. I'm sure he didn't understand everything that was happening, but suddenly my residence was populated by four children.

Fortunately for both Brendan and Scott, Jennifer loved being the big sister for three brothers. In some ways, she filled in as a mom, gaining wonderful experience in nurturing children and satisfying their needs. Though Jen would never have children of her own, she always used her instincts and acquired skills to be the best possible auntie to countless offspring of friends, siblings and future spouses. For Brendan and Scott, who were often ignored by busy parents, she was a lifeline.

A month after Scott came to us, Gloria started her own business, a communications consultancy with a specialty in medical device training and marketing. She called it Lindberg Communications, but soon changed the name to Integrated Strategies, Inc. (ISI), which better described the work she did helping medical companies integrate their often disjointed educational and marketing tasks. She began with a blue-chip client, Medtronic, a leading maker of implantable pacemakers and defibrillators.

Life in the Lindberg household became more complicated yet.

* * *

I had always envisioned our big movie project as a Paramount film, not an Indy. I wanted the big mountain at the beginning to serve as a kind of seal of approval that we had made a big-time film.

When post-production of *TWTTIN* was finished, John and I booked a screening room near Hollywood in which to show a workprint of the complete movie to distributors. No brass from any major studio came to the screenings. A few of the second tier and specialty distributors sent representatives—firms like Samuel Goldwyn, Cannon Group, DeLauentiis Entertainment, New World—but none of the elite.

I had promised investors that our movie—because it was based on a bestselling YA novel with a major teen star and supervised by an executive producer with an unbroken string of hits—would certainly attract a major distributor. We had offers from the minor leagues, but how could I explain why we had no interest from the major league?

I called Randy Phillips, now my go-to fixer, who said he would wrangle his partner, Arnold Stiefel, to get his close friend, the head of Paramount, to send the appropriate person to a screening. Arnold's connections were priceless. The next day, we were told to set up a screening for Barry London, vice president of the motion picture group at Paramount. Until Barry finally showed up, I still feared he wouldn't, and this would be the demise of one more dream. But he showed up.

Barry watched the movie and said he loved it. According to Arnold, he was also interested in *TWTTIN* for another more pragmatic reason. Paramount had booked a film in hundreds of theaters for the third week of October, which was coming up in just three months. That promised film, unfortunately, was behind schedule and would not be finished in time. Paramount had a dilemma—how to fill that open slot or lose it to a competitor. They had no credible replacement unless they could pick up our little independent film, which fortunately starred a hot young actor.

Paramount quickly sent over their standard distribution contract and asked us to sign it. Since I was responsible for getting the investors' money back with a profit, I thought it wise to read the fine print—which, it turns out, essentially gave most of the revenue to Paramount, not us. The agreement virtually guaranteed that we could never make money from our movie no matter how well it did.

Knowing that Paramount was counting on our film to plug a scheduling hole, I had some leverage and used it. I responded that we needed some changes in the standard contract. As expected, Paramount asked to get the changes for their review as soon as possible because of the pending release schedule. I brought an attorney from a Minneapolis law firm, Dorsey Whitney, to Los Angeles, and we worked through the problem issues. We needed a higher percentage of cable and home video revenues and also wanted to remove foreign rights from the agreement. My research had turned up a London-based film distributor, J&M Film Sales, that would give us a much higher percentage of foreign revenues.

During negotiations, we did a test screening at the Paramount back lot theater. The audience loved the movie but found the ending unsatisfying. Even in the script, the ending was weak, I thought, and I had never been entirely happy with the final scene as assembled by Chris. Paramount assigned an editor and editing room on its premises, and I supervised the reconstruction of the final scene.

This was a happy time for me. I had Paramount close to a signed distribution agreement, and I was officing on the Paramount lot, eating in the Paramount cafeteria and knocking around with well-known actors and crew. For this brief time, anyway, I was a real Hollywood producer.

After we presented our final cut, there was no time for another test screening, but Paramount executives approved the work. And we finally signed a distribution deal. Paramount agreed to our demands with a few minor tweaks. The marketing department shifted into high gear to prepare for the film's October release. In a flurry of activity, posters and ads were created, a 90-second trailer was produced, Randy pulled together a soundtrack album featuring Keith Olson's score plus a title song by Oingo Boingo, a popular rock group of the era. Prints of the movie were created for distribution to 850 theaters. This was a big opening for a low-budget movie.

I persuaded Paramount to have dual premieres in the Twin Cities. We coordinated staggered opening night screenings at the Grandview Theater in St. Paul and the Cooper Theater in Minneapolis. The governor and mayors attended, along with some of the movie's stars, movie reviewers, investors and other celebrities. Across the street from the Cooper, in a large ballroom, we held an after-show party. We rented all the available limousines in the area to transport celebrity guests. My entire family showed up, and we had a blast.

My son, Brendan (left), and stepson, Brant Zwiefel, with me at the premiere gala for *That Was Then... This Is Now*.

With the wide national release of our movie imminent, I was a wreck emotionally. In the movie business, you only get one opening weekend, and if crowds don't materialize, there is no way to recover the lost momentum. Opening box office receipts determine the success or failure of a movie domestically. Gloria and I decided to escape the stress by renting a bed & breakfast south of the cities on the Mississippi River.

The film opened on Friday, October 25, the day before my forty-second birthday, and on Saturday I received an alarming phone call from executive producer Alan Belkin. A major snow and ice storm had hit the eastern seaboard and most movie theaters had closed. Audiences were negligible there. Clean-up would probably soften receipts for Saturday and Sunday. Our opening weekend had been ruined by an act of God.

In truth, God had not caused this tragedy, and for all the snowplow drivers, this weather event was a magnificent gift of overtime pay. But for us, our film could no longer become a smash hit. Nevertheless, based on domestic box office receipts, *TWTTIN* still placed in the top third of all domestic films in 1985—not bad for a low-budget, seat of our pants venture.

Fortunately, Paramount sold the cable rights to Showtime and our take was two million dollars. Home video revenues were slightly lower than we had hoped, however, because those revenues are closely tied to box office performance. The biggest financial win came from foreign sales. Our insistence on retaining foreign rights and contracting with J&M Film Sales for non-domestic distribution had paid off. Most of our revenue ultimately came from foreign sales, for which we retained 80 percent of collected revenues. The picture had numerous four-star reviews but predictably some pans that called it "dumb" or "trite." Even then, it seems, we were living in a divided society with lots of different opinions.

A big hit would have tempted me to continue this career path, but I had to face the fact that I had reached this apex of my movie career too late. I was past forty, and I had four children still living at home. I had learned we just couldn't successfully build a movie company in Minnesota. This kind of career would require me to spend most of my time in California. Was I willing to uproot the children and move them to schools in Hollywood? Could I live separately from my family for long stretches?

The answer was no, I could not.

Tired of running businesses and not having time to do the fun creative part, I sought relief from management duties. I wanted to go back to my roots—creating content. So, I decided to work for my wife at Integrated Strategies. Admittedly, I suffered a moment of wounded pride going from Hollywood producer to my wife's employee. I never realized until recently that I had simply followed in my father's footsteps as he went to work for my mother's art gallery and never let pride get in his way. I could do that too.

Then I got a call from my ex, Karen, saying that Brendan wanted to return home to live with her. Losing my son again was a blow to my ego and my heart, and I blamed myself for being gone so much and not being truly present as a dad when I was home. I would have to find a way to make it up to him, and Scott too.

Mexico

Many things can be true at the same time. I wanted the relative stability of family life and a predictable income, but my heart was still thrumming with a passion for storytelling—and I had lived some of my best stories.

I wrote for some of Gloria's medical clients, which kept me semi-occupied, and the slow drumbeat of tracking down the Rockwell paintings continued under my sister's persistent eye. But then an opportunity presented itself, as so many times before.

David, an old friend who wanted to direct features, asked if I would write a screenplay for an adaptation of the original *Tarzan of the Apes* novel. "A more faithful version of the authentic origin story," was how he put it. I was intrigued because a decade earlier I had acquired an option on the original novel from the Edgar Rice Burroughs estate to do precisely that, but with a spin. Through a contact, I had received permission to use a new 3D technology owned by Blake Edwards, director of the *Pink Panther* movies and many others. But I couldn't get the project off the ground.

David said he had a rich investor in Houston who was interested in funding the Tarzan movie, and a potential star to play Tarzan. Could I fly to Houston with him to speak with the money man and the actor?

A week later, the investor, who was the biggest mattress seller in Texas, sent his wife, Doris, to pick up David and me at the airport. On the way to the meeting with her husband and the actor at a local restaurant, she noticed three Black men crossing the street. She shook her head at the sight and said matter-of-factly, "They look just like monkeys, don't they? That's what they come from, you know. Animals, all of 'em." Her Texas accent made the words sound sweet, but they scorched my soul. I could not make a movie with a bunch of racists.

At the meeting, I met her husband, Matt, who was very tall, and the actor, Greg Louganis, formerly an Olympic Gold Medal-winning diver, and his gay boyfriend. I could imagine Greg as Tarzan. He had the muscular build, the athleticism and the desire. I tried to reconcile Matt's and Doris's extreme bias against Blacks but apparent acceptance of gays, but I couldn't sort the many monstrous ways in which prejudice presented its ugly face.

We had an extremely cordial and productive meeting, but in a taxi back to the airport, I told David I couldn't work with Matt and his wife as key investors. He nodded sympathetically. They never did the movie.

A few weeks later, my friend Pablo, the Bolivian architect, asked me to lunch with yet another opportunity. He had just returned from Mexico City with a proposition. He knew a wealthy Mexican who would be interested in financing movies south of the border. Pablo had told his friend about me and my Paramount movie, and the friend had invited us to come down and discuss putting together an entertainment film company.

What interested me was the prospect of having a partner with money. Funding was always the hardest commodity to find in the movie business. I just hoped he was not a biased individual like Matt. If we were to do a deal with a Mexican, however, we would need some financing ourselves for travel and expenses. I could not ask Gloria to fund another of my pipe dreams out of her company. Fortunately, I knew a possible source for small capital.

Owen Husney, the man who discovered Prince and was the performer's first manager, was now running a management company with partner Ron Soskin. He had dabbled in the film business by co-organizing music for the John Hughes films *The Breakfast Club* and *Pretty in Pink*, earning gold album awards for each. I thought he might be interested in a film venture with a low cost of entry. I knew Owen from my Russell-Manning days, so I set up a meeting. Owen and Ron agreed to fund our attempt to get Pablo's friend into some kind of joint venture.

Pablo and I flew into Mexico City and set up camp at the InterContinental Presidente Hotel across from the National Museum of Anthropology. The person we would be meeting was Francisco Galvez, but Pablo could tell me little about him other than he was extremely well connected and very wealthy—certainly capable of financing movies made in Mexico.

The next morning, we hired a taxi to Francisco's office. Everything in Mexico City, I learned, was at least a half-hour drive from everything else. After forty minutes, we arrived at an unassuming office with no sign—the opposite of ostentatious. The windowless front door was made of plate steel. Two video cameras stared at us as we rang a doorbell.

A polite woman, the receptionist, opened the door and rattled off a string of Spanish words I didn't understand. Pablo smiled and returned some words, then translated what she had said into English. "She said that Francisco is expecting us, and we should wait for him in the conference room." I noticed that the front door was three-quarters inch thick and had a massive levered deadlock inside.

Realizing that my Spanish was almost nonexistent, the woman said in broken English, "Follow me, please." The offices beyond the lobby were larger than I expected. We took seats at a conference table, but as I looked at the wall opposite the door, I saw a series of large hanging panels that one could flip through to see various images and posted messages. Two of the panels were open and facing us, one of them showing pictures of missiles and the other one various automatic firearms.

I was not expecting this, and from Pablo's expression, neither was he.

I would learn that Francisco's main business was selling military and law enforcement equipment and supplies to the Federales and the Mexican Army and Navy. For some reason, these government entities bought from Francisco's company, which sourced whatever was needed from wherever it was—with a mark-up, of course. Clearly, this was how he had become so well-connected and wealthy.

After a few minutes, Francisco enthusiastically entered. He was in his fifties with graying black hair, and beneath his dark suit was a white shirt with an open collar. We stood, and he warmly embraced each of us while chattering in Spanish. I would learn that he spoke only Spanish and French, not English, so I would be relying on Pablo as my interpreter until I brushed up on my business Spanish. According to Pablo, Francisco apologized for making us late, but he had been on a long phone call with the secretary of the navy and couldn't get him off the line.

Suddenly, Francisco noticed that the hanging panels were open. He quickly closed them and apologized. His receptionist, he said, should not have exposed that sensitive material, but we should not worry—he was not an illegal arms dealer. Everything he did was legit.

For an hour, we spoke only about our backgrounds, our families, our passions and prejudices. I learned that he collected fine art, and he was excited that my family was in the art business. I learned that he had a beautiful wife—he showed me numerous photos of her—and an eight-year-old daughter, Perla ("Pearl") who had a ninth birthday coming up. We talked about music—he loved Mozart, and by coincidence, he and his wife were Yanni fans. My friendship with Yanni made a great impression on him, and he put on a Yanni CD in the conference room, likely to "prove" his fandom. He wondered aloud if I could get Yanni to accompany me on a trip to Mexico so Francisco and his wife could meet him.

I quickly learned that business in Mexico never got off the ground until relationships were established, which could take hours and sometimes days. My American tendency to get down to business only met with smiles and dismissals with Francisco saying things like, "Yes, yes, we'll get to that, but first we must have lunch!"

And that was the next order of business—lunch. Francisco wanted to take Pablo and I to a favorite restaurant, so he called his driver, who pulled around to the heavy front door. As we exited the office, I saw our vehicle for the first time—an armored van with surveillance cameras outside and soft leather seats and a small bar inside. We prattled merrily for about twenty minutes—he did most of the talking while Pablo admirably interpreted—until we arrived at a large, expensive-looking restaurant.

Pablo whispered in English to me, "He must like you. He's never taken *me* here."

The driver, who apparently also served as a bodyguard, judging from his sidearm, joined us at a table. Francisco ordered some kind of liqueur for each of us. I'm glad the cordial mellowed me a bit because the next few minutes would test my resolve.

For an appetizer, Francisco insisted that I try the "Aztec soup," a specialty of the house. I worried a bit when none of the others followed suit.

A few minutes later, a small, squealing monkey strapped to a wooden chair was carried out to the table. The chef approached the monkey with a small board that looked like an outhouse seat with a tiny hole in it and placed it over the monkey's head. The monkey's hairy skull protruded through the hole. Then, the chef produced a large knife and laid it flat on the board, its sharpened edge threatening the top of the monkey's head. With a deft stroke, the top of the head was effortlessly sliced off, revealing a tiny brain.

I almost fainted, as you might expect, but my Lindberg upbringing had taught me to never let them see you sweat.

As the monkey stopped twitching, the chef scooped out the brain and dropped it into a bowl of boiling water, apparently so I could watch it cook to the right doneness. Then the bowl was placed in front of me, and all my companions waited for my first taste of the delicacy.

My Lindberg upbringing failed me at this point, and I looked over at Francisco and simply said, "Sorry, I don't think I can do this."

Pablo started to translate, but Francisco stopped him and laughed good-naturedly. He lifted the bowl and handed it to the driver, who smiled and devoured the brain with a satisfied smack of his lips.

Honestly, I don't remember much else about that first day except that we never spoke about making movies in Mexico.

***

The next day, we got a late start because Francisco had important meetings all morning with the Federales—the national police force of Mexico. In the afternoon, after another hour of social chitchat, we finally started talking about movies. Francisco said he had been thinking about it and had concluded that we should form a film production company in Mexico. The company would be owned 51 percent by Francisco—majority Mexican ownership was required for all Mexican companies—and 49 percent by Pablo and I and whoever else we brought in.

We brainstormed company names for a while and settled on Cinematographica Internacional Venturas (CIV), which translates into International Film Ventures. We would choose which films to make together, I would write and produce them, perhaps even direct, and Francisco would finance them. All our films would be produced in Mexico where costs were considerably below Hollywood rates, and Francisco could use his influence to secure locations, extras and police cooperation at a favorable discount.

This seemed to be enough business for the day because Francisco then announced that he had planned a special evening for us. We left in his armored van for a long trek to the Xochimilco district at Mexico City's southern extreme. Through Pablo's able translation, Francisco used this time to tell us about the woman we would be meeting.

Dolores Olmedo was a friend of the most famous Mexican muralist and painter Diego Rivera and his wife, Frida Kahlo, also a well-known artist. Francisco believed the rumors that Dolores was also Diego's sometime lover and that there was some jealousy between Dolores and Frida, though over her lifetime Dolores collected many of Frida's artworks.

As Francisco remembered the story, Diego had first met Dolores when she was seventeen and on a visit to the Ministry of Education building in Mexico City where Rivera was painting a mural. Diego asked Dolores's mother for permission to paint a portrait of her daughter, which was granted. Over the years, he would paint many portraits of Dolores, some clothed and a few nude.

Dolores's father was a businessman who had died when his daughter was four, and her mother was a well-connected teacher who loved art and music. In Mexico, Dolores studied philosophy, law, music and art history, then relocated to Paris where she studied anthropology, museology and art history. After she returned to Mexico, she chose a more profitable career path in construction, shrewdly using her profits to invest in real estate, amassing considerable wealth in the process. Her lifelong passion, however, was collecting fine art, which she did successfully. She and Diego remained close friends, perhaps more, all their lives.

After Frida's death, Diego spent his final three years living with Dolores in her Acapulco home, painting numerous portraits of her and her children and numerous sunset scenes, most of which Dolores acquired for her collection.

Finally, the van pulled into a long, gated driveway leading up a hill. A tall attendant opened the ornate gate, and six unusual dogs immediately converged on the van barking loudly. The gatekeeper shushed them and waved us through. These square-faced canines looked like Egyptian hieroglyphs. Francisco said they were unique, hairless Xoloiztcuintle dogs, a rare pre-Columbian breed.

Our van was slowly climbing a hill called Tzomoloc, which in the native language called Nahuatl meant "the segmented hill," referring to the hill behind the house we were approaching. This was all Xochimilcas land during the pre-Hispanic period but had been transformed by Dolores into a wondrous estate filled with lush gardens of singularly Mexican flora inhabited by diverse animals, including geese, ducks and magical peacocks seemingly adorned with living jewels.

As the rambling stone structure appeared, I felt thrown back in time. Formerly known as the Hacienda la Noria, it dated to the sixteenth century with some colonial construction added during the seventeenth century. Single-story structures surrounded a courtyard on three sides. On the fourth side, the large, main house rose up, containing within it what was left of the small Chapel of Tzomoloc dedicated by the Spaniards to St. John the Evangelist.

Dolores had acquired the structure in ruins back in 1962 and for twenty-five years had been reconstructing the property to conserve the basic elements and materials of the original. She intended that the property would one day become a museum of her collected works. A decade after we visited, she finally achieved her vision when the Dolores Olmedo Museum opened as a showcase for the world's most important collections of works by Diego Rivera, Frida Kahlo and other important artists, plus a display of over nine hundred archaeological pieces representing Mexico's diverse ancient cultures.

The van parked in a designated space in the courtyard and the gatekeeper, who had followed us up the drive, escorted us toward one of the low-lying buildings with these words translated by Pablo: "While you wait for Miss Olmedo to be ready, she would like you to meet her protégé. Please follow me." Apparently, Dolores had decided to sponsor another artist.

We entered the structure, which opened into an art studio. Standing elegantly in front of a canvas with a brush in his right hand and a hooded falcon on his left wrist was Juan (I don't remember his name, so this one is made up). He was as good looking as my friend Pablo with a swirling moustache, a shirt unbuttoned to his navel and tight breeches that emphasized—what was that, a codpiece? I was looking at a living cover of a historical romance novel.

Juan and Pablo conversed briefly, and from Pablo's translation I learned that the artist had been provided room and board plus the promise that, as his skills improved, his work would find an audience. In exchange, he provided—well, that side of the bargain remained opaque. A percentage of the value of his work, perhaps? Personal attention and comfort from Dolores?

As I was contemplating the nature of this relationship, our docent wrangled us toward the main house, which was much larger than it looked. For about a half-hour, he guided us onto several floors displaying a magnificent collection of Diego Rivera and Frida Kahlo original paintings and numerous illuminated displays of pre-Columbian artifacts. I was dazzled to see so many wonders in a private home.

At last, we were called into the living room on the main floor, from which a spiral staircase rose gracefully to a balcony. The docent gestured to the balcony, and Dolores Olmeda suddenly appeared there. She was about eighty with blue-black hair, presumably colored, dramatically scraped backward and adorned with a sparkling tiara. She was bejeweled in spectacular ornaments complementing her flowing golden gown. Slowly, like an angel descending, she drifted down to our level. Gloria Swanson in *Sunset Boulevard* would have been envious.

Dolores called for drinks, and an assistant magically appeared carrying a tray of small glasses filled with a golden liquid. "What do you think this is?" I asked Pablo.

"Something very special, I'm sure."

We engaged in polite conversation burdened by the need for translation, and we slowly sipped the liqueur. By the time we finished drinking, I was already dizzy. Potent stuff! My empty glass was refilled, and by the end of the evening I had downed it again. I remember hardly anything beyond Dolores's stairway entrance and the first glass of golden oblivion. I must have slept all the way back.

By morning, I was not entirely sure the events of the previous evening had happened, but Pablo assured me they had and that I had not embarrassed myself in any way, though I had provided some amusement. With general agreement on the structure of the Mexican company we were going to form, Pablo and I caught an early afternoon flight home to start assembling the pieces.

This was going to be an adventure!

* * *

This was also going to get more complicated.

I had helped my friend Yanni review his first official recording contract with Private Music, a relatively new label specializing in new age music. Private Music's founder was Peter Baumann, who had found success as the keyboardist with the German electronic group Tangerine Dream. The label had other leading artists in its category but believed Yanni could be its silver bullet to big-time success. After a few tweaks, Yanni signed and Private Music immediately decided to do a music video to launch their new star's career. Yanni insisted that I create the video, and Baumann agreed, assigning a significant budget to the project.

I selected a track called "Forbidden Dreams" from Yanni's debut album, *Keys to Imagination*. I had heard all the tracks on this album many times in Yanni's basement studio, and this one struck me as unique, a highly percussive and kinetic track that lived up to its title. To me, it suggested a jungle adventure combined with an orgasmic fantasy, so I sketched out a dramatic video set at night in a jungle with a gorgeous woman being chased by unknown forest adversaries. She escapes numerous close calls but ends up in a stone canyon surrounded by her chasers who are performing odd, ritualistic dances. She steps onto a platform and performs astounding, balletic moves that can only be described as orgasmic. Yanni is seen in a tux beating on a marimba-like apparatus made of dinosaur bones and also seen naked and painted gold in a loin cloth while walking a leashed leopard.

Yanni beating on prop dinosaur bones as if they were the tone bars of a marimba, which the percussive synthesizer sounds mimicked.

Yes, it makes little sense but provides ample opportunity for magical images that reflect the music itself. And, after all, it's a music video, so it can be surrealistic.

Since there are no jungles in Minnesota, once the project was greenlighted, Pablo and I went to Mexico to scout locations. We were both familiar with Acapulco, so we went there first. Outside the city, we found a boat launch with access to an enormous bayou overgrown with cypress and its twisty roots—highly photogenic. We rented a long, narrow boat with a 70 hp Mercury outboard and an eighteen-year-old guide, Pedro.

The deeper into the backwater we went, the more exotic the locations became. But I couldn't imagine how to bring a full crew and cast with lights and generators, cameras and make-up artists to any of these hard-to reach locations, so with light disappearing, I asked Pedro to get us back. About ten minutes into our thirty-minute return trip, the motor coughed and stopped.

"Out of gas," the guide explained, confidently opening a red fuel container in the rear of the boat. Suddenly, his face grew ashen. He had forgotten to fill up the spare tank. We had no fuel to get home. And the single paddle that was supposed to be in the boat wasn't there.

I was amazed at how quickly it became dark in the bayou. We sat quietly for a few minutes, growing more fearful. I hoped Pedro had a plan for this, but he didn't. Within minutes it was very dark, and we could hear bats whizzing past us, sometimes feeling their wings brushing our faces. Occasionally, another small boat approached, but Pedro prevented us from shouting for help. "Drug smugglers," he explained. "The only ones out here after dark."

This did not calm Pablo and me. But then Pedro had an idea. He grabbed the boat's tie-off line and jumped into the water, which was only chest deep.

"What are you doing?" I yelled.

"I pull us back," he answered, suddenly tugging the boat in the direction of home. I admired his courage. I had no idea what kind of snakes or reptiles were in the water, but step-by-step we started making slow progress. Pedro may have been forgetful, but he was honorable.

After about fifteen minutes and maybe a hundred yards, we saw a light up ahead. The owner of the boat launch had organized a search when we hadn't returned. They hooked up to our boat and towed us back.

That's when I decided we were going to shoot the music video in a studio.

Pablo called Francisco for support in finding a studio, and he was delighted to help with a Yanni video. If Yanni was coming to Mexico, maybe Francisco could meet him? Of course. We quickly went back to Mexico City with Francisco's suggestion to visit Churubusco Studios. I'd never heard of it, but then I didn't know any studios in Mexico.

Churubusco was a major film production facility. Major films recently shot there included *Firewalker* with Chuck Norris, *Conan the Destroyer*, *Dune* (the David Lynch version,) *Amityville II: The Possession*, and one of my favorite films, *Missing*, directed by Costa-Gavras and starring Jack Lemon and Sissy Spacek.

We were given a tour of the extensive back lot, and I was excited to find many of the old sets from the original *Tarzan* movies starring Johnny Weissmuller. We found jungle sets, rope bridges, canyons—virtually everything we would need for the Yanni project. From a young age, Tarzan had been haunting me—from my Dad's first edition novels to my aborted 3D Tarzan movie to the mattress salesman's Louganis project to using the Tarzan sets for my Yanni music video. Maybe the spirit of Tarzan, a self-made man raised by apes, would safeguard my next venture, a music video by a self-made filmmaker raised by a magician and his assistant.

We were happy to learn that we could rent all the needed equipment on premises and book a full union feature film crew at a very attractive price. All I needed was a start date with enough advance notice for the studio to be available.

* * *

A few weeks later, I arrived in Mexico City with my wife, Yanni, my brother-in-law and cinematographer Bill Carlson, and Tara, a make-up artist I had used on *TWTTIN*. Everyone else was local. Peter Baumann from Private Music met us there, most likely to make sure we knew what we were doing. It was not so easy getting our prop dinosaur bones through customs. The agents thought they were real biologic specimens, which would have required special permits.

Mexico City sits high in the air at an average altitude of 7,350 feet. Jogging can be hard if you're not used to it, and nights can be downright frigid even in July. The temperatures were important because all our shooting was at night, sometimes with a mostly naked cast. We ordered numerous barrel heaters to keep people warm, and the locals, who knew better, wore parkas after dark. I wanted a leopard for a sequence, so we hired one with a trainer. Pablo and I cast a ballet troupe to play natives in the chase scenes and the final dance number. Out of this troupe, we found our female lead.

We shot every night from sundown to dawn. Despite some minor dustups with Peter, mostly misunderstandings regarding my way of organizing a shoot versus his, things generally went well except for the leopard. One evening, while we were all warming up during a break, someone asked, "Where's the big cat?"

The leopard had gotten loose in the dark. It was roaming around the shadowy set unseen. Everyone who was seated cautiously raised their feet off the ground. Everything got quiet as we listened for leopard noises. Then someone saw a flash of orange race under a craft services table. The tamer looked there, but it was gone. Then there was another blur and a few screams. The tamer saw the leopard's tail wiggling under a vehicle, then bravely grabbed the tail and pulled the big cat out of hiding. I would not have done that! Irritated, the leopard growled, then rolled onto its back and the handler rubbed its tummy. Everything went back to normal.

An Improbable Series of Risky Events

Yanni, painted gold, just prior to his leopard walk. Our translator, Susana, is next to him.

* * *

Because Francisco had helped us in many ways to organize the shoot, I persuaded Yanni to pay a visit to him and his wife at their villa in Acapulco when we were done shooting the video. Actually, it was more complicated than that. A year earlier, Francisco had bought a historic fourteenth-century fort in Acapulco. It was in disrepair and the roof was gone, so Francisco decided to turn it into an open-air night club, and he wanted Yanni to play there for the opening night two days after we finished shooting.

Yanni agreed. I kept Bill, my cinematographer, Tara and some film equipment, and we went to Acapulco with my wife for another adventure. I planned to give the footage to Francisco for promotional purposes. Francisco rented a bedroom at a villa for each of us.

For the midnight Yanni performance at the fort, the July temperature was well over a hundred degrees Fahrenheit. We all lost weight from perspiration and flopped exhausted into our beds afterward. The next morning, Bill Carlson and I had to take the rental equipment back to Mexico City, but Yanni, Tara and Gloria wanted to spend another day in Acapulco, so I let them. As someone said, bad decisions make good stories.

Mid-morning, Gloria wanted to go for a swim in Acapulco Bay. Yanni and Tara joined her. Gloria was a good swimmer, having grown up around the lakes in northern Minnesota. Yanni was an even better swimmer—at fourteen, he had set a Greek national record in the 50-meter freestyle swimming competition. Unknown to any of them, however, was the bay's reputation for rogue waves that could grab even a strong swimmer and pull them away from shore.

While Yanni and Tara relaxed on the sandy beach gabbing, Gloria headed into the water. She went farther than a comfortable distance for Yanni, who had assumed responsibility for her in my absence. As he was about to call out and ask her to come closer to shore, she suddenly disappeared—apparently grabbed by a fierce rogue wave—then bobbed to the surface, waving her arms and yelling. She went down again, then resurfaced in obvious distress.

Yanni darted into the sea and started swimming out to her. Fifty yards down the beach, an eighteen-year-old Mexican man also saw Gloria thrashing about and headed toward her. The two of them converged on my wife just as she was going down for the proverbial third time. With great effort, the two swimmers pulled her safely to shore.

But that was not the end of the day. By late afternoon, my troublemaking wife was lounging on the deck of a swimming pool with Yanni and Tara. After several Mai Tais, Gloria decided to stroll across the deck, which was slick with a mixture of water and suntan lotion. Suddenly, she slipped and went over backward, slamming her head on the concrete. A nurse by training, she recognized the signs of a concussion.

Yanni was deeply concerned but had no idea what to do with the injured lady, so Gloria barked out instructions. Since her room was next to Yanni's, she explained, he should get her to her bed. During the evening, she asked him to pound on the wall once each hour, and if he did not hear a return knock, he should call for an ambulance. All night, Yanni woke up every hour and pounded on the wall. Each time, Gloria pounded back so Yanni knew she had not slipped into a coma.

From the right, the Mexican rescuer; Gloria; Yanni; Tara; the Mexican man's girlfriend.

The next day, Yanni, Tara and Gloria caught a flight to Houston where Bill and I planned to meet them for the trip back to Minneapolis. When their flight reached the gate, Bill and I watched the jetway for our friends. Finally we saw them slowly making their way toward us. When Yanni saw me, he stepped behind Gloria, grabbed her by both arms, and pushed her toward me.

"Here she is," Yanni told me. "I don't want her anymore."

Drug Trafficking

After finishing post-production on the music video, I returned to Mexico City to move our film company forward with Francisco Galvez. I showed him the music video, which he and his wife loved. We signed legal papers, establishing the business. And then we got down to the important business of choosing our first project. Earlier, I had proposed a paranormal adventure film called *Soul Tracker* that I had already written and which was suitable for production in Mexico. But Francisco now said he wanted my script to be our second production. The first one, he said, should be a movie about a subject that he had great passion for—the problem of drug trafficking.

Francisco was deeply against drugs, which I appreciated. He didn't want his daughter to grow up in a toxic, drug-saturated society. The issue, as he saw it, was that the US blamed Mexico for its drug problems because Mexico supplied most of the product that was poisoning its citizens. But Mexico blamed the US because its demand for drugs produced an irresistible profit stream for smugglers. Francisco wanted to do a movie that addressed this issue head-on. His passion began to sway me. His movie would be the first one worth making.

"But I know nothing about Mexican cartels and drug trafficking," I explained.

Through Pablo's translation, Francisco replied, "You can learn. Just tell me what you need, and I will get it for you."

I told him that to start I would need sources of information, like contacts with Federales and people involved in trafficking. I would need access to the smugglers who were in prison and officials in charge of the prisons.

He just nodded and said, "Done."

Within two days, I had my first meeting with the most frightening and intimidating man I had ever met, the chief comandante of the Federales, who I will call Falco, the name I gave him in my screenplay. I spent hours with him, and he was remarkably forthcoming. I was also certain that he was ruthless in his single-minded endeavor to vanquish the cartels. He carried the burden of great authority in prosecuting his cause, but was paying a heavy price for it. His wife and children had been murdered by traffickers. His surviving mother lived in secrecy for her protection. Falco now lived a solitary life. Every week, he moved to a new location, making it difficult for the cartels to assassinate him in his sleep.

After my first meeting with Falco, I grew paranoid about my own surroundings. After the second meeting, I was afraid to be seen in public with him. But I knew that a fictionalized version of Falco would become the protagonist of my screenplay.

Falco arranged interviews with the warden of the grim Belem Prison in Mexico City and with smugglers who were incarcerated there. Some of the inmates were scarier than Ronald Steeves back in Minnesota. I learned through live demonstrations some of the torture techniques used to extract information. At times I wondered which were worse, the drug overlords or the Mexican authorities. Certainly, that issue would have to be explored in the screenplay.

I also learned about the extreme distrust between Mexican and American authorities, the frequent betrayals by both sides, the corruption of the police and the Federales who wore their uniforms while taking bribes from the cartels. The problems were so deep and complex, they seemed almost impossible to resolve.

Falco and I developed a good relationship, and my association with Francisco seemed to give the chief comandante extra confidence in supporting my research. "Maybe," he once told me, "you can do some good. I hope so."

Finally, it came time for the greatest test of our relationship. "Is there any way I could speak with one of the cartel leaders?" I asked.

Falco looked at me with such a penetrating glare that I was sure I'd crossed the line. Finally, though, he answered. "You should talk to the head of the biggest cartel," he said. "He spends time just north of Acapulco. We are at a stalemate, so he thinks he is invincible. Obviously, we have contact with him. Let me see."

His answer astonished me. It seemed that the cartels and Mexican law enforcement almost had a power sharing agreement. Falco knew these people. They hunted him while he hunted them, and yet there was some grudging respect for the power each held.

It took three days, but at last I received instructions from Falco to fly to Acapulco on Tuesday, stay overnight, and then at precisely ten o'clock Wednesday morning be at a specific location to be picked up by a helicopter flown by Federales.

The next day, carrying just a backpack, I was flown north from Acapulco over unbroken jungle that from our altitude looked like a dense, green carpet. About thirty miles from Acapulco, the helicopter set down in a small clearing. I was instructed to get out and wait for my escorts. The chopper took off and after a few minutes, when nothing happened, I grew worried that there may have been a mix-up. What would I do if no one showed up?

Then I heard rustling in the dense forest. Admittedly, I was frightened. In Minnesota, the noise could be from a bear, but in Mexico—a jaguar, perhaps? Unlikely as that seemed, my imagination was running wild.

Suddenly, three Mexicans stepped into the clearing with a saddled mule. They looked like movie banditos right out of Central Casting—untrimmed moustaches, slouchy sombreros, soiled shirts, crossed bandoliers slung sash-style over their chests. One carried a machine gun, and none spoke more than a few words of English. I suspected these men were of the lowest caste of traffickers used for benign missions such as picking up snoopy Americans.

I was urged to saddle up, and for about thirty minutes we followed a faint trail that finally opened up at the foot of a rise on the jungle floor. At the top of this small hill sat a large, white villa with surrounding gardens. The mansion would be the correct answer for a game of "What does not belong in this picture?"

I was introduced to the owner, who was the head of the cartel, a sixtyish man in sandals and an open-collared beige shirt untucked over expensive slacks. He greeted me with unexpected warmth, hugging me first, then leading me up some stairs to a veranda that overlooked the grounds. He spoke English, which would make my interviews easier. I had been told to expect a stay of a week, during which the cartel chief, who I will call Antonio, would answer my questions. Nevertheless, my nervous stomach reminded me that I was in the lion's den, and there were no guarantees for my safety.

For a week, I was entertained and fed like a celebrity guest, which confounded me until some off-handed comments by Antonio, such as "Make sure you get this right," and "Just use my family name" suggested that he hoped to become famous in our movie. Apparently, he didn't know my screenplay would be fictional, and probably thought it was going to be a documentary. I let him think what he wanted.

Antonio was amazingly candid about his business and the intricacies of "transporting merchandise undetected," but I'm sure the tactics we discussed were obsolete. He never used the word "drugs" but liberally talked about cocaine and marijuana as if they were aspirin and tequila, a beverage that flowed freely on the premises. Fortunately, after my experience with the mysterious golden liqueur at Dolores Olmeda's hacienda, I was no longer indulging in alcohol.

Antonio admitted that his business was illegal but attacked Mexican law enforcement as being equally illegal and immoral in their tactics. But it didn't matter, he pointed out, because he "employed" more law enforcement personnel than the government, so the two sides were almost indistinguishable. He knew Falco, and expressed admiration for his strategic gifts, but thought the man's obsession with putting the cartels out of business had blinded him to the realities of the world. He would take no pleasure, he confessed, in killing Falco, and hoped Falco would feel the same way should he kill my host first.

Like Falco, Antonio's disdain—hatred, even—for the American authorities was deep and festering. He called them hypocrites and self-righteous idiots. At least Falco, he admitted, was neither of those. It was Falco himself who had set up my week with Antonio with the assurance that during my stay there would be no attacks on Antonio's business interests.

Between conversations, we engaged socially in many activities, including a cocktail party with some local government leaders at which I was encouraged to conceal the reason I was there. I would be introduced, Antonio said, simply as an American business contact. Everyone would know what that meant. At first, I was uncomfortable with being considered an American cog in the smuggling business, but I convinced myself that I was acting as an undercover informant.

As the end of my week approached, I grew more apprehensive about my safety. On my final day, Antonio, in a white sport coat and blue shirt, sat with me during a leisurely breakfast of *tocino y huevos* on the veranda when one of Antonio's lieutenants approached nervously and whispered something to my host. Antonio immediately frowned and twitched his head as if indicating the man should bring the object of concern to him. The object turned out to be a bloodied and extremely frightened man. Obviously, this person had done something bad.

Antonio held up a palm to me as if saying, "Allow me just a minute to deal this matter." Then he nodded, and another man carried out a plastic drop cloth and unrolled it on the floor at the veranda's other end about thirty feet away. The bloodied man was dragged to the drop cloth and made to stand on it. On the man's head, someone placed a large mango about eight inches in diameter.

Antonio stood and removed a pistol that had been concealed beneath his white coat. Holding it in both hands, he aimed at the mango—at least, I hoped his target was the mango. It didn't matter, because the fired round struck the man in the face and he slumped to the floor, was rolled up in the plastic sheet and then dragged out of sight.

I was so shaken, I couldn't speak. Was Antonio's candor with me because he knew I would never leave the villa alive? Was I just a week's entertainment for a cartel boss?

As if nothing unusual had happened, Antonio sat down, put a forkful of eggs into his mouth and smiled at me sympathetically. He said, "So sorry you had to see that, but business is business. The man was a traitor—he knew the risks."

I still couldn't speak, so I just nodded and played with my food.

Early that afternoon, I said goodbye to my host, trying to fake a look of gratitude and confidence. The same Central Casting crew that had picked me up now led a mule to the foot of the stairs, where I saddled up for the half-hour march to the clearing where a helicopter was scheduled to retrieve me.

All the way to my destination, I kept wondering if I would be killed in the jungle where my body would never be found, and my wife and children would be left wondering what had happened to me. Having no cell phones in those days, I had not spoken to my family in about two weeks. They had no idea where I was, only that I was investigating drug smuggling in Mexico.

I reached the clearing intact, and about twenty minutes later, the Federales picked me up in a chopper and delivered me back to Acapulco where I caught a short flight to Mexico City. Grateful to be alive, I checked into a hotel, exhausted. I planned to recover for a day or two, then book a flight home. I was done with Mexico for a while. I had what I needed to write the screenplay.

About two o'clock the next morning, a phone call to my room woke me up. Who knew I was at that hotel and what room I was in? I had told no one.

A hoarse voice speaking very broken English said it would be much better for me if I was not there in the morning. In other words, I should get out of town right now. Had a mole with the Federales tracked me down? Had Antonio changed his mind about leaving me alive? Had a rival cartel been tracking me? Why would someone have warned me? Was leaving the hotel immediately an ambush?

I decided none of that mattered. I had to leave now, so I packed quickly and left the hotel. At the entrance, there were always taxis available around the clock, so I literally jumped into one and told the driver to take me to the airport. The terminal was open, but no ticketing windows had agents at that time of the morning, so I took a seat and waited nervously until I could purchase a ticket on the earliest flight home. I called Gloria from a pay phone and asked her to pick me up at the airport. She wanted a full report on what had been going on, of course, but I put her off. I was not ready to explain my adventures just yet.

* * *

At home, Gloria and I had quite a conversation. She was happy to see me but blunt in her assessment of my sanity. I had to stop this nonsense, she insisted. I nodded, but in truth wasn't sure I could stop. I had started something, and very possibly I was incapable of stopping before it was finished.

A few weeks later, I was reading the latest edition of *Time*, and on one left-hand page I discovered a story about the chief confidante of the Mexican Federales. He had been driving his mother from Mexico City to Acapulco for a holiday when a gang of gunmen ambushed his car and killed both occupants. Falco was dead. I wondered if Antonio had been responsible, and if so, had he taken no pleasure in it as he had promised?

I did write the screenplay, which was more fact than fiction. But by that time, my interest in moviemaking in Mexico had waned. Would I ever be safe working there, especially in a partnership with Francisco? Would I be happy traveling everywhere in an armored vehicle, always looking over my shoulder? Maybe Gloria was right.

We never made the movie, but occasionally I pull out the screenplay and read it just to remind me of the adventure… and the fact that if I could go to Mexico, Mexico could come to Minnesota.

Family Matters

Our children all learned to be independent and fiscally responsible. They each found their own path in the world, with only a nudge here and there from Gloria and me, yet they each had a distinctly different personality.

Jennifer, the oldest, was easily the most sociable, taking after her mother, Gloria. She made friends easily and was often the one who kept friendships alive. She always saw herself as a successful businessperson, so she attended St. Thomas University for two years, then completed her undergraduate studies at Normandale.

In early November of 1986, I asked her what she wanted for her eighteenth birthday. Her reply startled and touched me deeply. "Would you consider adopting me?" she asked. Over the coming years, she would again become close to her biological father, but at the time, she wanted a deeper connection to the man who was helping to raise her.

At the adoption ceremony, the judge legalized the adoption and then confessed that he didn't know what to do next. "I usually hold the young child on my lap for a photo," he said. Immediately, my beautiful daughter jumped up, ran to the judge and sat on his lap for a photo. The blushing judge just sat there grinning.

Because she had changed her last name to Lindberg, many of her friends thought she must have gotten married in a clandestine ceremony, which caused a lot of laughs. She worked briefly in a women's clothing store at Miracle Mile in St. Louis Park, ironically below the office of Marjorie Congdon's third husband, before going to work for my mother at Elayne Galleries, where she helped run two other galleries for the family business. Eventually she went to work in marketing for Microsoft, and after several job changes, wound up as chief marketing officer for Masonite, a Fortune 500 Company, at last realizing her career goal.

Jennifer's brother, Brant Zwiefel, wanted to retain his father's last name, so he remained my stepson. After barely graduating from Wayzata High School, he attended Arizona State University for one year where he excelled at learning to play guitar but little else. Though intellectually gifted, his motivation deficit continued until we enrolled him in counseling at the Institute for Motivational Development. In the first session, which Gloria and I attended, his counselor, John, made it clear to all of us that he couldn't fix anyone. The fixing had to come from the entire family unit. Gloria and I would need to learn new behaviors to provide the kind of support Brant needed.

We all found the process transformational, though it was difficult for each of us to change deeply established behaviors. This helped me become a better father and husband and helped Brant develop into a highly motivated individual capable of tapping into his God-given gifts. Like my brilliant friend Gary Hudson, the rocket scientist, Brant remained a college dropout, but used a job at IBM to obtain a better position at Microsoft and is now in a high-level position there. As a return on our investment in him, Brant gave Gloria and me two beautiful, intelligent and talented granddaughters.

My first son, Brendan, was always a positive force for good, possessing charisma and an abundance of goodwill. The divorce of his mother and me unfortunately caused him to bounce around between families and never establish a close relationship with his younger brother, Scott, who largely grew up separated from him.

Brendan attended the University of Minnesota but dropped out with six foreign language credits left to achieve. This, too, reminded me of my friend Gary Hudson, who had dropped out of college due to a low threshold of boredom. Brendan had started working for

Mom at Elayne Galleries when he was fifteen and then went full-time. He loved the art business and stayed in it until his untimely death in 2016.

My youngest son, Scott, lived through the turbulence of being dislocated to a family comprised mainly of a stepmom and stepsiblings. Because of our boisterous and chaotic family life in the Plymouth house, for which I take responsibility, he largely took cover from the domestic storms.

For much of the time that Scott lived with us, Gloria was victimized by multiple sclerosis (MS). Besides terrible pain and weakness, Gloria sometimes experienced bipolar-like emotional disruptions that must have seemed frightening to little Scott, especially since his father and chief protector was so often absent. Eventually, we converted the basement office into an apartment and moved Scott down there, and he enjoyed the privacy. Unfortunately, the rest of the family sometimes forgot about him.

Much later, Scott told me that he and Brendan often called themselves the "lost boys." Thinking about my role in their despair still throws me into anguish. When Scott graduated from Wayzata High, he received an award for being one of only five students out of a class of over 500 that never missed a day of school throughout their three years of high school. Every day, despite the weather or illness or fear of giving an oral book report, Scott got up, ate breakfast and caught the bus to school—and his father didn't even know how reliable he was.

Scott graduated with an associate's degree from a community college and worked for several of our family businesses as a self-taught computer coder and animator specializing in web-based learning systems, a career which he continues to this day as an independent contractor.

On good days, I often marvel at how well our children turned out—all of them caring and compassionate, smart and creative, responsible and independent. I wish I could take more credit for this outcome, but each of them is certainly a credit to humanity.

* * *

After I finally abandoned my dream of a career in entertainment, I returned with a head of steam to help Gloria build up her company, Integrated Strategies. An enticing project awaited. The company had landed a large training project for Rollerblade, which had struggled for several years to train the primarily adolescent sales staffs of sporting goods stores how to sell inline skates by introducing new product innovations to customers.

We were told that the traditional approach was to put on training camps regionally and bring salespeople together for lectures and fun skating events in adjoining parking lots. Testing had shown that the young adult audiences typically recalled only about 15 percent of what they had been taught at these daylong sessions, which means the training had failed. Could Integrated Strategies help?

Immediately, I recalled my army experience training illiterate and unresponsive draftees how to read and do arithmetic. The key to success, I had learned, was creating in each adult learner a desire to learn what was being taught. In other words, the key was RELEVANCE. If an instructor would clearly show the learner how and why the material was relevant to their lives or careers, the adult learners would snap into an active learning frame of mind. But if you established relevance and followed up with a lecture—which adults do not tolerate very well—you risk stopping the learning process in its tracks.

At our pitch to Rollerblade, I proposed producing a game-like series of mini-simulations in which each learner or "player" would play the role of a salesperson. Using carefully designed scenarios, the "player" would have to solve challenges and overcome objections provided by the customer. The scenarios would show the player why or how the learning would be personally useful. I showed a simple demo to the potential client, and they bit, which showed they were desperate to elevate the sales proficiency of this non-captive group of dealer salespeople.

We were partially bluffing, however, because we had never built anything like this before, and there were no existing tools to help us. Everything would have to be built from scratch, which was risky. Nevertheless, we plunged forward, and I invented rules for instructional design that disallowed long lectures and required the players to *request* any information they needed to solve the challenges. I believed that if a learner asked for help, they would be more likely to remember the help they received.

We insisted on rigorous follow-up to measure whether our new approach was successful. Rollerblade had done next-day testing of recalled information in the past with average results of about 15 percent—dreadful, actually—so they agreed to do the same thing with our course. Rollerblade purchased numerous computers and the one-day, technology-based sales simulation rolled out like a roadshow to each successive location.

On average, next-day recall of key information was a whopping 85 percent! This was much greater than any of us had expected. I knew we were onto something. Later, when we brought this demo and the test results to other organizations, many of them wanted to use this new methodology—which I was now calling HyperLearning—and I was becoming known as an innovator in adult learning with speaking engagements and workshops at large training conferences.

Integrated Strategies continued to grow, and we eventually had more than twenty full-time staff. Gloria even hired my ex-wife Karen, who had earned her Master of Education degree. The two of them became good friends and worked well together except for one thing... Gloria's emerging emotional swings. Gloria was more frequently experiencing significant muscular pain and occasional bouts of depression and irritability. The emotional swings were also causing some marital difficulties when stacked onto my workaholic nature. We both worried about the erosion of her physical and emotional health, but no one could tell us what was wrong. Her mother had suffered from lupus, so maybe that was it.

The problem with our company's continuous innovation for each project was that, because the products or services were in constant transition, the costs of development, experimentation and occasional failure used up the earned revenue. But it certainly was fun for a compulsively inquisitive person like me!

***

In 1988, I realized that I had reverted to the same kind of fee-based project work as I had abandoned at Russell-Manning. We were now doing more computer-based assignments than film or video production, but the business model was still the same. I started feeling trapped once more, but then another midnight phone call interrupted my gathering gloom and scattered some light on my path forward.

"Sorry to bother you so late," Bill Mack said. "But I need your help."

Bill Mack was a world-famous sculptor and painter based in Minnesota. He had been on *Lifestyles of the Rich and Famous*, the TV series hosted by Robin Leach, and his work was in galleries all over the world. My mother had given him his first gallery show, so he had known and trusted my whole family for a long time.

I met Bill at his art studio the next day, and he showed me a box of 265 handwritten letters—over 1500 pages of writing along with cards and envelopes with postmarks. The letters were all written to the same woman, Carmen Montez, who acted as a spiritual counselor to the writers, who were all major celebrities—Harry Belafonte, Tom Jones, Marlon Brando, and the biggest one, Elvis Presley. Bill had acquired an interest in the letters from the owner, and they wanted to write and publish a book based on the shocking contents of these letters.

I read through the correspondence and saw information that had never been made public before, content that measurably changed the story of Elvis Presley. The material revealed by these writers was so sensational that I wondered if the letters had been forged, but Bill had hired a world-famous handwriting expert to authenticate them. There were many story threads contained in the letters, but the major story was about how Elvis had been victimized by the producer of two Elvis Presley movies and a gang he had assembled for that purpose.

According to the letters, and corroborated by more than one writer, Elvis and Marlon had been kidnapped together by the producer's gang, which had then let Marlon go. Elvis then had been tortured nearly to death and gang-raped by up to ten men. This story was so incredible, I did not believe it at first. But later, I came to know a candy striper at the hospital where Elvis was taken after the assault. During his recovery, Elvis had befriended the sixteen-year-old girl, who had gone on to become a nurse practitioner. Eventually, she and I met, and she confirmed that Elvis had been admitted to the hospital under a pseudonym and was nearly dead when he arrived.

The details of this story and my participation in it are in my book, *Letters from Elvis: Shocking Revelations to His Secret Confidante*, so I won't cover many of them here, but there was an abundance of surprises.

Originally, a bestselling author and film director had been hired by the owner of the letters to write the book. Robert Slatzer had become famous for being Marilyn Monroe's first husband. Robert and Marilyn had been longtime friends, and after her first successful movie, they had run off to Mexico to be married. But when Marilyn told the studio about it, she was told by Darryl Zanuck, then head of 20th Century Fox Studios, that his most famous sex symbol could not be a married woman. The studio paid the Mexican government to destroy the marriage certificate, but ABC still did a TV Movie about the marriage called *Marilyn and Me*, which would be released three years later in 1991.

In 1974, Robert had written an international bestselling book called *The Life and Curious Death of Marilyn Monroe* and had followed it with two biographies—*Duke: The Life and Times of John Wayne* and *Bing Crosby: Hollow Man*. He also wrote a second book about Marilyn's mysterious death called *The Marilyn Files*. He had also directed several B-movies: *Bigfoot*, starring John Carradine, father of David Carradine, whom I had partied with in Los Angeles; *The Hellcats*, starring nobody I had ever heard of; and an anti-communist propaganda film called *No Substitute for Victory*, with John Wayne as host.

Robert Slatzer's writing credits had baited the owner of the letters into hiring him, and Bill Mack had paid a fee for his services. Unfortunately, because of health and other issues, he had been unable to make any progress. Bill wanted me to prod Robert and help organize an outline for the book, and I agreed. I built an outline, but later, when Robert still had made no writing progress, Bill paid off his contract, and I agreed to prepare a book proposal for publishers to review. If we got a publishing deal, I would become the sole author.

To assist us, I called in my good friend and previous talent agency owner Annemarie Osborne to attract New York's elite publishers to our proposal, and she did a wonderful job. Bill Mack and I assembled a coherent proposal with handwriting authentication, history of the project, photocopies of portions of the letters, an outline of the proposed book and two sample chapters. We also included some attorney summaries of copyright issues that suggested we had a legal path for the endeavor. With the proposal in hand, we flew to New York to meet with the publishers Annemarie had lined up.

The meetings were great fun. The publishers and editors we met were frankly astonished at the content of the letters. Several frankly said they did not believe the letters were genuine despite the handwriting analysis, and even if the letters were real, they feared blowback to their reputations if reviews criticized the authenticity. A couple said they had been sued by Elvis Presley Enterprises (EPE) in the past over published works and didn't want to get entangled again. "Those people are highly litigious. They will sue over everything they don't own a piece of," one of them told us. All, however, agreed that the biggest issue was copyright infringement because unpublished letters are copyrighted automatically in the name of the writer. Our submitted legal opinions did not sway their thinking.

One publisher, our favorite for this project, professed keen interest. We met with the editor-in-chief for dinner at his home and expected to work out details of a publishing agreement. He had promised to get back to us in a day or so, but after a week of silence, we reached out and were told that the firm had decided against the book. So sorry, they said. The risk was just too high. Much later, through other sources, I learned that news of the letters had leaked to EPE, which had squelched the deal with this publisher.

It would take nearly thirty years for me to find a way to publish the book. But once it was published, many doors would be unlocked to other astonishing Elvis secrets. Elvis Presley had become my new obsession.

* * *

Despite all the adventure, or perhaps because of it, I was at a pivotal point in my life. My mind was continually churning in search of something new, but I had lost any sense of direction. Religion, which for many people provided a sense of purpose, had failed to satisfy my need for answers. I had grown up Christian and had investigated Judaism, Islam, Hinduism and Buddhism, but in every case—particularly with Christianity—church leaders had spoon-fed me doctrinal clichés and discouraged me from asking hard questions, usually insisting that some issues were mysteries not meant to be understood. For a naturally inquisitive person who thrived on asking questions and figuring things out, this seemed insulting, as if the church did not trust me to be an intelligent, rational human being.

But then, one evening, Gloria and I attended a friendly meeting at the home of one of my chief rivals during the time I was running Russell-Manning. Since we were no longer competitors, we could now be friends and had a lot in common. Fred, a wise Persian immigrant who owned a large film production company, was a member of the Baháʼí Faith, a religion I had never heard of.

A talented Baháʼí pianist performed some music and spoke about the relationship of music to spirituality, which my wife and I found interesting. When the presenter invited questions about the Baháʼí Faith or its perspective on any of the issues in the world, I asked what the principles of this religion were. The other members of the group, which included scientists, mathematicians, educators and other highly educated people from numerous cultures, all had something to say.

What most impressed me was the simple statement that a basic tenet of the Faith was the need for everyone to conduct their own independent search for truth and make their own decisions without coercion by anyone else. This was one reason, I learned, that the Bahá'í Faith had no clergy—no priesthood to claim special knowledge or have superior authority. The spiritual teachings of the Faith, I was told, were based on the principle of the oneness and unity of humanity in all its wonderful diversity. All religions, according to this Faith, were but different stages of one universal religion of God, so we must respect the basic spiritual teachings of all religions, which generally agree with each other on spiritual matters despite differences that have evolved due to human intervention over time.

Frankly, I was flabbergasted that there was a religion that gave me permission to think and ask questions. Gloria and I walked away with an armful of books, but I took seriously the mandate to study ALL religions including the Bahá'í teachings and then see what made sense to me.

Gloria registered as a Bahá'í six months later in June of 1990, but I felt a responsibility to read as many of the Bahá'í Writings as I could before making a decision. Finally, on New Year's Day of 1991, I told Gloria that I was a Baha'i. Signing a Declaration Card was just a formality.

For me, this was the best decision of my life. But being a Bahá'í didn't remove all my difficulties. It just gave me new tools and perspectives with which to deal with them, and a clear purpose for my life—to help bring greater truth and unity to the world.

* * *

While Integrated Strategies continued to grow, Brendan was beginning a summer of full-time work at Elayne Galleries. Each day, he took the public bus from south Minneapolis where he lived with his mother to the gallery in St. Louis Park, a twenty-minute ride. At eighteen, he had now been working part- and full-time for a couple of years.

On one bus trip, he had sat next to an attractive young woman named Kathy, who was about twenty years old, and struck up a conversation. By coincidence, she was returning to her home, which was about three blocks from the gallery. Soon, they became friends, and she invited him to her small home after work. They didn't date, just had interesting conversations, until suddenly one day she seemed to snap and became very possessive of my son. He had never given Kathy his phone number or address, but she knew this information, which disturbed him.

Then he started getting phone calls from her wanting him to come over and see her, which was even more disturbing. Things escalated when Kathy said she was coming to see him at his house, which he shared with his mother and her husband, Rich. Brendan tried to shut down the relationship, but the more he tried to cut her off, the more she tried to intimidate and finally threaten him. She was behaving like Glen Close, the violently possessive woman in *Fatal Attraction,* the highest grossing movie in the US three years earlier.

When Kathy sent a note to Brendan at work saying that she was prepared to blow up the gallery if he didn't restore their relationship, he went to Bonnie, my sister, who had previously worked with the local police on the Rockwell Heist. The police told Bonnie that they had a file on Kathy, who had previously spent time in a mental institution and was on their watch list. I knew from my relationship with Ronald Steeves how these domestic issues could quickly spiral into tragedy, so I was worried.

The police investigated Kathy and uncovered adequate grounds to arrest her. She spent some time in jail, but then was placed on parole and started harassing Brendan again in violation of a court order. Again, the police arrested her, and another trial date was set. She didn't have money for a defense attorney, so the city assigned a young public defender to her case. While working with her defense counsel, Kathy unexpectedly shifted her obsession from Brendan to her attorney and began harassing him at home and during strategy meetings.

This did not end well for the young lady, but Brendan and the gallery were finally freed of Kathy's frightening threats. For quite a while, Brendan lost interest in dating, filling his time with work at Elayne Galleries, his sanctuary. There he would be safe. After all, his warm and generous grandma had a track record of arresting brutish criminals. And, if anything appeared that she couldn't handle, well… his grandpa, the magician, could make anything disappear.

Black Hole

The first half of the 1990s was a black hole of uncertainty, stress and financial insecurity. At times I felt like I was living through difficult tests of my newfound faith. Today, in hindsight, I can see that it was indeed my Bahá'í Faith that helped me survive these dark days by giving me something much bigger and more important than me on which to focus.

After a period of growth, the economy had taken a downward turn, competition had increased, and business had fallen away. Unfortunately, our overhead at Integrated Strategies had not declined with falling sales. Simultaneously, Gloria's undiagnosed malady worsened.

We personally concluded that she was suffering from fibromyalgia, a chronic disorder that causes pain and tenderness throughout the body, as well as fatigue and trouble sleeping. Fibromyalgia was a new diagnosis—not even a "thing" until 1987. Some people, even healthcare providers, considered it to be mainly psychosomatic, but Gloria's misery argued against that.

Starting in January of 1993, I began journaling my experiences for the first time. Some short excerpts from this journal aptly describe the chaos, conflict and pain of our lives during this bleak stretch when I was struggling to use my faith and some old-fashioned rational thinking to fend off my personal fears and frustrations.

January 23, 1993

> Gloria had the flu today and could not attend the Scanticon "After Hours" show at the Radisson. I came home right afterward. I am worried about her—both for her sake and mine. It affects me deeply. I must work on being independent of her moods instead of reacting to them... I am amazed at how much the age of 49 seems like 39—and 38—and 37—and 30! I cannot remember most of those years. They seem wasted... unrecollected as they are. Perhaps remembered lessons of these years will be taken advantage of in the future. Gloria, I love you.

By February, things had not improved, but I found I could give myself a pep talk by journaling.

February 3, 1993

> What an emotional rollercoaster ride. I'm feeling very blue tonight. Writing may help me figure out why. Maybe it's because Gloria is having a major fibromyalgia attack and is in misery. I hurt for her. It's hard on the rest of us too, though. She is on the verge of tears much of the time. I can't share my feelings of fear or depression with her because I'm afraid it might bring her down even further... Actually, I'm tired of being the one who is "up" all the time. I just want to rest. And be depressed. Thanks for listening, Journal, you help me focus. Now I realize I have good reasons to be depressed.

Gloria's pain at times was unrelenting. I just didn't know what to do. Maybe it wasn't fibromyalgia but something worse.

February 4, 1993

> Gloria was hurting so bad this morning at the office she could hardly move. Then Deb suggested a masseuse, who came in with table and all. It worked a temporary miracle! For a time, the pain was virtually gone. Maybe I should try it. Past midnight now, always so much to do.

More frequently, Gloria's pain and depression seemed to redirect her frustration and wrath on me. I was an imperfect husband, I admit, and her barbs stung. Little by little, I started to withdraw from the relationship rather than finding a way to be more supportive, which was what she needed. Increasingly, it seemed, I was becoming the target of Gloria's blame for everything that was wrong in her life. Half the time, I felt blameworthy. During the other half, I was indignant. All the time, however, I felt guilty because I could not find a solution to our abundance of problems.

February 15, 1993

> Gloria is somewhat distant tonight. Her muscles ache and she's been upset that Brant has been grousing about everything lately. For some reason, she thinks I'm to blame, even though I'm working 70-80 hours a week.

March 17, 1993

> A wild, bizarre time we just had. Gloria's fibromyalgia has been bad. Two days ago we had a major blow-up in a Rollerblade project post-mortem meeting. Gloria stormed out and never came back. At home that evening, she threatened to walk out of the marriage. Talk about ups and downs. This is more than depres-

> sion, but she can't see that... She says I don't help out enough at home. I know I should help out more, but I don't know how I'll do it. I worked tonight until 10:30 at the office and then came home and cleaned up the kitchen and dining room. I can't write any more tonight and tomorrow is a hectic day.

Other disturbing events were also contributing to the chaos. My sister, Bonnie, had been suffering for years with painful rheumatoid arthritis and had undergone replacement of the knuckles in her feet and hands. Suddenly, she was hospitalized with a serious foot infection. At the same time, my stepson Brant had been hospitalized with a disturbing heart condition.

April 7, 1993

> I went to visit Bonnie in the hospital tonight. As I walked in, she told me that Jen had called to say that Brant had just collapsed and they were rushing him to Urgent Care. A few calls later, Jen told me that Brant's EKG showed signs of a heart attack. Gloria and I are both feeling guilty about this poor kid working himself so hard practically at our command.

Fortunately, Brant was eventually diagnosed with a chronic genetic condition called brugata, which mimicked the symptoms of heart attack. We learned that Jennifer also had this condition. Back home, Gloria's strange illness continued to complicate our relationship, and with its ebb and flow I drifted further away, leaving Gloria, I fear, feeling abandoned and hopeless.

June 9, 1993

> Yesterday, Gloria blew up at me when I tried to give her some good news about how some restructuring of

> responsibilities at work were finally giving me some relief so I could have more time for family. I think Gloria feels left out of things because with the funeral of her father and her chronic illness, she's been away a long time, and now when things are happening it must seem like she was the obstacle. Not true, of course.

In the fall of 1994, the company had continued to survive—was growing, in fact—and to make more room we leased the entire first floor of the Strom Building on I94 in Minnetonka, Minnesota. This was a bold move with Gloria's condition worsening and our home stress escalating, but that was the family way. Put your head down and seize the challenge.

* * *

Gloria was also keeping a journal at the time, and she generously shared it with me. In a September entry she wrote:

Gloria, September 24, 1994

> Another day of trying to work but developing spasms and weakness within a couple of hours. Couldn't help the guys move out of the computer room and into the new building. What a struggle it is. I'm so afraid of losing my mind with whatever this is. How does one know God if the mind goes?

After a series of tests following that entry, Gloria's condition was formally diagnosed on my fifty-first birthday, October 26. She was not suffering from fibromyalgia after all. Instead, she had a disease called remitting relapsing multiple sclerosis. It was comforting to finally have a name for her illness, but MS is a frightening disease. It is incurable and usually progressive, meaning it only gets worse. It produces not only excruciating pain, weakness and fatigue, but also emotional disturbances like uncontrollable anger and depression, though these negative emotions can also be heightened states of emotions already present.

Gloria started giving herself a daily injection of a drug that produced nasty, flu-like symptoms for a few days, leaving her with only one or two days of relief before another injection was due. The average period between flare-ups was extended slightly but not enough to make the terrible side-effects worthwhile. The doctors urged Gloria to quit working altogether.

A bright spot emerged, however, when Gloria's doctors proposed a novel, experimental treatment for her MS symptoms. It was thought that a monthly injection of a huge dose of steroids could shock the immune system, causing it to aggressively respond in a way to significantly relieve the symptoms. Would she be willing to try this treatment? She was more than ready. Her condition was deteriorating rapidly. In December, she quit working.

* * *

One evening before Christmas, I woke up and discovered that Gloria was not in bed. I heard clattering downstairs, so I put on a robe and walked down the steps to the kitchen where I found Gloria going through drawers like a madwoman. I startled her, and she grabbed a butcher knife, then came at me, apparently meaning to stab me. I caught her arms and tried to wrestle the knife away, but she was unusually strong and fought me off, so I fled into another room, frightened. She disappeared into a different room, so I was able to call 911.

The police arrived within a few minutes, and I met them at the door. After a brief search, they caught Gloria, who was incoherent, and put her in the locked back seat of a squad car. After taking my statement, the police said they would take her to the psychiatric unit of Abbot Northwestern Hospital in Minneapolis where she would be admitted for her own safety. I called Brant and Jennifer to explain what was happening and promised to keep them informed.

The next morning, I drove to the psych unit where Gloria had been locked up overnight. I found her in an open sitting room talking to some other patients. A psychiatrist on duty told me that they had found her absolutely calm and coherent in the morning, and since breakfast she had been counseling other patients the way she had assisted staff during her three months of nurse training at a mental institution. Gloria was happy to see me, but she couldn't explain what had happened to her. She said she remembered watching herself from a position outside of herself and wondering, "What is that crazy woman doing?" We were allowed to leave the unit with phone numbers to call just in case.

A month later, I woke up again because of strange noises. This time I saw the light switched on in our large, walk-in closet, but the door was almost closed. I stepped quietly to the door and slowly opened it. Gloria was holding my .370 elk hunting rifle and loading live rounds into it.

"What are you doing?" I asked. It was a stupid question as I could plainly see what she was doing.

Surprised, she swiveled, pointing the barrel toward me. I grabbed the rifle and we wrestled fiercely. She screamed at me. Like before, she was astonishingly strong, but she couldn't get the weapon out of my hands, so she scurried around me and disappeared somewhere in the dark house.

I called 911 again and the same officers showed up. I was even more frightened this time. How could I continue to live with a woman who seemed intent on killing me?

The next morning, I arrived at the psych unit and again found Gloria patiently talking to other patients. When she left, she warmly thanked the staff for keeping her safe, and they in turn thanked her for assisting. The whole incident was surrealistic.

I called a family meeting without Gloria to discuss the problem. We debated whether we should try to have her committed for the protection of herself and me. No one wanted to take such drastic action, but one family member volunteered to investigate the process… just in case.

Then, in February, a third incident occurred. After struggling to sleep, I had drifted off with Gloria beside me, but woke up and found her gone. The temperature outside was in the teens. No lights were on, and in my search of the upstairs rooms, I couldn't find my wife. I went downstairs and started turning on lights. I found Gloria barefoot and wearing a thin nightgown in the living room. As I approached her, she looked frightened and ran. I chased but couldn't catch her, so I called 911 again.

Hearing me call 911, Gloria suddenly bolted for the front door and ran into the frigid night, racing toward a woods across the street. There was snow on the ground, so I feared her bare feet would suffer frostbite.

The police arrived within minutes. Using a searchlight, they found her crouching behind some brush in the woods. They got her into the squad car and wrapped her in blankets. For a third time, she was taken to the psych unit. This time, I sobbed as the police pulled out of our driveway. I had lost my wife to this dreaded disease—that much seemed certain.

I couldn't sleep after this episode, so I thumbed through a Bahá'í prayer book looking for some comfort or assistance with my difficulties. I found this prayer, which has become my favorite.

> **O God! Refresh and gladden my spirit. Purify my heart. Illumine my powers. I lay all my affairs in Thy hand. Thou art my Guide and my Refuge. I will no longer be sorrowful and grieved; I will be a happy and joyful being. O God! I will no longer be full of anxiety, nor will I let trouble harass me. I will not dwell on the unpleasant things of life. O God! Thou art more friend to me than I am to myself. I dedicate myself to Thee, O Lord.**

I read and prayed until I finally fell asleep.

My drive to the psych unit the next morning seemed almost routine now. But as I watched Gloria happily talking to patients in the sitting room, something new happened. The psychiatrist on duty said he wanted to speak with Gloria and me in his office.

The doctor told us that Gloria's unusual episodes had caused him to take a deeper look at her medical records, and he had found that a couple days before each meltdown, Gloria had been administered a massive, experimental dose of steroids to treat her MS. He asked if we had been warned of any potential side effects of this treatment. We had not, which the doctor found alarming.

"I have no doubt, Gloria, that you have been the victim of steroid-induced psychosis," the doctor explained. "The steroid injections you've been given coincide with your psychotic episodes over the past three months. You need to stop these experimental treatments immediately."

Gloria cried at this news, and do did I. She wasn't irretrievably crazy after all. There was an external reason for her loony behavior. It was wonderful to get some good news for a change.

Unfortunately, that year was going to get even worse.

* * *

Tensions remained high as I tried to manage the company, which I had vowed never to do again, and simultaneously guide the creative processes and product development. Then, as the year was just getting underway, Gloria's mother died, unleashing a period of grief. Shortly after that, the One Stop gas station/convenience store that Gloria's sister and brother-in-law owned in Longville burned down. A few months later, her brother-in-law had a serious car accident in Canada while hunting and almost lost his leg.

On December 30, a major tragedy struck. Gloria and I were relaxing between Christmas and New Year when I received a call in the morning from an office holder in the Strom Building where Integrated Strategies occupied the entire main floor. The caller told me that he had gone to his third-floor office to pick something up and noticed that water was seeping into the hallway from our back door.

Assuming it was likely a backed-up toilet, I grabbed some rubber boots and a plunger and headed for the building, which was about ten minutes away. Before I entered from the rear, I saw more than a trickle of water emerging from the exterior door. I walked to a main floor exterior window and looked into one of our offices. Horrified, I saw it was flooded, which meant the entire floor was flooded. A switched-on computer that should have been standing on the floor was now floating in water at least eighteen inches deep, its lights still shining brightly in the dark room.

I called 911, which sent out a fire truck, then called Gloria, who was at my side shortly after the fire department arrived. The fire chief warned us not to enter the office because there was a real danger of electrocution. Two firemen opened the back door and a tsunami gushed out of our offices and flowed across the rear parking lot into a swamp, taking chairs and trash containers with it. We felt like our entire company—everything we had worked so hard to build—had just been washed away. The event had been caused by a burst water main under the concrete slab floor. The explosion had blown a sizable hole in the floor and filled our suite with water.

In 1995, there was no Internet cloud in which to store and back-up digital records, so all the company's documents were on paper now destroyed by the flood. The computers had suddenly become junk. The furniture was ruined. We were wiped out.

Our insurer sent an adjuster to the site, and he stayed a week. Initially, he told us that we were not covered for losses due to rising water, which would have required a special rider. We were crestfallen. But I thought this adjuster was a reasonable man, so I proposed another way of viewing the incident. It was not a matter of rising water, such as a traditional flood where rivers and creeks can rise up to destroy property. Our event, I argued, was really an accident—a water main had burst—and thus we should be covered under protections we had paid for.

The adjuster wrote his assessment using that argument, and amazingly, the insurance company agreed. Even so, the settlement covered only a portion of our tangible assets and none of the costs of lost project files and progress. At this point, we didn't even know which projects were in process!

Friends of the company and even some vendors came to our rescue, helping us locate temporary office space, rent furniture, and move into the new quarters. We were candid with our clients, and they stood by us as we restarted many of their projects from scratch, which meant some delays—and for us, additional expense, which was the last thing we needed.

*　*　*

It took a heroic effort by our staff to reestablish some business equilibrium. As we all worked overtime, rehab efforts were underway at the Strom Building, and about six months after the flood, we were able to move back in. This was a positive development, but another company move, which meant reorganizing all the equipment and workspaces, took its toll on staff members and Gloria.

Shortly after we settled into our rehabilitated offices, I noticed that Gloria, who had been off the high-dose steroid program for a few months, was again struggling with intense pain and depression. She was doing her best to help at work but spending most of her time at home.

One evening, after a terribly rough day buoying up drained and disheartened employees at the office, I arrived at home about nine o'clock and found Gloria in a red-faced rage, evidence of a full-blown flare-up. She stood up angrily, got in my face and said she knew I was having an affair with one of our female employees and that was why I was late. She made other terrible accusations.

Totally drained by the day's stresses, I lost my temper, hoisted a rolled-up newspaper from a coffee table and swatted her in the mouth with it. She lost her balance and fell backward onto a soft couch.

She glared at me and shouted, "That's spouse abuse. I'm calling the police."

Furious and out of control myself, I said, "Fine. Go ahead," and stormed into the kitchen to get away from her. I was already feeling guilty about my behavior, which was hardly mature. I had already calmed down by the time the police arrived several minutes later. Gloria, still raging, told them how I had swatted her, and she had fallen. What she said was true, so I agreed with her.

The police filed spousal abuse charges against me, and three weeks later I was in court facing a judge. Gloria had recovered from her flare-up and was feeling bad about reporting me. She hoped to drop the charges, but in cases of spouse abuse, the victim cannot drop charges because too often charges are dropped under threats by the abuser.

The judge said that the simple act of swatting my wife with a newspaper qualified as abuse and asked if the report of my behavior was correct. I said yes and received a sentence of six months parole with the caveat that if I had no more charges during my parole, my record would be expunged of the misdemeanor.

The event actually brought Gloria and I closer together. She started to realize how serious her mood swings had become, and I realized that I was indeed capable of performing an act of violence. Both insights were important.

My first meeting with my parole officer in North Minneapolis, a high crime area, was enlightening. In a suit and tie, I sat in the waiting room with a group of addicts, drug dealers and prostitutes. My parole officer was a Black man about six-three and two hundred fifty pounds. He reviewed my offense and shook his head, staring at me. "Not a terrible thing you did," he said. "But it was wrong."

I agreed.

"The irony is…" He paused for a moment, then continued. "I'm married to a woman with MS. Love her to death. But when she's in a flare-up, whoo-eee! She can really trigger me. So, I know what you were going through, but you can't let your anger take control like that. Here's what we're gonna do."

Normally, he said, I would be required to come into Minneapolis and visit him once a week to make sure everything was going well. But, in my case, he was willing to have a short phone call with me every two weeks. I was relieved—and grateful for his understanding. It turns out, I wasn't the only spouse of a person with MS going through hell. The disease affected entire families. I gained a new perspective that I hoped would make me a better and more supportive husband.

I really did hope for that.

New Ventures

For the next couple of years my life was still a blur. With Gloria seldom able to work, I allowed my focus to shift from Integrated Strategies to a shiny new opportunity that literally got phoned in. Phil, a friend of mine and Marc Kramer's, had co-founded an employee assistance program (EAP) several years previously, and this new model for providing workplace counseling on an as-needed basis was taking off. UnitedHealthCare (UHC), the largest health insurer in the nation, had acquired the business, and I had developed a series of marketing videos that launched the new entity now branded as Optum. Today, Optum is the largest and most profitable business in UHC's portfolio.

Phil called to say that Microsoft was preparing to launch a new Internet-based platform called Microsoft Network (MSN) that would provide a host of authoritative content and wanted UHC to anchor the healthcare section. Would I become the content developer and technical lead?

Integrated Strategies needed a contract like this, and while most people did not yet know what the Internet was, it clearly was exploding under the radar. I said yes, and Microsoft provided me with technical training in Seattle. We set the entire healthcare strategy up as a partnership between giant UHC and baby Integrated Strategies, so we would be involved long-term in this exciting new venture that had unlimited potential. With both Microsoft and UHC behind it, what could go wrong?

An Improbable Series of Risky Events

Well, we invested hugely in the deal, and were well on our way to launch, when Phil called to explain that Microsoft had just abandoned MSN because it had become clear that the open Internet was going to overwhelm closed platforms like MSN and AOL. I proposed that we continue the partnership on the open Web, and Phil stammered his way through the discouraging news that UHC was going to do just that but had decided it did not want a partner. The healthcare goliath wanted to own the whole thing.

I quickly pulled together a plan to develop a healthcare platform that would not only provide authoritative content but, for the first time on the Internet, provide collaborative chat rooms staffed by nurses to provide live consultations. I called this new platform Prime Health. But I needed a healthcare partner for nurses and content, so I called on HealthPartners, a Minnesota-based company that had developed the world's first Health Maintenance Organization (HMO).

As a spring-loaded entrepreneur, I started a new company called InSite Health to capitalize on becoming the first health information and services company on the Internet. Fortuitously, HealthPartners had just begun a new venture capital arm that was looking for projects to fund. They loved our idea and agreed to finance the development. With HealthPartners co-venturing with us, what could go wrong?

Just before we were to receive HealthPartner's final quarter-million-dollar investment, they called to say that all their venture capital projects had just been terminated. HealthPartners was no longer partnering on new concepts—no reason given. But I suspect the slumping financial performance of its main HMO business had a lot to do with it. Once more, we almost made it to the finish line before a blizzard of bad news hit.

* * *

The Rockwell mystery suddenly reemerged in 1995. Mom received a call from the curator at the Rockwell Museum in Stockbridge, Massachusetts, who said that a letter had been received from a man in Brazil claiming that he had the stolen paintings and wanting to know the legitimate owner. He was willing to sell back the artwork.

Bonnie had heard that before and was not interested, so she didn't follow up, assuming it was Minetti again. Several months later, Bonnie received a fax from a Florida attorney saying he knew someone who had information about the stolen paintings. She ignored that fax too, but the attorney persisted until one day Bonnie took a call from someone who said, "I have a friend who has been trying to contact you about the Rockwells, and you won't respond." Before Bonnie could hang up, the caller explained that he was a South American living in Washington, DC. His job was installing draperies at embassies around the world—an odd occupation for someone calling about stolen art.

The caller went on to say that he had a college friend named Luis Palma who lived in Florida and had information about the paintings. Bonnie called me and said, "I don't know—but this guy sounded different—more sincere. Still, I'm afraid of starting this search all over again when I thought it was done."

Like me, Bonnie is a drama junkie, so we finally decided to give this adventure one last go. Bonnie spoke with Luis on the phone, and he told her he represented the man who had purchased five of the Rockwells from a Brazilian immigration official. He said the owner was willing to sell them back, but the price would not be so exorbitant, and Luis would collect a small broker fee.

In later conversations, we learned the paintings had been brought into Brazil by a man who had arrived on an international flight at the Sao Paolo airport. A customs agent discovered the paintings. The traveler was not detained, but the paintings were personally confiscated by the agent. In essence, the paintings paid for the traveler's entry into Brazil, a country that does not extradite its citizens to other countries, so fugitives often seek entry and citizenship there.

A customs agent turned some of the paintings over to a corrupt federal policeman who unsuccessfully tried selling them through his underworld contacts. Finally, the policeman found a reputable art collector who was interested in five of the Rockwells. The other two paintings apparently were used as collateral for a loan. None of the

Rockwells were listed as stolen on the Art Registry, an international listing of stolen artworks.

After taking possession of the paintings, the art collector became worried that the paintings might be stolen but not registered as such. Under Brazilian law, the artwork, even if stolen, was protected against seizure by the country in which it was stolen, but the collector was concerned about his reputation. Later, the collector discovered that the Art Registry had not been formed until the year after the Rockwell Heist and works stolen before then, like the Rockwells, had not been appended to the list. Eventually, he asked Luis Palma to check further, and the Rockwell Museum told them the works had been stolen from Elayne Galleries. These conversations occurred over many months.

At last, Bonnie asked Luis for proof that the paintings were in his possession. She asked for one of the paintings to be sent to Minneapolis for authentication. "That won't happen," Luis replied. They agreed on photographs of the paintings with the obligatory dated newspaper. Soon, several photos arrived. In each one, a Rockwell painting was seen in front of a steep hill in a rainforest that looked like Brazil. Bonnie and Dad saw telltale stretcher marks on the largest painting and judged the work to be authentic. Surprisingly, next to that large painting stood a slender man holding that day's current Rio newspaper. We were told this was our middleman, Luis Palma.

"Is this the world's dumbest man?" Bonnie said to me. "He's in the picture next to a stolen painting. He must feel protected by the lack of extradition in Brazil."

"It seems like Luis has been truthful with us, though," I replied.

We decided to try something even bolder as a further test. Bonnie contacted Luis and invited him to Minnesota for a dinner party at her home. This would present an excellent opportunity to establish a deeper relationship, she told him. To our amazement, he accepted the offer.

The afternoon of the party, Luis Palma arrived at the MSP airport. Dad picked him up and brought him directly to Bonnie's house in Minneapolis where her husband and I were joined by my sister's friend, Dee Dee, a producer for KMSP-TV, and Dee Dee's husband, Jim, the corporate attorney for the station's owner, Hubbard Broadcasting. Bonnie and my former partner, Bill, had previously divorced. She had married a wonderful man named Kevin, who had been running the frame shop at the gallery for a few years.

Dad and Luis arrived, Dad introduced Luis to the other guests, and we quickly entered into pre-dinner small talk. I was nervous about how this intensely awkward event would transpire. After all, in Bonnie's home we were now entertaining the frontman for the person who possessed our stolen paintings. That alone would have made this dinner party memorable, but the strangest part was that the topic of the Rockwells never came up.

Luis proved to be a charming and sociable dinner guest. He showed us pictures of his girlfriend and his apartment in Miami. He told us how he had come to be in Florida, what kinds of jobs he'd had, what kind of car he drove. Oh—he showed us a picture of his car too. It all seemed, well… almost too natural. At the end of the evening, Dad drove Luis to his hotel and arranged to meet him at the gallery in the morning to discuss business details. And that was it.

About a week after the dinner party, Luis revealed the name of the art collector, José Carneiro, an art historian and gallery owner who lived in a town north of Rio de Janeiro. Because Luis had vouched for us, we were now allowed to communicate directly with Carneiro. In 1998, twenty years after the theft, we finally arranged our first face-to-face meeting in New York City with the gallery owner who possessed the missing Rockwells. I could hardly wait!

Bonnie insisted I accompany her on the trip to New York. We were to meet Carneiro at a particular bar in a certain hotel at a specific time on the day we arrived. The circumstances created the atmosphere of a mystery novel. As we entered the bar, a portly man with bushy eyebrows stood up from his table and waved, smiling. He must have recognized Bonnie from her photo on the Elayne Galleries website.

We sat down and ordered drinks. Immediately, Carneiro began talking about his long history in the art business which brought him to New York several times each year. He wanted to make sure we understood he was not a black-market dealer but an honest collector and gallery owner, so he stressed that he also owned an affordable private school in his Brazilian town to make up for the poor public education provided by the government.

He persistently repeated his claim that he had not known the Rockwells were stolen when he acquired them or that the policeman who sold the paintings was a corrupt official. He had traded a Rolls Royce, other valuable items and considerable cash for the paintings, so he had a large investment in the Rockwells. He wondered if we understood that in Brazil he legally owned and possessed these works, and US law had no jurisdiction over them.

We agreed that Brazilian law provided these protections. "But nevertheless," I said, "the paintings were stolen from our gallery, so there is a moral responsibility to return them, isn't there? What would an honest man do in this case?"

Carneiro stared down at his wine glass. Obviously, he did not like my polite challenge to his claim of honesty. Finally, he looked up and stared at me, saying, "We were *both* victimized, weren't we? I think both of us are owed restitution."

If Carneiro had purchased the paintings without knowing they were stolen, he had a point. But if the only parties in this discussion were each a victim, who would provide restitution? I could see he was leading us to an agreement in which we would buy back the paintings.

"If you are expecting some compensation from us," I said, "we would need to physically see all the paintings to be sure each one is genuine. I know you've already rejected the idea of sending a painting to us for authentication, but what if we came to Brazil? Would you show us all the paintings?"

He slammed his hand enthusiastically on the table, scaring Bonnie, then said, "Excellent idea! You will see that they are genuine. And then we can do a deal."

After the meeting, Bonnie and I debriefed. I explained that we needed more contact with Carneiro to establish trust. She had an idea that expanded the usefulness of the Brazilian trip.

"If we're going all the way down to Brazil," Bonnie said, "we should bring a TV news crew to document the end of the Rockwell mystery." That idea came from my wonderful sister—always thinking. If we were to reclaim the paintings, onsite news coverage would increase the reputation of the paintings and consequently raise their value.

Back in Minneapolis, Bonnie contacted Rick Kupchella, a news anchor for KARE 11. She knew that Rick was a Rockwell fan and had avidly followed the mystery of the Rockwell heist. Rick decided to cover this amazing development himself. So, a few weeks later, Bonnie and Kevin joined Rick, a cameraman and me on the long flight to Rio de Janeiro. Carneiro had approved bringing along a TV crew and had even agreed to an on-camera interview, perhaps seeing it as positive publicity for an honest businessman doing the right thing.

Our fivesome stayed overnight at a Rio beach hotel. Late the next morning, two SUVs pulled up at the hotel, one containing Carneiro. We caravanned to Teresópolis, about an hour north of the Rio city limits, stopping once for lunch at a Brazilian barbecue that was truly a carnivore's paradise. In the city, we pulled up at a large commercial building containing four floors of condos with retail shops on the street level. Carneiro had our luggage and video equipment sent up to the fourth level where he occupied the entire floor and then he led us excitedly to his gallery on the main floor.

Carneiro was proud of the gallery and told us about all the wonderful works on the walls. Then he described his gallery in Lisbon, where he was born, and how he traveled to Portugal several times per year. He never explained what had brought him to Brazil, and we didn't ask.

When we eventually arrived at his condo, he introduced us to his wife and the caterer he had hired to make us a delicious Brazilian dinner. His condo contained as much hanging art as the downstairs gallery, and on an extended tour of his space we heard the story of each piece. It was strange, after twenty years of chasing the stolen Rockwells, to be in the home of the man who possessed five of them, including the two paintings owned by Elayne Galleries. But the Rockwells, we discovered, were not in this condo. They were in Carneiro's villa in the rainforest north of Teresópolis. We would be going there in the morning.

After dinner, we had more polite conversation and Rick, the news anchor, tried to extract some information about the Rockwells, but Carneiro continued to say things like, "That's for tomorrow. You will see all the paintings tomorrow. Tonight is for friendship."

We were all exhausted after flying to Rio and driving to Teresópolis. Bonnie finally suggested it was time for everyone to get a good night's sleep. As our team members headed for their bedrooms, Carneiro reached for my arm and said, "Let's talk for a few minutes, OK?"

I agreed.

He poured me another drink, and one for himself. He seemed oddly diffident in contrast to the confidence he had radiated throughout the evening.

"Is something troubling you?" I asked.

He sighed deeply and said, "I have decided not to do the interview with your TV people."

I was staggered. How could I tell Rick that he and the cameraman had come all the way to Brazil for an interview that was not going to happen? They could still get some B-roll background footage, but the Carneiro interview was expected to be the centerpiece of their story.

I saw something new in Carneiro, something I had not seen before. I saw a man who felt my disappointment in his decision—a man with some empathy, despite his inflated ego and professional bluster. I also saw a man I believed wanted to do the interview but was afraid of something, so I pressed him further.

After much more conversation, I learned that Carneiro was afraid of how his connection to stolen paintings would affect his reputation in the art world and even in his ownership of the local school, of which he was so proud. I pointed out that the news story would only be seen in the Minnesota region, so it was unlikely that anyone beyond that viewing area, especially outside the country, would ever see the interview.

We went back and forth on the issue. I nursed my drink so slowly I didn't get drunk, but Carneiro poured himself several. Probably, I just wore him down, but at four in the morning he agreed to do the interview.

The next morning, SUVs transported all of us except Carneiro to a destination in the hilly rainforest about forty-five minutes north. Finally, we drove through an ornate gate into an exotic compound smaller than the Hacienda la Noria in Mexico but just as fabulous. Peacocks strutted the grounds, exotic jungle birds excitedly called to us, and the native flora had been meticulously landscaped. Carneiro's villa sat on the grounds, but we had been instructed not to enter it until Carneiro arrived.

As a past filmmaker, I assisted Rick and the cameraman as they captured B-roll footage showing the grounds, the villa exterior, the roaming creatures, and a few "stand-ups" of Rick providing narration for the show itself but also for several promos that would advertise it.

Carneiro was late. I worried that he had backed out of the interview and didn't have the courage to tell me. But at last, he arrived. With the cameras rolling, he unlocked the villa's front door and guided us into the main foyer, which opened into the front room. As we entered that larger space, Bonnie and I caught our first glimpse of five Rockwells we had not seen in person for over twenty years. We had finally found the stolen Rockwells in the rainforest of Brazil!

Bonnie immediately recognized distinctive marks on the backsides of the paintings and stretcher creases the Elayne Galleries staff had noted before the theft. She and I embraced and cried a little. The adventure of finding the paintings was over, but another adventure—getting them back and dealing with the insurers, was going to be a new adventure. We could not legally bring the paintings back to the US because they were listed as stolen, and we would be arrested if caught. The FBI was uncooperative. Carneiro, in the end, put his trust in us to auction the paintings and split the proceeds after repayment of amounts reimbursed by the insurers. It took another two years to sort everything out, but we did it.

I only wish Mom had lived long enough to see the return of the Rockwells. KARE 11 broadcast a two-part series about us solving the mystery of the biggest art heist in Minnesota history. And the full story, including the identities of the thieves who broke into the gallery in 1978, was exposed in Bruce Rubenstein's book, *The Rockwell Heist*.

Surprisingly, one of the thieves who stole the paintings was Kent Anderson, the brother of beloved comedian Louie Anderson. When Rubenstein's investigation uncovered this fact, I was shocked, because Louie and I had once co-written a comedy screenplay that never got off the ground. Many people have said Kent was funnier than Louie, but there was nothing funny about what he and his cronies put my family through for twenty years.

* * *

In the midst of all this activity, I was asked to step into an exciting TV special that a producer friend of mine, Perry Schwartz, was attempting to get off the ground. The project had a sponsor, Starkey Laboratories, the world's largest maker of hearing aids. The musical nature of it immediately attracted me.

A Musical Christmas Card
To The World From

Featuring
TONY SANDLER &
CRYSTAL GAYLE

Perry was set to direct the special, and he wanted me to help audition Georgian talent to be featured in the show. Tony Sandler, a popular singer, was signed to co-star with country music star Crystal Gayle. To be honest, I had to research Georgia and found it situated on the eastern coast of the Black Sea between Ukraine to the north and Armenia to the south. Georgia had recently parted with the Soviet Union and was still going through separation anxiety.

Perry, Tony and I, along with a small entourage, flew to Moscow, where we caught an Aeroflot plane to Tbilisi, the capital of Georgia. During our two-week stay, folk and classical music artists and dancers came to Tbilisi to audition for a part in our Christmas special. Tony Sandler, who had performed with symphony orchestras around the world, was astonished at the artistry of these Georgian performers, and the local people were friendly and supportive, though political tensions were still high.

This boys' choral group from the Caucasus region of Georgia gave a stunning performance at their audition.

Of all the excellent auditions, my favorite was performed not in Tbilisi but in the small town of Gori, the hometown of Stalin, a harrowing hour's trip from the capital as driven by one of our guides at breakneck speed over rutted and congested roads. Still standing in the town square, a statue of Stalin remained fixed in place, the only one that had not been pulled down in all the previous Soviet bloc countries.

We entered a small theater building and were ushered into hard seats as a women's choral group in cheap, fake-satin robes took their places in front of us to perform their a cappella repertoire. Our hopes were not high for a world class performance in this third-rate hall, which resembled an American high school auditorium from the 1950s.

The choir director told us that the first and last pieces were the first public performances of music written by a local Georgian composer. And then he struck a note on a piano so the singers could get their pitch, and the women began to sing. Tony Sandler had brought with him a high-quality, handheld cassette recorder or we would not have preserved one of the most remarkable performances I had ever heard.

The Georgian harmonies were different than what I was expecting, and the method of singing was from deep within each singer's body without tremolo. The effect was stirring, deeply emotional and overpowering even as the director coaxed the choir into near silence. The first number had me by the throat, and tears streamed down my cheeks. *So, this is what a spiritual experience feels like*, I thought. I glanced at Tony Sandler, the world weary and sometimes cynical performer, and his eyes were moist as well.

The fourth song was an unexpected, avant-garde piece in which the women wordlessly created sounds and harmonies that at times sounded like a jet aircraft taking off, only to transform into the sweetness of high angelic voices that suddenly dropped into impossibly low tones and rhythmic chanting. This tone poem seemed impossible for womens' voices to produce without electronic augmentation, but there they were, fourteen women of various ages with no instrumentation or sound support taking Tony and me on a stirring ride into unseen and unheard worlds. After the performance, both Tony and I were breathless. I could hardly wait to figure out how to weave some of this unworldly magic into our Christmas special, which was my job.

As with so many adventures and wonderful projects, this one too crashed. Political updrafts first caused our sponsor to drop out and then discouraged other sponsors from signing up. It had simply become too risky to produce a complex musical special in Georgia.

* * *

After the collapse of Prime Health and despite our success on the Rockwell adventure, I was feeling disappointed and depressed by all the hard work at Integrated Strategies with so few tangible results. Gloria and I decided to sell the company—a hard decision. We found a willing buyer, a sales incentive firm that wanted to supplement its incentive offerings with sales skills training—a logical service extension. But they would only buy the company if some Lindbergs stayed on board to run it. So, Gloria and I "sold" our children, Jennifer and Brant, as company assets to satisfy their demands. In truth, Jen and Brant were happy to finally have adequate financing and a sales force to grow the business.

I split off. My adult learning insights from the army had grown into a successful adult learning model I now called HyperLearning. I thought this model could become a stand-alone business. The HyperLearning concept excited many people, including some fundraisers, and led me to another partner, Alan, who had been an executive with a national firm that provided testing services, the tail end of training. The concept was to provide adult learning courses using the HyperLearning model delivered on the new platform called the Internet. Never mind that no one had ever done this before and that most businesses still did not know what the Internet was.

Unfortunately, we had no technical platform to create the Internet-based courses. All we had was an amazing and proven methodology. As if by fate, an amazing opportunity with Hewlett-Packard (HP) to advance this business presented itself to us. When we presented the HyperLearning model to HP, they went crazy over it, agreeing to fund the entire cost of developing a course-building platform plus four comprehensive courses for HP's hardcopy (printer) business. We were allowed to own the platform, and HP owned the courses, which were highly successful when delivered. My son, Scott, joined the company as lead course developer and doubled as our quality assurance department.

Using our new, proprietary platform, we started calling on large companies with training needs, which was all of them. But we found that most training departments didn't know what the Internet was, and even if they did, they didn't have computers. We also learned that existing trainers believed Internet-delivered training would make their in-person training skills obsolete so they were mostly obstacles instead of allies.

Still, we found some believers. IBM used our methodology for training sales staff in Latin America. An aircraft company signed a contract along with a few others. It was clear, though, that sales training was the big market because training costs could be justified by increased sales revenue from sales-ready staff.

I came up with the idea of licensing sales training content from the leading, name-brand gurus—Brian Tracy, Tony Allesandro, Jim Cathcart and others. We signed deals to use their content and convert it into HyperLearning courses. I began teaching the HyperLearning methodology to roomfuls of trainers who had doctorates in instructional design.

What we learned once again from all our efforts was that a company can be too early in its offering. It turns out that Internet acceptance by business and industry was slower to develop than we had anticipated. We were easily three to four years ahead of the product acceptance curve.

In the years that followed, many other training companies would pirate our methodology, which could not be patented. Their timing was much better than ours. I remembered that Gary Hudson and I were at least forty years ahead of the curve in private space commercialization. Patience was never one of my virtues.

Despondent again, not by failure but by the inability to push forward a wonderful concept, I joined my daughter, Jennifer, in another startup called Threewire, which intended to provide Internet-based marketing services to medical companies. We came up with the idea to build websites that would attract patients with specific medical conditions like prostate cancer or erectile dysfunction so we could present sponsored solutions. The Google search engine was still in its infancy, and people were now using it to find relevant content. The problem, of course, was the difficulty of getting any webpage to rank high enough in search engine results to produce a significant number of prospects.

After a few weeks of study and testing, I invented a patentable method of search engine optimization—a particular set of tactics for content and technical creation of web pages—that would predictably produce high rankings for meaningful search terms. Jennifer and I also patented our new web-based marketing strategy, which we called Slipstream Marketing. Though patented, it was essentially unprotectable, so it is now ubiquitous on the Internet because it worked so well.

At this point, I could not have been further from my original goal of making Hollywood movies, but I was having fun and doing things no one else had ever done.

After an ethical issue caused by the founder, Jen and I left Threewire. In 2004 I agreed to create and manage a digital agency for a friend. The new agency was affiliated with a well-known video post-production and special effects firm. During several years there, our staff took my adult learning concepts even further. We started developing high-end, immersive business simulations in which managers and executives would be challenged to run a business or solve business problems or test new business concepts in an environment that resembled the real world and provided realistic consequences for mistakes. I had finally pushed my adult learning theories to the max.

Near the end of my tenure, my good friend, the multi-talented Annemarie, asked me to co-produce a demo for a new TV series that actor Levar Burton hoped PBS would fund. Levar had begun his long career as the young Kinta Kinte in the popular ABC mini-series *Roots* based on author Alex Haley's family history. Levar went on to play Geordi La Forge, a human Starfleet officer, in all seven seasons of the series *Star Trek: The Next Generation* and its four feature films. After this, Levar was the beloved host and executive producer of *Reading Rainbow*, the most-watched PBS program in the classroom. The show ran for twenty years. We hoped that Levar's longstanding PBS experience would help our chances of getting our proposed series greenlighted.

Film and television star Levar Burton.

We called our series *The Science of Peace*, and the primary focus was to depict the many ways that science can promote the advancement of peace for our planet. As interviewer/host, Levar would probe various areas of science with innovative scientists to discover how science can be used for more than inventing horrifying weapons of war. We chose two provocative topics to demonstrate our treatment of the subject. The first was based on investigative work by a scientist who was studying a Dutch family in which every member had committed a serious, violent crime. The scientist had been searching for a missing or broken gene in the family that could explain the violent behavior, which could lead to gene therapies to resolve the violent tendencies. The second story presented conclusions by

Dr. Bruce Lipton whose epigenetics research had taught him that human cells have intelligence located not in their nuclei but in their membranes. These trillions of sentient entities live in cooperative communities, working together in response to the signals they get from their environment, including beliefs about that environment. In other words, Lipton established that cells are a microcosm of the human world from which we can learn a great deal about peaceful coexistence.

I thought our finished demo was riveting and provocative. Unfortunately, though PBS loved the demo and the show concept, it wanted to own all ancillary rights and we wanted to exploit the web-based and educational markets independently. We were not able to reach a business compromise.

I was now past normal retirement age, but my brain was on fire with more ideas. I still craved having mysteries to solve, stories to tell, concepts to test. But I was tired out. So, I retired from the agency, abandoned the stressful film business and decided to complete the last thing on my official bucket list—the great American novel.

Books

I had written two books previously. Neither was a novel, but I learned that writing a book takes a lot of work. My first book was a Bantam paperback called *Betty Crocker's More for Your Money*. Betty got the credit, but I was the hired ghostwriter. The book was a compilation of tips about how and when to intelligently buy everything from appliances and food to insurance and houses. Yes, for a few moments, I was Betty Crocker— at that time, with a beard.

I co-wrote my second book with my mother. Titled *The Power of Positive Handwriting*, the book was an instruction manual for how to change strokes in one's handwriting that would affect one's personality traits. It was a family project. Mom provided the know-how as a Certified Graphoanalyst, Dad generated the handwriting samples that illustrated the text, and I wrote the words. The book turned the tables on the typical use of handwriting analysis to reveal existing traits. Mom's theory was tested, though controversial, proving that no Lindberg was ever afraid of controversy.

Now it was time, however, to write a novel, a new adventure that would take me two years. I decided to craft a historical novel based on the true story of the birth of a new world religion, a story that few people knew. At the end of my first draft, I had a nineteenth-century saga that took place in Persia, Regency England and New York. Yes, it was a bit long—actually *quite* long at 336,000 words (the typical novel is 80,000 or fewer words)—but was riveting, in my opinion.

Dad was my official reader. For years, I had read his poetry and commented on it. Now he was reciprocating by critiquing my literary work. As I finished sections, I emailed them to Dad and eagerly awaited his approval the way a young son looks for approval on new endeavors from his father. I cherished each response. Sometimes he just gave approval and encouragement to keep going, but other times he offered meaningful, third-party advice. This collaboration reminded me of how we had bonded earlier in a way that he found comfortable by playing guitars together, and how much I appreciated his guidance then. Writing is a solitary business, and Dad was my companion through the loneliness of words.

Because of his health issues, Dad was living with Bonnie and Kevin. He had always told us that he wanted to die alone, not with family sitting around and watching. One day, my sister took him to a doctor's appointment and then left for errands. While she was gone, during a conversation with the doctor, Dad simply went to sleep and never woke up—just the way he would have wanted. The loss of my father haunted me for a long time because we could have been so much closer. I had missed that opportunity. That's why our time chatting about my book was so important to me.

At last, I finished the manuscript and sent it out to publishers as first-time authors are told to do. I waited for a publishing deal to be offered, but none came. In fact, only three out of scores of publishers even acknowledged receipt of my doorstopper of a manuscript, which could not be missed because of its size. One of those three responses courteously said the reader had enjoyed the first few pages, but that there were far too many pages after those. In other words, the manuscript was *way* too long.

Considering myself a fast learner, I cut the manuscript in half by eliminating many characters and entire sub-plots, which is harder than you might think. Then I went to a workshop for new authors, and the publishing expert advised me that long books by unknown authors—mine was still twice as long as a typical manuscript—are particularly difficult to get published. Maybe, he suggested, I should write something shorter and in a more commercial genre.

I backed up my epic novel and set out to write a thriller. I had grown up on genre fiction, so I thought this would be fun. My first effort, an action-adventure thriller, was still long but shorter than *The Da Vinci Code*, a highly successful book in the same genre. This time, my daughter suggested I self-publish the book instead of enduring two years to find a publisher and then wait for the book to finally emerge into the marketplace.

Since I had all the requisite skills to edit, design the cover and interior, produce the printer files, make a Kindle version and then market the book—well, why not just do it myself? I created an imprint name, Calumet Editions, named after a small Minnesota town Gloria and I were driving through while brainstorming names. The purpose of an imprint was to make my book appear less "self-published" on Amazon. I published *The Shekinah Legacy* in December 2011, then figured out how to leverage a clever marketing technique to obtain visibility on Amazon and waited to see what would happen.

If my book was as good as thrillers by the famous, bestselling authors, then getting high visibility on Amazon should sell as many of my books as the big guys. Right? By the end of January 2012, *The Shekinah Legacy* was the #1 bestselling thriller of any type on Amazon, which suddenly ranked me as #4 on its "Movers and Shakers" list of authors with the fastest growth in sales.

Other self-published authors noticed my success and asked if I would help them publish and market their books. Since I was now retired, I took on several other authors under the Calumet imprint. But mostly, I was urged by readers to write another book in the series.

Series?

I had never imagined *Shekinah* as the first book of a series, but there was another unwritten part of the saga that I could develop, so I started on a sequel. In the meantime, reader reviews for Shekinah on Amazon were pouring in, and despite excellent sales not all reviews were flattering. Just as the movie reviews for *TWTTIN* ranged from 1 to 4 stars, *Shekinah* was getting more 1-star reviews than I had expected. The average review ranking was still 4+ stars, but every bad review stung!

Gary Lindberg

I noticed a disturbing trend among my reviewers. Many of the bad reviews were posted by evangelical Christians who were offended that I dared write about a search for the bones of Jesus. They believed Jesus had ascended bodily into heaven, so no bones could ever be found. These reviewers seem to have missed that I never claimed the bones existed, only that certain forces were searching for the bones to prove that Jesus had not ascended bodily. The reviewers also seemed to miss that the book was fiction, not fact. Everything in it was made up. Finally, when checking other reviews posted by my haters, I discovered that the preponderance of these reviewers only posted negative reviews, seldom positive ones for *any* book.

Instead of feeling wounded, I decided to find entertainment value in these reviews because they exposed the small minds that had conceived them. I wrote a blog called "My Favorite Bad Reviews," which went viral. Naturally, this helped sell more books to people who wanted to see what the controversy was all about. Many reviewers who loved the book publicly pummeled the bad reviewers with comments. Here are excerpts from that blog post.

> Like most authors, I always wanted to be seen as a good writer. Before long, however, I got my comeuppance in this review:
>
> > This book feels like it has been written by a 13 yer (sic) old. The writing is simpistic (sic)...
>
> At least I'm good at spelling. Another writer summed up my deficiencies in just three words, a master stroke of economy:
>
> > Too many words.
>
> The statement reminded me of my favorite scene in the movie *Amadeus* in which the king feels compelled to come up with a criticism of Mozart's most recent work and settles on "too many notes."

Fortunately, most of my readers seemed to agree with the reviewer who wrote:

> **The author describes everything in perfect detail so that the reader feels like they are right there.**

This is what thriller writing should do, I think. As for the plot of my story, which I spent countless hours researching and developing, one early reviewer broke my heart by complaining:

> **Too much development and not enough story for me.**

What? Not enough plot? But at least I kept the story moving, right? Apparently not for the reviewer who wrote:

> **It started out very slow and just got worse from there.**

This kind of stuff can make an author tear his hair out. A thriller has utterly failed if it doesn't have ample action and a fast-moving pace. My ego was salved, however, by a rush of other reviewers who wrote things like:

> **There is great action in this story. Mesmerizing! Action Packed! Terrific detailed storyline!**

I had taken pride in creating three-dimensional, interesting characters, until I learned that I had failed:

> **No character development to speak of.**

I wondered if that reviewer had read the same book as the one described in this review:

> An exceptionally creative story with well-defined characters and story line.

What stunned me even more, though, are those reviewers who felt threatened by the beliefs of my made-up characters in this work of fiction. It turns out that within my thriller, according to some reviewers, was hidden a treatise that attempted to debunk the central principles of Christianity. Who knew? Not me. I thought it was just an entertainment about misguided people with conflicting points of view about religion. Sort of like real life. My favorite review of this kind was:

> There is great action in this story, but it is filled with twisted religion and history. I kept thinking that some readers would take this garbage as truth. This could have been a great book if the author's personal agenda hadn't blocked the way.

I still don't know what my agenda was. Something nefarious, apparently. One reviewer went even further, using my story as a pulpit for her own beliefs:

> I believe in the resurrection, our righteousness before God comes through Christ's work on the cross.

To be honest, I was not in agreement with the beliefs of ANY of the characters in this story. They are assassins, defrocked priests, CIA and Mossad agents and terrorists. But I never felt the need to publicly state my disagreement with this unsavory group of people. At last, though, another reviewer expressed his dismay with this string of one- and two-star reviews by stating:

> Will all you fundamentalists give it a rest? This is not a history book and neither is your blood-soaked Bible.

So now my reviewers were arguing among themselves. All I had to do was sit back and enjoy the food fight.

My all-time favorite review is too long to print here. Naturally, it was absolutely glowing and full of praise—except for one thing. The reviewer gave my book a 1-Star review (worst possible rating). Go figure.

Today, I have written numerous books and received many more reviews. I have learned that an author can't please everyone and that all readers have personal opinions, relevant or not. I've also learned that the only sure way to know if a book is satisfying to you is to buy it and read it, because the book your neighbor hated, you may love.

My *Shekinah* sequel, *Sons of Zadok*, became the #1 bestselling technothriller on Amazon. For my third book, I novelized my old screenplay, *SoulTracker*—the movie I wanted to make in Mexico with Francisco Galvez—and retitled it *Deeper and Deeper*. It became the #1 paranormal thriller on Amazon. Finally, I refined my first attempt at writing fiction, my historical novel, which I retitled *Ollie's Cloud*. It quickly became the #1 bestselling British historical novel on Amazon.

At about this time, I was receiving many more requests from authors who wanted my assistance to edit, design and market their books. I was in peril of running yet another business, but I was loving every minute of being an author and a publisher. One of my authors had been taught by a talented author coach named Ian Graham Leask and suggested I meet him as we seemed to share the same philosophy about the publishing business.

Within several months, Ian became my partner in Calumet Editions, and to this day remains the best partner an eccentric old guy like me could possibly have. For a couple of years, we successfully worked to build up the business, and then, one day, I happened to tell him about my adventure with the Elvis letters and the frustrations of encountering only timidity among publishers.

I was astonished when Ian replied, "Why don't *we* publish that Elvis book?"

I reminded him of the risks identified by other publishers and numerous attorneys, but Ian was insistent that we could find a path to publishing this book of Elvis secrets. But I would have to write the book first, he reminded me. So, I began.

* * *

Then, life intervened again. My oldest son, Brendan, became very ill and was diagnosed in May 2015 with Stage 4 esophageal cancer. During a meeting with Brendan, Scott, Karen, Gloria and me, his oncologist told us she did not expect him to live much past Christmas eight months later. We were all devastated by this news, of course, but my devastation was deepened by personal remorse and guilt. I had squandered decades of opportunities to establish a closer relationship with my son, failing to close the unnecessary gaps between us. This failure was just like the one between Dad and me. Somehow, we Lindberg men had been miswired for making connections even though we longed for closeness.

During the next eight months, I decided to shatter the old patterns and get to know my son. I drove him to most of his chemo appointments and on the way home we stopped for walks around the lakes or through the Rose Gardens near his apartment. We talked a lot and swapped unshared stories from our lives. The more we talked, the more we felt comfortable expressing our feelings, regrets, even our love for each other. It was cathartic for me, and I hope for Brendan.

In November, the primary tumor had not shrunk as expected so they started high doses of radiation, which was difficult for Brendan to tolerate, but he never complained. His last dose was on Christmas Eve, and we all celebrated at Bonnie's home. Brendan was gracious but clearly wiped out. He said he was needing to rest for a few days to get some strength back.

The next time I heard from him was after a Vikings TV game on January 10. He called and said, "Dad, I'm not feeling so good."

He sounded worried, which was not like him.

"Do you want me to come and pick you up so we can go to the ER?" I asked.

"I think so," he said.

I packed up Gloria, who was a retired ICU nurse, and we drove the half-hour to Brendan's apartment. We walked up the three flights of stairs, and I knocked on the door. No one answered, and my heart started beating hard. I knocked again, and when the door did not open, I tried the handle. In expectation of our arrival, Brendan fortunately had unlocked the door.

Gloria and I entered and look down the hallway to his bedroom. He was lying on the floor in his underwear. He'd had a coughing fit and the esophagus, weakened by the radiation therapy, had ruptured and he had bled out on the carpet.

I called Karen and Scott, his brother, and they arrived after the first responders and medical examiner. As they were preparing to remove Brendan's body to the morgue, Gloria performed a remarkable act of mercy. Knowing that Brendan's mother and brother had not seen Brendan for the last time, and that the sight of his body was very disturbing, she asked the medical examiner to wait for a few more minutes. Gloria, who was Brendan's stepmom, somehow went into nurse mode and cleaned up Brendan's bloodied face, put a pillow under his head to cover the blood stain and make him look asleep, and covered him with a blanket. Then she invited Karen and Scott into the bedroom. I had never loved my wife as much as I did at that moment.

The grief was unbearable. I cried for a week. The geology of love can sift the heart's strata from granite to tears. At the funeral service, I was astonished to see a huge number of his friends whom I had never met. Our family was stunned at the wide circle of influence he'd had on so many people. They turned out for him and told stories about how he had helped them and affected their lives in so many wonderful ways. There was much that I didn't know about my son, that I had missed out on. But I was catching up now.

Five months later, I found myself in the hospital preparing for open heart double-bypass surgery. Gloria said I had a broken heart, and I don't doubt that.

The surgery was supposed to be a routine, three-hour procedure, and I was expecting a year-long recovery. About five hours into the surgery, Gloria knew that something must be wrong. It was taking too long. At last, a surgical nurse came out and told friends and family that there had been complications, and they would keep everyone informed.

Later, we would learn that I had died twice on the operating table, and each time, obviously, they had brought me back. But they were concerned that I may have lost oxygen to my brain for a time, which could result in brain damage.

As I awoke in recovery, protocol required the nurses to ask if I knew my name, my wife's name, my address, and other personal information. Frighteningly, I had no memories at all. For two days, I could not remember my wife's name or my telephone number. Then, slowly, I started getting back some of the numbers. On the third day, when my surgeon paid a visit, he asked hopefully whether I remembered my wife's name.

"Yes!" I said, overjoyed at the return of my memory. "It's Fletcher!" This was the name of our dog. At least I remembered *his* name. Over time, my memory grudgingly returned, but the recovery process was grueling. I had been filleted during surgery, my chest propped open for almost eight hours and all my muscles stretched to the limit. Recovery was slow and painful for the next year, but my business partner, Ian, was understanding and supportive.

Aware of how close I had come to all my memories evaporating without a trace—"All those moments… lost in time like tears in the rain"—I vowed to recollect my experiences and present them as a gift to my son so he would know his father's life better than I knew my father's. It would take me eight years to fulfill that vow, and during that time there would be still more stories to add.

Elvis

I used my recovery time to work on the Elvis project, a sure cure for boredom. Gloria assisted me every day with walks and other medical assistance, essentially operating as my personal nurse, something for which I never properly expressed my appreciation.

When I had a complete draft of the Elvis manuscript, Ian did an extensive edit, making it better. We hired an expensive but experienced literary attorney in Beverly Hills, Jonathan Kirsch, to approve every word, hoping to avoid any legitimate legal violations should we be sued as expected. Kirsch also helped us find an insurer who agreed to provide two million dollars of liability coverage for the book, protection I had thought would be impossible to secure.

All this time, my wife was distressed over my obsession to publish a book she considered a legal nightmare. For her, I'm sure, my insistence on releasing this dangerous book was more than she could bear. I had previously burdened her with my monstrous Russell-Manning debts, then my serious medical issues, and now I was setting us up for surefire lawsuits. I didn't know then, but she had already given up on our marriage and secretly sought solace from another man, a former classmate who lived in northern Minnesota.

Over a hundred people turned out for our book release gathering at the Barnes & Noble in Edina, Minnesota. I couldn't understand why Gloria resisted attending her husband's breakthrough book event, but eventually she relented and sat solemnly through the event. It would be the last of my book signings that she would ever attend.

The available copies of *Letters from Elvis* sold out quickly. Thirty years after I had first read the letters in Bill Mack's studio, my book about them was finally published, and I was immensely grateful to my partner for his courage and relentless pushing for completion of the project. I thought that my Elvis saga had finally reached its conclusion, but I was wrong. The release of this sensational book provoked three unexpected events that would shift my life again.

* * *

The first consequence of the release of *Letters from Elvis* was a torrent of hate, libel and abuse directed at me. Certain avid Elvis fans who were deeply invested in the traditional legend of Elvis Presley—the hardcore Elvis fundamentalists—were deeply distressed by my revelations, particularly the details about Elvis being kidnapped, tortured and gang raped. Some believed I had no right to violate their idol's privacy, though his right to privacy died with him in 1977. Others simply found these details implausible and accused me of forging all the letters and making up false stories. Some couldn't believe the claim made by Elvis that Vernon Presley was not his biological father, which suggested that his mother, Gladys—worshipped almost as a Madonna figure by fans—had been unfaithful. I started getting written death threats, some with photos of my townhome with my wife and dog in the front yard.

A discussion group on the internet called the Elvis Collectors Forum organized a series of hateful reviews on Amazon to discourage sales of the book. Despite my exhaustive research, fact-checking and authentication of sources, I was labeled a heretic and a charlatan online. The Forum, comprised of collectors of Elvis music and memorabilia, had a more pragmatic reason to dislike my book—the fear that my book's revelations might tarnish Elvis's reputation and diminish the value of members' collectibles. In fact, this book provided a much more sympathetic picture of Elvis than the traditional legend did.

I received many irrational criticisms and attempts to discredit me by members of this group.

> They lost me at the assertion of rape: that alone renders this project an absurdity.

This same statement in different words has been expressed countless times by those who previously disavowed the claims of rape by clergy in numerous Christian churches around the world. The charge of Elvis being raped—made by both Elvis and Marlon Brando in handwritten letters—was not absurd, but catastrophic.

> It's a known fact that Elvis hardly wrote anything. His signature was copied by others and on a stamp.

Only an ardent Elvis fundamentalist believes this. Numerous authenticated letters (some with long text), cards and other correspondence have been authenticated and auctioned. He had no difficulty writing fluidly and did so often, including a famous, long letter to President Nixon.

> ...none of the dates or facts add up. He was fully surrounded virtually every minute of every day of his life yet this seems like a life in some weird other plane... I think the author is disgusting and to blame.

Actually, ALL but two facts in the abundance of letters I was given "add up." I scrupulously researched all dates, places, people in attendance at events, concerts, and everything else that was checkable and found that everything but the two exceptions lined up with other historical sources. And the exceptions I noted could have easily been mistakes of memory. Regarding Elvis being surrounded every minute by his handlers, that certainly is absurd and impossible ("every minute of every day," really?) though an oft-repeated bit of fantasy, as we now know.

> Elvis's cousins and friends have made statements that contradict "facts" in this book.

It's interesting that people are so willing to take at face value what Elvis bodyguards and Priscilla and even biographers have written about Elvis without a single word of corroboration on many of these matters by Elvis himself! It's as if hearsay were the truth. Until now, granted, it is the nearest thing we've had to "truth," but with the discovery of all these authenticated letters, we have Elvis's own first-hand testimony. Amazingly, those who loved him best and studied the hearsay most are the fiercest critics of his own handwritten words. That is a fascinating but very sad phenomenon.

The easiest thing for "fans" to do upon the release of my book was to shoot the messenger, but since the messenger in this case was Elvis himself, it was time, I suppose, to shoot the mail carrier, which was me. Well, I'd been shot at before.

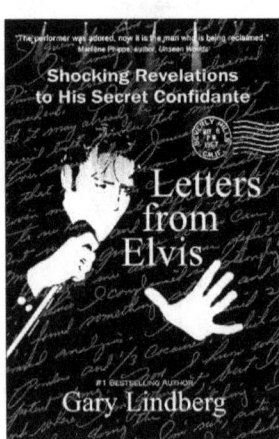  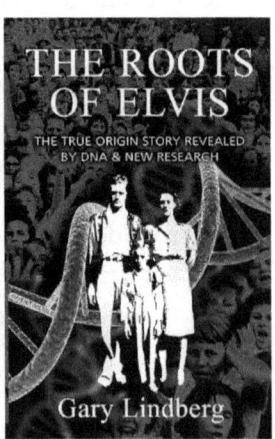

My three Elvis books, which I refer to as *The Unknown Elvis* series.

* * *

The second event that followed the release of *Letters from Elvis* was a phone call from Salt Lake City, Utah. A man named Brad said that he had read my book about the letters and believed he had some additional letters from the same writers—Elvis, Belafonte, Brando and Tom Jones. I was highly skeptical and thought maybe he had somehow found photocopies of some of the originals in our cache. I had ordered transcriptions of all our letters, and they were on the computer for ease in searching for specific text, so I asked Brad to read aloud parts of his letters.

Brad indeed had letters that were missing from my set, about a half-dozen from each of the writers. I immediately flew to Salt Lake City and spent the weekend with Brad and his wife. Brad also had private papers, correspondence and banking records from Carmen Montez, the secret confidante to whom all four celebrities had written. The complex story about how Brad came into possession of this material originated with his first girlfriend's parents, who owned the apartment building where Carmen Montez and her Russian-Cuban husband, George Ramentol, had lived.

I bought the publishing rights to all the materials in a briefcase that had been abandoned in the apartment building after the death of Carmen and George. The Elvis letters were especially illuminating. They revealed yet another kidnapping of Elvis with a startling conclusion. I was already working on a sequel to *Letters from Elvis* to be called *Brando on Elvis*. This book was intended to reveal the full text of Brando's letters about Elvis. Now I could include this new material as well. The discovery of these additional letters along with a trove of personal information about Carmen Montez increased the credibility of the still-evolving Elvis saga.

* * *

A third result of the release of *Letters from Elvis* was yet another phone call, this one from Julian Riley, a resident of Tupelo. In a hoarse voice, speaking words bent out of shape by a Mississippi drawl, Julian tactlessly said, "I just read your book about Elvis. I thought you should know you made some mistakes in it."

Thus started an unlikely friendship between an old, conservative, southern man who flew the Confederate flag and a northern Yankee independent who more often politically leaned left. Julian, a lifelong resident of Tupelo, the birthplace of Elvis, had been researching the performer for many years. He was particularly interested in the family history and genetic connections of the Presley ancestors. He gave me access to an Elvis family tree he had assembled with over 42,000 names.

He taught me how to match DNA data from one person to over a hundred samples he had collected voluntarily from Elvis's relatives to determine precise family connections where they existed.

Julian knew just about everyone in Tupelo and its environs. A few years earlier, he had self-published a book called *Roots of Elvis*, which was poorly written and designed and now obsolete. We decided to continue the research and co-author a first-class, updated volume that debunked many popular myths and revealed newly acquired information. We called the new book *The Roots of Elvis*, and it replaced the older version. The back cover stated some of the books startling findings this way:

> Elvis's public origin story is a mess of myth and factual errors that is finally corrected. In *Roots of Elvis*, you will learn, among many other things, startling new facts about:
>
> - Elvis's Cherokee and Jewish ancestry—fact or fiction?
> - The Presley matriarch who had 9 children but never married.
> - The identity of Elvis's unknown great-grandfather.
> - The identity of Elvis's biological father.
> - The mystery of Gladys Love Presley's middle name.
> - The secret of Elvis's birthplace.
> - The genetic mutation that may change Elvis's origin story.

This book again stirred controversy, but also led to some changes in the Elvisphere. For example, by revealing that Elvis's famous birth house in Tupelo was a replica, not the original, the Elvis Museum on the grounds replaced the wording on the placard next to the "birth house" with text that no longer boldly stated "This is the house where Elvis was born."

We also built the case for our determination—with 90 percent certainty—that Elvis's biological father was not Vernon Presley, but Rev. Lawrence David Riley, Sr., a Baptist minister in Tupelo who was married to Glady Presley's best friend. Rev. Riley also was my co-author's uncle, making Julian Riley an unknown first cousin of Elvis. It turns out that Elvis was not a Presley after all. He was a Riley but never knew it. These facts also explain why Julian had invested so much time researching the family ties of Elvis.

* * *

The fourth major event triggered by the release of *Letters from Elvis* was the most surprising phone call of all, this one from northeastern Texas. The call was arranged by Guy Cooper, an intermediary in Phoenix whom I knew well. I had asked Guy to have an acquaintance of his, one who said he was interested in speaking with me, call my cell phone at four o'clock on a Saturday early in December 2018. Before the call, I set up a second iPhone to record the incoming call on my primary iPhone.

Right on schedule, I received the call in the kitchen as my wife was making spaghetti for dinner. I flicked the Accept Call button and tapped the Speaker button so I could talk hands-free and record the call on the second phone. I said, "Hello, this is Gary."

The caller replied, "Hello, I was told to call at four o'clock. Is this OK?"

The voice startled me because the rich baritone sounded so much like Elvis. In real life, Elvis had a three-octave vocal range, so he could reach astounding high notes but could also sing lyric baritone with unexpectedly rich, low tones.

The caller and I exchanged smalltalk for about five minutes. I learned that Guy had sent him my *Letters from Elvis* book, and the caller claimed to be a member of the Presley family. I started the call expecting a rant about my invasion of Elvis's privacy and the phony claims of gang rape, but that didn't happen. The call was friendly and folksy due to the caller's Texas accent.

Finally, I asked, "So how are you part of the Presley family? A cousin or something?"

"No sir, I'm Papa's little secret."

"Not sure I understand."

"Well, truth is, I'm Elvis's firstborn son. My name is Joshua Presley."

Gloria dropped the sauce spoon on the floor. The call was on speaker, so she was hearing everything that was said. She pointed her index finger to her temple and made a circling gesture indicating the caller was a lunatic.

"Excuse me," I said, "but I thought Elvis had just one child, a daughter—Lisa Marie."

"No sir. He has a few other children, but I'm his oldest son."

"But not a son with Priscilla?"

"No sir. He met Mama when he was on the 'Lousiana Hayride'—she was in Gladewater, Texas. Originally from Alabama. They had a, you know, a fling, and she got pregnant and had me and my brother nine months later."

"You have a brother?"

"We're twins, just like Elvis had a twin named Jesse."

"I see." I'm sure I sounded skeptical because I was. "So what do you want from me?"

"Well, I want you to tell my story, and the true story of Papa, cuz it's never been told. I'd like you to write it. You were respectful to Papa in your book, even with all that ugly stuff, and I liked that. You told the truth, mostly—what you knew, anyway. But there's way more."

I suspected that this Elvis soundalike was working a con, but I couldn't figure out his game. How would he try to get money from me? Maybe persuade me to buy the rights to his story? Perhaps cover the costs of publishing and marketing the book?

"How much would this cost me?" I asked bluntly, cutting to the chase.

"How much would what cost?"

"The rights, or whatever I'd need to pay to be involved?"

"No, no… I don't need any money. I'm coming into a lot of money soon. I wanna pay you to write the book."

I had pitched him a slow strike for a home run swing, and he had passed on it. We continued to talk for close to an hour. The longer we talked, the more compelling information he shared, almost none of which I could independently verify. Finally, I said, "What you're telling me is kind of hard to believe. As an investigative writer, I need evidence, like photographs, documents…"

"If you agree to tell my story, I can prove everything that I tell you. I can send you some samples now."

Within a few seconds, text messages with images started coming to my iPhone. Some of the pictures were astonishing. For the next few hours, Joshua texted me a mountain of information I had never heard before, and that changed nearly everything I had learned about Elvis and his family. My brain hurt from the intake.

Finally, I called Joshua back and said, "Listen, if we're going to work together, I need to come down to wherever you are so we can hole up for a week and figure this thing out."

"I can get you a ticket," he said.

"No, I can't take a penny from you. I can't do this as a work-for-hire or I'll be seen as your publicity guy. I'll pay my own expenses, and if we end up working together, I will write the book without pay. I need to be financially independent on this or the story will have no credibility at all."

It occurred to me that I may have done a con artist's job for him by agreeing to work for free without his asking. But I would have a week in Texas to sniff out any foul stuff before committing. We agreed that I would come to Gladewater for the first full week of January 2019. By coincidence, I would be there for Elvis's birthday on January 8, the day he would have turned eighty-four if he had lived.

I announced the plan to Gloria, who simply said, "Are you crazy? How do you know this isn't the guy who was sending us death threats? What do you really know about him? His stories are crazy." I told my partner, Ian, of my plan. He and the Calumet staff all agreed with Gloria—this was a foolhardy journey that could easily have a disastrous conclusion.

So, I bought a round trip ticket to Texas. I was too old to die young.

* * *

On Sunday, January 5, I arrived at the Tyler airport after dark on the last flight in. With only a handful of passengers aboard, my suitcase appeared quickly. As I headed down the ramp past the vacant security checkpoint, Joshua met me with a warm embrace. He was shorter and heavier than I had expected, but I recognized him immediately from texted photos. He grabbed my suitcase, and we headed for the parking lot where he put my suitcase in the trunk.

I can't disclose much of our conversation on the way to my hotel because of a handshake arrangement between us. We had agreed, purely based on trust, that he would not withhold any information or evidence from me and truthfully answer all my questions. In exchange, I would not publish any of the information he shared until one of two events had occurred, neither of which I am at liberty to reveal at this time.

I can disclose certain sensitive information Joshua told me about himself, however, because it does not affect other family members, and I was able to verify the facts of his statements later. Prior to my travel to Texas, Joshua had been forthcoming about spending seven years in a Texas prison for sexually molesting his two-year-old stepdaughter after marrying the girl's mother. He claimed that he had been framed by a drug ring in Upsher County, Texas, which had threatened and bribed his wife into falsely testifying against him. The judge who tried him, he claimed, was involved in the drug ring along with her son, and she had suppressed evidence of his innocence during the trial that she presided over.

During his stay in prison, Joshua told me, he had been illegally kept under the influence of psychotropic drugs to maintain his silence and had suffered several strokes, which had not been treated in a timely fashion. He still suffered from some of the effects. During my stay in Texas, Joshua presented me with official documents proving the truth of these facts. After seven years of incarceration, the suppressed evidence establishing his innocence surfaced, and Joshua was released on parole pending a legal settlement. The state offered him more than thirty million dollars because he not only had been falsely imprisoned but mistreated while incarcerated.

Joshua's personal story itself was bookworthy, but family entanglements made it currently unpublishable because to tell the story would also reveal other fiercely held family secrets.

During my stay with Joshua, the first of many, I was literally overwhelmed with information so extraordinary—most of it corroborated by other people or documentary evidence—that my mind was spinning. The debunking of Elvis myths in *Roots of Elvis* barely touched the surface of what Joshua exposed to me that first week. As he was dropping me off at the airport for my return home, he said, "Keep in mind that what I've told you is just the tip of the iceberg. There is so much more."

Seeing the Beginning in the End

Gloria picked me up at MSP and quietly drove me home. Her behavior struck me as unusual because "quiet" was not a word often used to describe my talkative wife. In the car, I was quiet too. I had to process everything I had learned in Texas, some of which would have seemed outrageously unrealistic if I had not seen and heard so much evidence. At home, I briefly summarized some of what I had been told. She listened, nodding but not saying much. Exhausted, I went to bed.

The next morning, I was following up on emails in my basement office when Gloria's voice came down the stairs: "Can you come up? We need to talk."

Those four words spoken by a spouse—"We need to talk"—always means something unpleasant is about to occur. I trudged up the stairs, steeling myself for a fit of rage or accusations about my selfishness in leaving her for a week or her desire for a trial separation. "I suppose you're thinking about ending the marriage," I said.

"It's more than that," she replied ominously. "I've been having an affair for the past five months."

I metaphorically saw my life pass before my eyes. Everything we had shared, the good and bad, the kids and the friends, and our faith and business and counseling and once-upon-a-time love—it all whizzed past and evaporated into nothing but pain. We were standing and facing each other, but my legs suddenly grew too weak to support me, so I sat down. She did too, facing me.

I could only manage one word. "Who?"

"John. You've never met him, but I've told you that occasionally I would stay at his farm rather than rent a hotel when I was monitoring Land Trust property up north."

"You mean that 'crusty old classmate' who was just an old friend? You lied to me about that?"

She nodded. "The crusty and old part was true."

"You've been having sex with him?"

"Yes."

"So, these past fifteen years, when you've been telling me the MS had taken away your desire, had deadened the nerves, and sex caused too much pain—all that was a lie because you didn't want sex with me? Clearly, you've had your desire back for the last five months."

"I'm not proud of my behavior," she said, "but I was desperate. In the beginning, yes, the MS took a lot away from me, but then the feelings came back."

"But you didn't think to tell your husband?"

The conversation had come to an end for now. So much of my life suddenly drained away that I couldn't even replace it with anger—until later. I felt gutted, not so much by her wanting to leave the marriage, but by the sense of betrayal. I had trusted her implicitly, and she had knowingly cheated on me, not just once but continuously.

I took three gut-wrenching years before we finalized our divorce. I tried hard to win her back—somehow, I was still in love with her—but as my cousin, Verna Lee, told me, "Once a woman decides to leave a marriage, it's over. There is no going back."

During this painful period, three women in my life kept me going—my cousin, Verna Lee; my sister, Bonnie; and my ex-wife, Karen, the mother of my sons. I thank them all for helping me stay sane, keep a measure of my self-esteem, and stay socialized. They also helped me appreciate that all of us make mistakes—even me—and that forgiveness can be more a gift we give to ourselves than to the person forgiven. Without these wise women, I would not have made it.

I chose to use those three years post-Gloria to question what was wrong with me. I was now a three-time loser in marriage. Clearly, much of the fault was mine, and those faults were not hard to identify. Once I admitted them to myself, I worked hard to overcome them. I think I've been partially successful. I also learned that once I was removed from an atmosphere of persistent anger and resentment at home, I was almost immediately more peaceful and relaxed.

Just as I was reaching my loneliest point, something wonderful happened. For a multitude of reasons, my son, Scott, who had become estranged from me, was suddenly living with me. I am sure that if I hadn't worked on overcoming my most harmful traits, this restored relationship could not have happened. I was able to help Scott through some personal difficulties, which made me feel useful again. In return, Scott taught me how to be a truly independent man living without the support of a wife. In a way, I should probably thank Gloria for setting in motion one of the happiest times in my life.

One day, when the conditions of the pledge of secrecy I gave Joshua have been fulfilled, I will write the true story of Joshua Presley and the truly astonishing story of Elvis and his family. Until then, I find fulfillment in my writing and publishing work and in finding the truth behind the myths of fascinating and perplexing mysteries.

* * *

I just got a call from a person who recently acquired a cache of small Picasso paintings and drawings that are unknown to the art market. Are they authentic? Most have a letter of authentication signed by Maya Picasso. At the time of the signings, Maya was the official authenticator of her father's works. But are these letters authentic?

The story of how these artworks left the studio of Pablo Picasso, passed through the hands of many colorful and influential people and ended up at a nonprofit foundation in South Africa is long and convoluted—just my kind of project. I may have to live long enough to sort this out and write a book about the true story. If I don't live long enough, all is not lost, because then I will finally learn the truth of the world's greatest mystery of all—*what happens next.*

Acknowledgments

I wish to thank the many people who assisted me in recollecting my past and helping to produce this work. My two wives, Karen and Gloria, generously helped to reconstruct forgotten episodes and timelines, and they permitted me to publicly present some painful memories. Scott Lindberg delivered a unique perspective as the author's son. My sister, Bonnie, fortunately remembered facts about many family adventures and tribulations. These individuals also contributed many of the photographs contained in this book.

I also wish to thank Rick Polad for his thoughtful and expert copyediting; my partner Ian Graham Leask for his advice in structuring the book; Josh Weber and Beth Williams of Calumet Editions for their assistance in publishing the work; and my dog, Joey, for giving up too many walks so I could work on this seemingly unending project.

There are many others who contributed indirectly through their accompaniment on my numerous adventures; these are referred to in the text.

About the Author

Gary Lindberg has spent his entire adult life as a screenwriter, movie director and producer, author of fiction and nonfiction, and book publisher. He is the author of four Amazon #1 bestselling novels. His first two books about Elvis were *Letters from Elvis*, based on a large cache of unpublished correspondence to a secret confidante, and *Brando on Elvis*, a detailed account of letters written by Marlon Brando about Elvis Presley. A third Elvis book, *The Roots of Elvis*, unearths the true story of Elvis's ancestry. He co-wrote and co-produced the Paramount motion picture *That Was Then, This Is Now* starring Morgan Freeman and Emilio Estevez.

www.ingramcontent.com/pod-product-compliance
Lightning Source LLC
Chambersburg PA
CBHW050515170426
43201CB00013B/1968